THE HUMAN ECONOMY

« « « · » » »

BY

Eli Ginzberg

McGRAW-HILL BOOK COMPANY

New York   St. Louis   San Francisco   Düsseldorf

London   Mexico   Sydney   Toronto

Library of Congress Cataloging in Publication Data

Ginzberg, Eli, 1911–
The human economy.

Bibliography: p. 254
Includes index.
1. Labor economics. 2. Manpower policy. I. Title.
HD4901.G43   331   75-45490
ISBN 0-07-023283-0
1 2 3 4 5 6 7 8 9 BPBP 75432109876

The editors for this book were Thomas Quinn and Cheryl Love, the designer was Christine Aulicino, and the production supervisor was Milton Heiberg. It was set in Times Roman with display lines in Times Roman, Perpetua, and Palatino by Rumford Press.

Printed and bound by Book Press.

CONTENTS

PREFACE

DURING THE LAST THIRTY-SEVEN YEARS, the Conservation of Human Resources Project at Columbia University has been engaged in research on human resources and manpower. During this extended interdisciplinary effort, my colleagues and I have sought to illuminate, primarily through empirical investigations, critical aspects of the development and utilization of human resources in both developed and developing nations. We have investigated the effect of unemployment on individuals, the underdevelopment of potential among minorities, the causes of ineffective performance in the military, talent and performance, the life styles of educated women, and other facets of human resources in economic and social life. Because the human resources factor had not previously been explored in depth, we made a major commitment to empirical research.

Our efforts to construct theory were limited. In the early 1950s, our work entitled *Occupational Choice** carried the subtitle *An Approach to a General Theory*. In the mid-1960s, our study entitled *The Pluralistic Economy* provided a new framework for studying the enlarged entrepreneurial roles of both government and nonprofit institutions. The complementarity among the three sectors—private, nonprofit, and government—suggested this new approach for studying the functioning of the American economy. In 1971, the introductory and concluding chapters of *Manpower for Development: Perspectives on Five Continents* called attention to the lessons which could be extracted from the efforts of developing nations to force the pace of their economic growth by improving the quality of their human resources.

It is questionable whether, without the prodding of my junior colleague and collaborator Alfred S. Eichner, I would have ventured on the present effort. He not only insisted that I explicate the theory which I have

*See bibliography for detailed citations.

v

used in my teaching and research and in my work as a government consultant but he also offered to assist me in every way. It has taken me almost a decade of continuous but interrupted effort to reach this point, and it is primarily because of him that I have done so.

A close friend, Arthur H. L. Rubin, prematurely dead at a loss to us all, made me promise shortly after World War II that I would not flinch at undertaking a major work on human resources. Had he been able to read this manuscript, it would be a better book, but except for the promise he extracted, there might be no book.

My wife, Ruth Szold Ginzberg, has been the third member of the troika. In her quiet way she let me know, not once but repeatedly, that no number of publications was the equivalent of the one book that should command my best efforts. And she did much more to encourage me. She put aside her own work and committed her limited free time to polishing the manuscript, not once but twice. The reader, as well as the author, is in her debt.

The final manuscript has been improved through the help which I received not only from Professor Eichner but also from the other members of the Conservation staff—Ivar Berg, James W. Kuhn, David Lewin, Dean Morse, Beatrice Reubens, and Borhs Yavitz. In addition, I profited from the careful reading of the draft by five friends: Juanita Kreps, Wilbur C. Munnecke, Howard Rosen, H. J. Szold, and George Tobias.

For fifteen years, the Conservation Project has received substantial funding from the Office of Manpower Research and Development, U.S. Department of Labor. It is proper, therefore, that I take note of this relationship, since the present effort at synthesis draws directly on our earlier research.

Sylvia Leef typed and retyped multiple drafts of the manuscript from handwritten pages which nobody but she could decipher, always with efficiency and good humor.

During the past years, when the scale of the Conservation Project's activities increased substantially, Ellen McDermott took over responsibility for all the fiscal and personnel activities of the Project, thereby enabling me to protect my time for research and writing.

And during these same busy years, it was my good fortune to have Elizabeth Tang as my personal assistant. In her calm and effective manner, she kept everything under control and, in the process, protected me from the stresses and strains which otherwise would have threatened the completion of the manuscript.

Anna Dutka assisted in checking the sources and in preparing the bibliography.

Prospectus: The Human Resources Approach

THE WORLD OF IDEAS lives in a stormy relationship with the world of experience. The disciplines of economics, sociology, and political science must address the pressing problems of the day. Moreover, the manner in which the problems are analyzed depends in no small measure on the stage of theory development. The recent emergence of human resources as a new arena of scholarly inquiry can be understood by briefly reviewing the role of manpower* in the affairs of nations, particularly the United States, during the present century. Many dimensions warrant attention. We will consider six: mass unemployment, shortages of scientific manpower, the expansion of educational opportunities, the drive for equity, the trade-offs between full employment and other economic objectives, and the changing expectations about work.

The record indicates that except for immigration, no manpower issue commanded attention in the United States prior to World War I, although, interestingly, the concept of the "conservation of human resources" was put forward early in this century by President Theodore Roosevelt as part of his broad program to protect all the nation's resources.

The years between World War I and World War II were marked by severe and prolonged unemployment in most of the advanced economies,

---

*The use of "manpower" and "men" as generic terms for both men and women reflects long-established usage. There is no question that sex discrimination is characteristic of our tradition and our language. I have sought to use neutral alternatives such as "person" or "individual" wherever possible, but in many instances "manpower" or "men" is preferable. In my view, the revolution in the role of women is the most important societal change of the twentieth century, of greater potential import and impact than the establishment of communism or the emergence of the atomic era. But it will take time for language to adapt. In the interim, a sympathetic male can only avoid semantic innovations that are artificial.

so severe that it paved the way for Adolf Hitler to gain the Chancellorship of Germany in 1933, the same year in which Franklin D. Roosevelt inaugurated a broad program of economic and social reform in the United States, a move directly related to the antecedent and continuing high level of unemployment. Keynes's *General Theory,* published three years later, provided the intellectual rationale for the interventionist programs which both Hitler and Roosevelt designed to start their economies moving again by putting the unemployed back to work. The initial studies of the Conservation of Human Resources Project focused on the causes and consequences of large-scale and prolonged unemployment, first in the coal-mining valleys of South Wales, where up to 90 percent of the labor force in some communities had been unemployed for a decade, and secondly in New York City, where many men had been on relief rolls for at least five years.

With the exception of chronic unemployment, no other manpower issue surfaced until the outbreak of World War II. Since then, those issues that have come to the fore are important in their own right and further important because of the challenge they present to both theory and policy.

World War II marked the first time that nations with advanced economies had to mobilize all their human resources. The United Kingdom and the United States responded more effectively than Germany, whose Führer did not encourage married women to leave their homes for paid employment. However, Hitler was able to use millions of "slave laborers" commandeered from among the people who came under the control of his armies.

In the United States, the dominant view was that the millions of married women who had responded to patriotic appeals by donning overalls and going to work would leave the labor force when hostilities came to an end. Of course, many did just that, but war permanently altered the attitudes and behavior of married women toward work outside the home. Many social scientists, ignoring this reality, still use the prototype of a male worker who remains attached to the labor force from his late teens or early twenties until he retires and who, in the absence of adversity, works full time, full year. Nevertheless, the patterns followed by women workers continue to undergo changes with respect to both their attachment to the labor force and the number of hours they work, not only in the United States and other developed countries but also in many developing societies. In many countries, women have been the principal source of the growth in the labor force in the last quarter century.

With the onset of World War II, a second manpower problem emerged, one never before on the agenda of industrialized nations. Because of the interfaces among science, technology, and national security, all the major powers were faced with shortages of talented manpower. Early in his chancellorship, Hitler ignored this relationship, with the result that many non-Aryan scientists fled from Germany and settled abroad, primarily in the United States, where they made a major contribution to military technology, including the development of the atomic bomb. In the post-World War II decades, the superpowers, primarily for reasons of national security, and the industrialized countries of Western Europe and Japan, primarily for reasons of economic growth, devoted increasing attention to expanding their supply of scientific, professional, and technical personnel. Since these individuals are educated and trained in institutions of higher learning, these countries expanded their colleges and universities. Moreover, since the proving ground of research and development is the laboratory, governments assumed the primary responsibility for financing scientific research.

Economists were slow to address the issue of highly trained manpower, since they believed that shortages of people, as of goods, would lead to a rise in price, which in turn would evoke a larger supply. Consequently, they felt that there was no pressing need for social intervention, a position reinforced by their unwillingness to see government play a direct role in the labor market. But only a national effort could provide the new sources of funding for higher education, expand the supply of qualified students, and provide career prospects for many of the new graduates—all issues for which the market could offer little guidance and fewer solutions.

The third dimension of manpower grew out of the experiences of the developing countries. When a large number of countries in Africa and Asia gained their independence in the late 1940s and 1950s, they set about to modernize their societies and speed their economic growth. They saw their retarded development as the direct consequence of their earlier status as colonial dependencies and, once freed from this constraint, they looked forward to accelerating economic development. These countries' leaders believed that development requires an increased number of trained persons. One technique that had been used by many colonial powers to reinforce their control was to limit the numbers of indigenous persons who could attend school, especially institutions of higher learning, the principal route into administrative positions. In many less-developed countries (LDCs), only a small number of people, mostly urban males, had learned to read and write, and few were qualified to fill the demanding positions in government or in the modern sector of the economy.

Because of the long period between the time when a child first enters school and when he emerges as a high school or college graduate; because of the acute shortage of facilities and teaching staffs; because of the high dropout rate in many LDCs, where for every hundred who start school only ten complete the tenth grade and only one obtains a college degree; and finally, because of a shortage of governmental resources for education because of competing demands, all the LDCs encountered difficulties in designing educational and training structures geared to facilitating their economic and social development. With the advantage of hindsight we can identify many shortcomings common to the educational structure of most LDCs, from the overproduction of university graduates to inordinately high dropout rates in the first three grades of elementary school. Nevertheless, despite errors in planning and execution, most LDCs are probably further advanced than they would otherwise be if they had not made a concerted effort to increase their pool of educated and trained manpower.

A fourth issue that came to the fore in both developed and developing countries after World War II was the pervasive pressure for broadened opportunities for the masses so that the best jobs with the most prestige and the highest salaries would no longer be preempted by the small minority who had had access to advanced education which controlled entrance into preferred careers. This drive for equity was reinforced in developed nations by the rising demand for scientists and engineers, whose ranks could best be increased by widening opportunities for able young people from low-income families, many of whom had formerly been unable to acquire a higher education.

The drive for equity had additional dimensions. In some developed countries, such as Sweden and the United Kingdom, it was expressed in the compression of wage rates and in the reduction of the gap between the disposable income available to upper-income groups and that available to lower-income groups. In the United States, the principal thrust was to reduce and remove the discriminatory barriers which had so long handicapped the black minority. Recently, a rising consciousness among women about the multiple aspects of discrimination which limit the opportunities in their lives has opened a new front against discrimination.

Considerations of equity have also come to the fore in the LDCs as they have scrutinized their development records. In the early 1950s, it was widely believed that the key to raising the standard of living of the masses in the LDCs was rapid economic growth. But the anticipated growth in the GNP was not achieved, and the rate of population increase did not slacken. Moreover, what improvement was achieved tended to be restricted to the modern urbanized sector and redounded primarily to the advantage of the small numbers who belonged to the establishment and who were able to take advantage of the new opportunities. In recent years, economists, planners, and aid officials have begun to question the trickle-down theory of development. As they reviewed the record, they found that a small minority were the principal beneficiaries; the masses continued to be mired in poverty.

Since both the democratic and communist ethos place importance on broadening opportunity and reducing inequalities in income, the tension between doctrine and reality has increased. Improvements in communications have made an ever larger number of men and women, including many living in out-of-the-way places, aware that somewhere conditions are better, often much better. The pressures produced by this growing awareness overhang the politics of nations, rich and poor, since the leaders increasingly understand that they must address the demand for equity.

The fifth manpower issue that has surfaced since World War II is the need of developed nations to reconcile their search for full employment with other economic goals, such as reasonable price stability, increased productivity, and the protection of the individual's freedom to choose his work and place of residence.

No government of an advanced nation can be insensitive to the public's insistence that there be jobs for all who are able and willing to work. In light of the mass unemployment in Western Europe and the United States in the 1930s, the accomplishment of most countries of the Atlantic community and Japan in achieving and maintaining a high level of employment throughout most of the post-World War II period must be considered a major achievement.

But every year proves once again that for every social goal that is achieved, another demands attention. The market-oriented economies of the West are plagued by nagging inflation which continues to elude effective control. The dilemma runs deep. The conventional methods of controlling inflation by forcing a slowdown in the economy are no longer acceptable to societies that cannot renege on their commitments to maintain a high level of employment. Their only alternative is to experiment with reforms aimed at reinforcing the market's ability to keep increases in wages and prices within bounds. Since the solution requires reforms in the political structure, market mechanisms, and the distribution of power among interest groups, it will come slowly and only after some false starts.

We must quickly add that the centrally controlled economies are caught in a different dilemma in their attempts to operate a full-employment society. The evidence suggests that they pay the high cost of lower productivity and restrictions on the freedom of workers to choose their work and place of residence. The repeated efforts of communist countries to introduce wage premiums may provide a partial answer to the lowered productivity, and their increasing use of special incentives to attract people to industries and regions which lack appeal reflects their awareness of the limitations of a policy based on the coercion of workers.

The sixth and last manpower issue to be reviewed here is the most difficult to define and assess. It has been subsumed under the rubric of changing expectations about work. Many social scientists believe that the combination of higher levels of education, employment, and income, reinforced by new sexual mores, heightened individualism, and an antiestablishment ethos, is leading more and more young people in the developed nations to turn their backs on careerism and the work ethic. They argue that today workers are less interested than those in earlier generations in getting ahead as fast as possible and earning as much as possible and are increasingly concerned about the nature of the work they do and the satisfactions they derive from it. We might have anticipated that expectations with respect to work would change in light of the changes that have taken place in the way in which people are reared, work, and live. What remains obscure are the trade-offs that workers are willing to make; they may be interested in less routine assignments, but not necessarily at the cost of reduced wages. Certain assumptions about a changing work ethic may prove to be premature, but changing expectations and realities in all developed nations will certainly affect the behavior of people in the work arena.

This selective review of six important manpower issues which have surfaced since the Great Depression and the difficulties that both developed and developing nations have experienced in dealing with them helps to explain the burgeoning interest in manpower among both policy makers and scholars. The fact that neither economics nor any other social science is capable of responding adequately to these manpower phenomena suggests both opportunities and dangers. A long period of exploration, experimentation, and development is required before the new discipline of human resources can mature. Economics can provide considerable help, but the new framework must be broader, since manpower problems are not rooted in the market alone but involve such diverse institutions as the family, government, and the educational system.

The purpose of this book is to contribute to the task of discipline building by analyzing the principal institutions and mechanisms which shape the development and utilization of manpower. This effort has several aims: to delineate the key roles which each of the major institutions plays in the process, to analyze how the institutions interact with one another, and to identify the principal sources of manpower waste and suggest where remedial action should be focused. While the analysis is predicated on the experience of the United States and the advanced economies of Western Europe, considerable attention will also be paid to the LDCs to determine whether the human resources approach has broader applicability. Only occasional reference will be made to the communist societies because we do not have detailed knowledge of their experience.

Part I starts with an analysis of the differences between human resources and other resources and the consequences of these differences for theory construction. It then proceeds to make explicit the relation between social theory and social action with reference to the manpower arena. Here the emphasis is that all investigators, are committed to a value position which they can deny but cannot escape. Next we present a framework for studying the principal institutions involved in the development and utilization of skills and competences. The concluding chapter in this Part delineates the interactions among the principal components of the manpower system, thereby providing a dynamic perspective.

Part II analyzes the processes through which people acquire skills and competences in developed and developing nations. The focus is on three basic institutions—family, school, and employing organizations. Next to the cycle of growing a stand of timber, the production cycle for specialized competence is the longest. Some medical specialists do not complete their training until their thirties; on the average, then, their preparation is longer than their working life! Attention is directed to two critical variables in skill development: the influence of the family on the career aspirations and outcomes of its children and the extent to which the individual's characteristics and societal changes modify the influence of social class.

Part III focuses on manpower utilization, that is, the factors which determine the opportunities which developed and developing nations provide their members to work and obtain income, the ways in which these opportunities are distributed among different groups, and the types of manpower imbalances that characterize different societies and the prospects of containing them.

Part IV is concerned with large organizations which increasingly dominate the economies of developed nations. Consideration is first directed to the manpower strategy which these large organizations pursue to assure that they have the people they need for current and future operations. A second concern is the career objectives of individuals who seek employment in large organizations. Since the goals of employers and employees are partially congruent but also in conflict, attention is directed to the manner in which conflicts are compromised.

Part V uses the building blocks that have been put into place and presents a summary of the conceptual foundations of the manpower system. Next an effort is made to use the conceptual foundations to show how the broadening of options can contribute to the well-being of the individual and society. The last chapter points directions for manpower policy.

For

The Staff of the Conservation of Human Resources Project,

Columbia University,

who, following Adam Smith, recognize that the wealth of a nation

depends on

". . . the skill, dexterity, and judgment with

which its labour is generally applied."

On the bicentennial anniversary of the publication of

The Wealth of Nations,

London, March 9, 1776

PART I

« « « · » » »

FRAMEWORK

In civilized society he stands at all times in need of the co-operation and assistance of great multitudes, while his whole life is scarce sufficient to gain the friendship of a few persons. In almost every other race of animals each individual, when it is grown up to maturity, is entirely independent, and in its natural state has occasion for the assistance of no other living creature. But man has almost constant occasion for the help of his brethren, and it is in vain for him to expect it from their benevolence only.

—ADAM SMITH, *The Wealth of Nations*

· I ·

The Human Resource

WHEN THE INTERNATIONAL LABOR ORGANIZATION was being established immediately after World War I, the American trade union representatives refused to agree to the draft charter until it was amended by replacing the phrase "labor is a commodity" with "labor is not merely a commodity." By taking this stand, American labor leaders underscored the importance they attached to treating labor differently from other resources.

This first chapter will set out the principal assumptions which underlie and the implications which flow from a human resources approach to the study of the economy and society. The parameters of a human resources approach will be established and its basic characteristics identified by contrasting it with the commodity approach, which has served as the model for economic analysis during the past two centuries.

First, attention will be directed to the limitations of the model of the competitive market for analyzing the employment relationship. Next, the multiple dimensions of the employment relationship will be explored for the purpose of developing an appropriately enlarged framework which will be responsive to the range of forces influencing the behavior of employers and employees.

The commodity approach has been so generalized by economists that they now analyze all human behavior, including marriage, child rearing, divorce, crime, and even preparation for the hereafter in terms of a utility-maximizing model. They predicate that people seek to reduce their costs and increase their benefits and that the best way to understand human behavior is to apply the economic model used in the study of commodity trade.

he human resources approach considers human behavior as more diverse. It contends that although men devote a great deal of time and energy to economic pursuits, only a framework that makes room for the values and goals that inform their behavior, the governmental system which enables them to live together and pursue common goals, and the educational-training institutions which provide the basis for skill acquisition can encapsulate the many ramifications of men's behavior which transcend their pursuit of material goods.

The contrast between the two approaches can be sharpened by considering differences in the nature of resource, the reach of the market model, and the arena of work as a source of satisfaction. The economic model deals with commodities which, by definition, are passive and inert. The coal mine owner sells his output at the market price, not knowing and not caring whether the coal will be used to heat a church or a brothel. Specifically, the coal involved in the transaction is totally inactive. It is different, however, when human beings rather than commodities are involved. People are active participants in any transaction that involves them in any of their several roles—as workers, citizens, or parents or as individuals seeking to realize their personal goals. Their actions are molded by their experiences, their expectations, and the options they confront.

The commodity approach treats the employment relation in the same manner as any transaction involving inert resources. It postulates that buyers seek to purchase labor of a standard quality at the lowest possible wage; workers seek a job that will yield them the best combination of earnings and collateral benefits.

However, there are reasons to question the appropriateness of treating people as if they are commodities. To mention only a few: although higher wage rates can induce workers to move, Adam Smith's dictum that, of all luggage, man is the most difficult to transport still holds. Over time, employers can shift the site of their operations to take advantage of a more favorable labor supply, but the key words here are "over time," since the relocation of plants with heavy capital investments seldom is accomplished in less than a decade.

Traders in wheat, coffee, newsprint, chemicals, and a thousand and one other commodities and products operate within a broadly defined system of specifications and standards. Both the buyer and the seller have a clear idea of the commodity that is being traded. But in an employment transaction, the employer has only an imperfect idea of the skills, competences, and other qualities of the person he is about to hire; the worker in turn knows little about the job he is accepting beyond the wage, the hours of work, and a few other broad characteristics.

Moreover, the treatment of inert resources in the production process is determined by technical considerations. For example, one chemical is combined with several others in set proportions to produce the desired output. Unless there is a change in technology, the batching treatment, precipitation methods, and the production processes are the same one day after the other. The commodities act and react in accordance with their inherent, inert characteristics.

Unlike commodities, people respond in different and often unpredictable ways. Different people respond differently to the same stimuli, and their responses are often unpredictable when they are exposed to new stimuli. Most employers devote considerable effort to eliciting desirable responses from their workers, and this concern is subsumed under the concept of improved motivation.

The human resources approach contends that the application of the market model to the buying and selling of labor is even more questionable than the limitations of the constraints of mobility, information, and motivation would indicate. Most job applicants seek to establish an "affiliation" with an organization which will enable them to look forward not only to a job and a wage in the short term but also to job security, skill development, promotions, and an array of fringe benefits, including a pension at the end of their working lives. Their primary concern is not with a single transaction but with a long-term affiliation.

Although most workers seek such an affiliation, or its equivalent, as do professionals or journeymen who in the usual course of a working life can also anticipate higher earnings and uninterrupted work, not all workers succeed in achieving one. A significant proportion must settle for jobs that are not secure and that do not lead to skill enhancement and higher earnings. When both workers and employers are exposed to the rigors of competition, the market model comes closer to describing the realities that bound the employment relationship.

In an advanced economy, however, many workers do succeed in making an affiliation by virtue of the dominance of the large organization in the profit, nonprofit, and public sectors, where management seeks to develop and retain a stable work force. The desire of workers for a long-term affiliation is matched by the desire of employers for a stable work force which can be trained to meet the skill needs of the organization and which can provide a pool of experienced persons available to move into successive levels of supervision and management.

The nub of the confrontation between the human resources and commodity approaches is the unjustified extension of the market model. The human resources approach recognizes that a market for labor approximating that for inert resources exists even in advanced societies, but it contends that the model is applicable to at most about a third of the full-time work force. It therefore emphasizes the importance of the affiliation process as critical for understanding the behavior of workers in their employment relationships.

The foregoing consideration of the limitations of the market model for the study of employment leads to a further difference between two approaches. Basic to the commodity approach is its emphasis on the role of the market as a clearance mechanism. According to this approach, the market ensures that, through price adjustments, either surpluses or shortages of a commodity will be rectified sooner rather than later. If demand is in excess of supply, enterprises will expand output; if demand lags, a reduction in price should lead to increased sales.

Clearly, the market operates to some extent to equilibrate the demand and supply of labor, but the critical question is to what extent. A few illustrations suggest that the area is relatively restricted. Manufacturers adjust to slack market conditions by building up their inventories or by shutting off part of their production facilities. Under boom conditions, they meet part of the soaring demand by reversing the process above; they reduce inventories and bring high-cost capacity back into use.

Half a century ago, J. M. Clark pointed out that the furlough or discharge of workers in a depression enables the employer to reduce his costs; nevertheless, these workers and their families must be fed, clothed, housed, and otherwise provided for. A related formulation notes that the labor of unemployed workers runs to waste. Labor cannot be stored, and the skills that people have accumulated may begin to obsolesce or atrophy. Moreover, unless workers have jobs, they cannot add to their competences; this in turn reduces the future productivity of the work force. The longer people are unemployed or underemployed, the more serious are these wastes.

The failure of the market to serve as a clearance mechanism with respect to workers and jobs was a key element in Keynes' revision of economic theory. Writing in the mid-1930s, Keynes recognized that even in the absence of trade unions, workers would be unwilling to accept lower wages since they knew that this would not necessarily lead to greater total employment. This led to his emphasis on alternative mechanisms for expanding demand.

The post-World War II efforts of the governments of all developed nations to play a leading role in establishing and maintaining a high level of employment speaks to their collective judgment of the inability of the market to perform its clearance function in the employment arena. The fact that the developed nations have faltered on the way to meeting this goal does not weaken the validity of their having taken action. Today, no statesman and only an occasional scholar would advocate relying on the market to bring about the full employment of a nation's human resources.

The commodity approach, which treats labor as similar to inert commodities, applies the theory of marginal productivity in explaining how manpower is both allocated and rewarded. There is no need or intention to challenge the theory in its entirety, but its unwarranted extension to the entire economy must be questioned. Clearly, in particular circumstances, employers do consider the relative costs and gains of using more capital or more labor and do make decisions on the basis of a rough analysis of their respective marginal productivities.

On the other hand, it stretches the theory very far to apply it to the approximately one-third of the work force in an advanced economy who are employed in the nonprofit or governmental sectors. So little is known about productivity in these sectors that output is measured in terms of input. Furthermore, to extend the theory uncritically to the large segments of the private sector where production and prices are controlled is also suspect.

The relevance of the market model for explaining the earnings that people receive from their work is equally suspect. The noncompeting nature of the labor market, first analyzed by the British economist John Cairnes over a century ago, warns about the complex processes involved in balancing trained people and work opportunities. A decade will intervene between the planning of a new medical school to reduce a shortage of physicians and the graduation of its first class. The pervasive tendency to produce an oversupply of arts graduates grows out of the time span involved in career decisions, the distortions introduced by the educational and training institutions, and the dynamics of the economy and the society.

The human resources approach suggests that the prototypical large organization, characteristic of developed societies, organizes its work among groups and that there is no direct way of measuring the contribution of the group, much less the individual within the group. This is not to say that evaluations are not made or that they are haphazard. The consideration advanced here is less extreme. It starts with the recognition that every hierarchical organization has a ladder of positions with graded skill and experience requirements geared to a scale of wages or salaries. It notes that incumbents are paid the accepted rate for the position, rather than in accordance with the quantity or quality of their output. True, those whose performance is judged to be better than others are more likely to be promoted. But the person making the selection will usually choose from among those he knows and likes or act on the recommendations of those he trusts. Under so constricted a system of selection and promotion which provides ample opportunity for favoritism and error, it is inevitable that many managers are either overqualified or underqualified for the work they do. More to the point, what they are paid is not closely related to their marginal contribution.

This brings us to the last major confrontation between the human resources approach and the commodity approach. The issue centers around work as a source of satisfaction or dissatisfaction to the worker.

The founding fathers of economics viewed work as a disutility, an activity which men and women prefer to avoid but must engage in if they are to obtain the necessities of life. People would prefer to be free of the pressure to work so that they might spend their time and energy as they desire, but they agree to work because this is the only way through which they can survive and prosper.

Alfred Marshall, the doyen of British economists at the beginning of the century, was uneasy about this formulation, since he realized that many men enjoy working. But he reconciled his insight with the established doctrine by pointing out that since men must work longer than they would like—for a full day instead of a few hours—it is analytically justifiable to consider their total labor input as a cost. Thorstein Veblen's view that men have an instinct for workmanship and that the degree to which they exercise it and the ends to which they direct it are culturally determined never received credence. Had his opinions been taken seriously, a basic restructuring of economics would have been required.

Even if one postulates that men seek to avoid work and work only because they must, and then only up to the point where they prefer additional leisure to more income, the main-line approach fouls its line. When a man works for himself on his own farm or in his own store, we can assume that he will find his own crossover point between more work and more income versus more leisure or more consumption. But most men in industrial societies work not for themselves but for others. Accordingly, the individual seeking employment must fit himself into the existing employment pattern which, over large sectors of a modern economy, has been determined by a complex set of institutional arrangements and articulations involving corporations, trade unions, and government.

The human resources approach does not consider the principal activity in which men engage, namely, productive employment, solely as a disutility significant only for the income which people derive from it. It does not claim that most people enjoy their work, or even that it is possible to so restructure a society that most people would find their major satisfactions in their work. Freud believed that work and love provide structure and meaning to human existence, but he also thought that civilization itself is the source of most discontents.

Work binds men to one another by enabling them, through cooperative activity, to build a house, clean the streets, assemble an automobile, launch an advertising campaign, treat a patient, and engage in other forms of paid work. These activities help to shape the lives of the participants by giving them roles which help to define who they are to themselves and to others; their work also establishes the framework within which they interact with their fellow workers for eight or more hours every day.

Work is, above everything else, a social activity, and however routine or enervating the specific tasks that command their time and attention, most workers derive considerable satisfaction from the social interactions that are integral to every work setting. Consider, for instance, the feelings of loss and deprivation that are the typical concomitants of a man's losing his job and having to endure a long spell of unemployment. The social context of work helps to explain J. M. Clark's observation that the most important output of modern industry is its impact on those who produce the product. The human resources approach postulates that work has always yielded direct satisfactions and that clarifying and extending its capacity to do so represents a major challenge to all societies, especially those capable of producing large surpluses.

What implications can be extracted from this juxtaposition of the commodity approach and the human resources approach? First, we found that since men do more than make a living, we cannot rely exclusively on the utility-maximizing model to explain their behavior even in terms of their employment relationships. Their behavior in the job arena is affected by their other roles as well, as members of a family, a community, and a nation. An analytic framework which seeks to account for their job behavior must make room for the principal determinants which affect the totality of their actions. The commodity market model is too restricted.

Secondly, to consider human beings as if they were inert resources leads to error because the analysis ignores the extent to which men, as individuals and particularly as members of groups, strive to alter the institutions they have inherited in order to make them more responsive to the goals they seek to realize. Inert resources have no capacity to respond to the forces acting on them, but man is an active factor concerned with molding his own future.

Thirdly, commodity trade is focused on the isolated transaction. One person wants to buy what another wants to sell. If both agree on the price, there is a transfer of money for a commodity and that is the end of the transaction. The employment relation is different. Most workers seek a permanent job, and many organizations in turn seek a permanent work force. Consequently, the tender and acceptance of a job offer is not a single transaction but, rather, the first step in a long-term affiliation involving mutual responsibilities and commitments that may stretch over forty years. That people must eat even if they are unemployed, that labor cannot be stored, and that reductions in wage rates will not necessarily increase the demand for labor point to the limitations of the market's performing the same clearance function for people and jobs that it performs for commodities.

The fourth finding suggests that although the theory of marginal productivity is useful in explaining relative wages in the competitive sector of the labor market, it throws little light on the wage and salary structures of large organizations where work is organized on a group basis and where the specific contribution of the individual cannot be measured.

Finally, we found that the underlying assumption of the market approach that work is a disutility and that people work only because of the money they earn lacks credibility. Clearly, most men find some satisfaction from different aspects of their work, from participation in social relations in the work setting to the specific activities they carry out.

In sum, the commodity approach has limited applicability for illuminating what transpires in the job market, and its indiscriminate extension is unwarranted. Since there are a great many facets of work, employment transactions, and the supply and demand of labor which it cannot explain, there is a need for a broader framework with a different methodology. The human resources approach is proposed in place of the market approach.

This brings us to the second theme which this introductory chapter addresses: the multiple dimensions of the employment relationship. They will be explored with the aim of delineating the parameters and elements that must be included in a framework that has been enlarged to make room for the underlying realities.

When a man accepts a job, he does more than promise to put forth certain efforts, physical or mental, for a stipulated number of hours per day. By entering upon an employment relation, a man implicitly restricts and limits his most valued possession—his freedom. During the hours he works, what he does and how he does it are largely determined by his employer. Since people in advanced societies usually work forty or more hours per week, to which must be added the hours of their travel to and from work, the total time involved represents a substantial segment of a person's waking hours.

People who work for other people find not only that their time and energy are no longer under their own control but also that they have accepted the role of subordinates. They must follow the instructions and orders of those who supervise and direct them. Those who wield power over others often, either unwittingly or deliberately, criticize or disparage their subordinates, which diminishes the self-esteem and self-respect of the latter. The risk of being abused by one's supervisor is inherent in every employment relation. Many supervisors get satisfaction from the power they wield over others, satisfaction which they may not be able to acquire in any other way.

Human beings live with their memories and are supported by their dreams. Some people spend years preparing themselves for work and look forward to putting their skills and competences to use. Often, their anticipations are frustrated. The work to which they are assigned makes a demand on only a small part of their capabilities, and these individuals inevitably feel diminished.

Frustrations may result if their work gives them little or no opportunity to add to their knowledge and techniques, which prevents them from increasing their competences. In both democratic and communist societies, many men look forward to improving their skills and thereby advancing up the job and income ladders. Unless they are given this opportunity, they feel trapped. For those who seek their principal satisfactions from their jobs, the conditions they confront in the arena of work take on special significance.

Finally, a concern over equity is a critical dimension of every employment relationship. A person who agrees to work for another receives in exchange a wage and other benefits. No matter how high his wage or salary, he will consider himself entitled to more if he knows that others no more skilled or experienced are receiving more. Moreover, workers often see little justification for the wide gap between what they are paid and what managers receive, since they are convinced that the profits of the company largely reflect their efforts. While most workers, even in Western Europe, are not Marxists committed to the doctrine that they are entitled to the whole of the surplus, they are concerned with receiving their fair share. As long as others receive a great deal more, they feel cheated and will struggle to increase their share. Since no man knowingly is party to his own exploitation, the continuing struggle for equity is inherent in the employment situation.

This recapitulation of the concomitants and consequences of the labor bargain, involving the basic elements of human life—freedom, health, self-esteem, self-development, security, and equity—helps to clarify why human beings cannot be analyzed in the same manner as inert resources. Although employers in the pursuit of profits are often able to substitute between human and other resources, this does not justify equating the two. The "human" aspect of labor is not a minor difference; it goes to the heart of the employment relation.

The principal dimensions of the human resources approach can now be summarized. The first stresses the active and responsive role of human beings in all decisions that affect them, now or in the future.

It was because men refused to be treated as instruments that slave revolts occurred, that immigrants were willing to brave the unknown to start life over, and that workers risked their lives to form unions to protect themselves from being abused by their employers. Less dramatically, as every supervisor knows, the work which an employee agrees to perform in exchange for his wage and other benefits can never be extracted but must be elicited. Workers generally accept the work norms of the group they join, and every group reaches, at least for a time, an understanding with the employer as to their work norms. Men and women never see themselves as instruments. Each person views his life as an end in itself, not a means for other people to reach their ends.

Secondly, since all human beings have multiple roles, they are guided by different values as they seek to realize their several objectives. No theory which holds that men are concerned solely with improving their material well-being is attuned to the complexities of the human condition. Most men are strongly motivated to increase their income and wealth, but they are also concerned with the interactions between their economic role and the rest of their lives.

The third postulate is that human beings are born into and live all their lives in structured social situations. Thus, every analysis must take account of the potent institutions which shape and give direction to their lives. To engage in social analysis with the individual as the sole datum can lead only to distortion and error. Of course, enlargement of the individual's scope for decision making or the broadening of choices open to him may be among the most important objectives of social action. But freedom for the individual postulates the existence of powerful institutions which must be included in the analysis.

Fourthly, the human resources approach takes into account the fact that men, by virtue of the passage of time and the acquisition of experience, continually engage in a learning process whereby they can gain new understanding about both themselves and the institutions to which they are bound. No individual can avoid this challenge of ongoing reassessment. Since no society can immunize itself completely from new and unsettling forces from within and without, and since modern societies are particularly exposed to such forces, it is essential that all social analyses take account of this inherent dynamic.

Finally, the pervasiveness of change implies continuing instability as the result of the lack of alignment among the values and goals of different groups and the reduced effectiveness over time of the society's dominant institutions. The search for solutions that can moderate this inherent instability is the overriding challenge to statecraft.

This work is directed to elaborating how goal-directed people acquire skills and competences and seek satisfactory jobs and fulfilling lives and in the process alter the institutions that their society had erected to serve earlier generations.

· 2 ·

Values in Social Theory

THE HUMAN RESOURCES APPROACH emphasizes the instability of the values and institutions that shape the goals and activities of nations, especially advanced nations. A reading of modern history, and particularly the history of this century, delineates the discontinuity and change which are the common elements of their experiences. Implicit in the human resources approach, therefore, is the search for a model that can accommodate this dominant dynamic of social existence.

A second element of social inquiry relates to the research agenda. The founding fathers of social science, especially the British and French leaders in the late eighteenth century and at the beginning of the nineteenth century believed that they were engaged in an effort directed to contributing to the betterment of man. *The Wealth of Nations,* Adam Smith's opus, was written to guide the legislator and the statesman in the realm of political economy. Smith's followers, Bentham, Malthus, Ricardo, and James Mill, who put a firm foundation under classical economics, were directly concerned with the bearing of their work on the formation of public opinion and policy. They addressed the critical issues of the day—agricultural tariffs, welfare, population policy, noninterference with business, free trade, income distribution, emigration, and trade unionism. The work of their continental colleagues—Helvetius, Holbach, Rousseau, Diderot, and Voltaire—was given credit for hastening the French Revolution. In its formative years, social science was sensitive to the dynamics of societal change and sought new and improved knowledge in the expectation of directing that change to desirable goals.

The initial success of the founding fathers of social science led to later difficulties. This was particularly true with regard to economics, where Smith's model of the competitive market was used as a basis for policy prescriptions which did not necessarily fit the changing reality. *The Wealth of Nations* did not justify Parliament's slow response to the evils of industrialization. However, Smith's theory of laissez faire came to be invested with a transcendental value. The captains of industry and finance and their followers used the theory to ward off efforts at social intervention. Faced with a choice between directing their efforts to elaborating and refining the inherited corpus or coming to grips with the unanswered problems of a rapidly changing reality, more and more of the economics fraternity opted for the former. The primary explanation of this is to be found in the process of institutionalization; practitioners of economics and the other social sciences became the captives first of the higher educational establishment, later of government and of business.

The importance of this institutionalization can be seen in the contemporary role of the social sciences on the American scene, the leading center of large-scale research. A large number of social scientists are employed in a staff capacity in government, nonprofit institutions, and private enterprises where they assist decision makers by assessing trends and pointing up alternative policies, but they function primarily as specialists who work on problems that others set for them. The decisions about which goals are to be pursued remain the prerogative of the politician or the executive, not the social scientist, who seldom challenges them. The analyst thus employed makes his technical skills available in exchange for a salary and career. There is little to distinguish the social scientist from the large number of other professionals and technically trained persons who, in an advanced economy, constitute an ever-larger segment of the hired work force. These professionals literally belong to the establishment.

What of the numbers who are based primarily at colleges, universities, and research centers where they instruct the young and pursue research? First, it should be recalled that it took the universities the larger part of a century to capture the social sciences, but captive they now are and are likely to remain.

The dynamism of the modern university is shaped by the intellectual orientation of the natural sciences which, with their emphasis on models, quantification, and prediction, early came to serve as prototypes for the social sciences. The success of experimental science was so impressive that social scientists opted for imitation.

This scientific ethos was reinforced when, shortly prior to World War I,

Max Weber's advocacy of "value-free" social research won the day. According to Weber and his followers, the social scientist must leave *his* values, politics, and social preferences behind when *he* studies society. The value orientations of groups and nations are very much within the orbit of inquiry. But the investigator must not permit *his* personal values to intrude. The description, ordering, analysis, and evaluation of social institutions, it was believed, should proceed according to the rules of inquiry prevailing in the natural sciences with their emphasis on hypothesis formulation and hypothesis testing, using empirical data wherever possible.

Even a cursory inspection of post-World War II developments in the social sciences attests to the continued dominance of this approach. Economics, sociology, political science, and social psychology are increasingly dominated by mathematical model building, sophisticated statistical methodology, and hypothesis testing. As social scientists became engrossed in problems of methodology, their concern with policy lessened. Their principal preoccupation has been to improve the models that engage their attention. For them, "relevance" has increasingly become the improvement of the scientific apparatus with which they work. Relevance in terms of social policy has receded into the background.

Although the Weberian prescription of value-free social science has been challenged by an occasional analyst, it has escaped serious attack since its most likely opponents, the Marxists, did not want to undermine their own claims that dialectical materialism was a "scientific" theory. But, as will soon be made clear, value-free social science is a contradiction in terms, since no social scientist can escape his own values.

Men create institutions to help them accomplish their collective aims, but once created, institutions take on a life of their own, and in the process both the goals that men pursue and the means that they employ are modified. At each stage, the members of the body politic must consider whether the existing social structures are responsive to their current needs and aspirations. Judgments about the effectiveness, efficiency, and equity of existing structures differ according to the qualifications of each evaluator. But no evaluator can be neutral in making assessments. As Aristotle noted, man is by nature a political animal, which means that he cannot stand outside the society to which he belongs.

Since there is always a less-than-perfect fit between the institutions that men have created and the effectiveness with which these institutions function, social inquiry is value-laden, not value-free. The investigator must select one rather than another problem for inquiry; likewise, he must decide how much time and effort to devote to exploring the subject he has

   The complex considerations involved in the search for equity and freedom confront the theorist with a stark choice. He either includes these values in his analysis or he accepts the fact that his work will be unable to talk
to these critical issues. Since men live only in societies, since cooperation
among them is critical for their survival and welfare, and since their willingness to cooperate depends in no small measure on their sense of equity,
a meaningful social analysis cannot skirt the distributional problem.
   The value position underlying the present analysis can now be formulated: a society must strive to reduce gross inequalities in the distribution of
opportunities and rewards for distinct but related reasons. The first relates
to the principle of stability. A society that values its survival must be able to
contain its dissidents. If an ever-larger number of its members come to view
the existing arrangements as inherently unjust, they will strive to topple the
existing structure, and eventually they will succeed. Next, justice is a value
in its own right. If we believe that all men are children of God, we must
view as inhuman and immoral a situation where one man's life is shortened
by lack of food while another's is prematurely ended by excessive self-in-
dulgence. Thirdly, a society concerned about its future must consider how
changes in the distributional pattern can contribute to the fuller development of human potential through the broadening of opportunities.
   Freedom presents a parallel challenge. Freedom has both a negative
and a positive connotation. Freedom implies that a person's inalienable
rights—to use the words of the Declaration of Independence—are not arbitrarily denied by those in authority. Positively, freedom implies that individuals have sufficient resources to enjoy broadened options.
   Some theorists hold that as long as men do not transgress the rules
which a society has established for its own protection, they are entitled to
accumulate as much property and power as they can. But here, too, as in
the case of justice, the stability principle, the common bond of humanity,
and considerations of social efficiency and effectiveness come into play. To
paraphrase Anatole France: to say that a poor man is as free as a rich man
to attend the opera conveys very little. The enjoyment of broadened options, a cornerstone of freedom, involves control not only of one's time but
also of resources without which people become bound to the unending task
of surviving. A society must ask whether the restraints on personal freedom
are so pervasive and oppressive that more and more persons will challenge
the existing arrangements and seek to upset them. As the long struggle over
slavery made clear, the right of every human being to control his own labor
takes precedence over the property rights of the slave owner. Finally, the
freedom of men to think, discuss, and publish what they believe should be

broadly tolerated. This freedom should not be arbitrarily constrained by those who exercise political power; no society can prosper if new and different ideas are arbitrarily repressed.

If justice and freedom are the goals of the good society, and we stipulate that they are, then the search to realize them must be seen for what it is—a process in which intermediate goals and mediating mechanisms are not fixed but are subject to continuing change as the society seeks to learn from its experiences. The third premise on which this work is predicated is the role of critical thought in the process of goal clarification and the selection of means to accomplish the stipulated goals. The dominant view holds that the social sciences have nothing to contribute to the clarification of goals; the position held here is the diametric opposite. It postulates that the principal tasks of the social scientist are to evaluate both the immediate objectives the society is pursuing and the institutions it has established and is modifying to accomplish them and to assess whether these objectives and methods are congruent with the ideals of a just society of free men. The contributions of investigators who perform these tasks with insight and responsibility will themselves become part of the ongoing process of goal setting and institution building, which is, and must remain, open-ended as long as men use critical thought to help them pursue their goals.

The thrust of this position is that social inquiry can justify its role and function only if it contributes to illuminating the problems and solutions which will enable a society to expand both social justice and individual freedom. The basic propositions so far delineated can be briefly recapitulated:

All social inquiry is concerned with values, since the investigator relies on his own values to help him to select his problem, determine his approach, and place his findings in context.

The twin objectives of decreasing inequity in opportunity and income distribution and enlarging the scope for the individual to shape and lead his own life are the hallmarks of social development.

The institutional structures which enable a society to pursue these primary goals cannot be specified once and for all, but must be continually redefined and reformulated in light of each society's experiences.

Critical thought has a unique role to play in these clarifications and redefinitions, including the specification of intermediate goals and the mechanisms to achieve them. A social science which limits itself to tracing how existing institutions function is twice deficient. It fails to contribute to the clarification of goals and thereby helps to reinforce those in place. It further deprives the society of the criticism it needs to make the existing institutions more responsive to a changing reality and changing aspirations.

The human resources approach emphasizes the time-conditioned nature of all social goals and institutions. No matter how well each has served the society, in a world in which change is endemic, critical thought must be brought into play to help redefine the goals and redesign the institutions so that they can become more responsive to changing circumstances and aspirations.

The following chapter demonstrates that the processes of manpower development and utilization can be effectively analyzed only within a broad framework that includes four major systems—the value structure, the government, the economy, and the manpower development institutions. The concern of the present chapter is to explore the values that inform these major systems on which a society must rely in its efforts to expand justice and freedom.

We will consider each system in turn.

First, only a society that has reached a certain stage in its development will recognize the desirability of pursuing the ends of expanding justice and freedom. Unless it has reached such a stage of commitment, the ensuing analysis of the reinforcing values that can assist in implementing these objectives is irrelevant.

A second premise relates to the society's basic stance toward experimentation. Unless it looks upon change as more than a threat to its established ways and sees it also as an opportunity to narrow the gap between its goals and their realization, it will hesitate to alter its basic institutions.

Thirdly, a society must be sufficiently sophisticated to appreciate that not every ill that it faces justifies its intervening, that interventions can fail, and that even if they prove successful the initial policies and programs will require modification as experience is accumulated.

Finally, the society must have reached a point in its development where it knows how to temper strong emotions with disciplined analyses in deciding among alternatives by weighing the evidence and seeking a balance between risks and returns.

These, in brief, are the basic conditions that must characterize a society if it is to have a reasonable chance of success in its pursuit of greater justice and freedom. Assuming that they are in place we can proceed to explore the value orientations that must inform the three other major systems to assure a favorable outcome.

A first requirement of government is that it be capable of eliciting a consensus among its members without resort to violence and under conditions that assure tolerance for an opposition that abides by the rules. A people who live under a government which can arbitrarily deprive them of their lives, their freedom, or their property will plan accordingly and deploy much of their energies and substance to protecting themselves from untoward consequences. Men must enjoy reasonable security of person and property if they are not to be diminished in spirit and action.

Government is a precondition for social development. Only through government can men accomplish common objectives that require collective action. If they participate in the selection of those who govern them, they may broaden their freedom by expanding the tasks of government. Unless they believe that enlarging the scope of government will result in a gain to themselves, they will hesitate to add to its powers. They may err and find that, having enlarged the powers of government, their opportunities have in fact been not broadened, but narrowed. But a citizenry that makes laws can also, on the basis of experience, change them. The critical issue is whether they are able to play an active role in the political process. A government that is chosen and controlled by the electorate is an extension of the individual citizen. Such a government does not stand in opposition to the individual, as a constraining influence on his freedom, but as a collaborator capable of enlarging his opportunities.

If all power were concentrated in the representatives elected by the voters and in the officialdom that operates the state apparatus, there would be reason to fear that those in control of the decision-making mechanisms might sooner or later succeed in pursuing primarily their own interests. The larger the scope of governmental decision making and the more technical the issues being decided, the greater is this danger; witness the difficulties of the legislature, even more those of the public, in attempting to assess alternatives in the arenas of defense, intelligence, scientific research, and nuclear technology. Since effective power depends on many elements—organization, knowledge, money, control of opportunity, and the distribution of rewards and punishments—a society concerned with the enhancement of justice and freedom must prevent the few from gaining control of the levers of power.

If the use of force to gain consensus is proscribed by tradition, the only alternative is persuasion based on freedom of discussion and dissemination of information. Therefore, a critical test of the integrity of government is its approach to communications. If those in power are able to put forward their views and deny this privilege to others, the decisions of the electorate will be uninformed. If men are prevented from hearing opposing opinions and arguments, they are not free to make a meaningful choice. They will be puppets whose opinions and votes are manipulated by those who control the flow of information. Reasonable access for all groups to the communications system is an essential precondition for the proper functioning of a good society.

There is one other foundation of effective government. Every society needs a feedback system which will enable it to alter or reverse earlier decisions. Since the outcomes of social intervention in the form of new laws, new regulations, and new procedures are always problematic, and since the conditions which evoke such intervention are subject to change, it is essential that a society have built-in mechanisms through which it can reappraise the results of earlier actions and decide to continue, modify, or rescind them.

Effective evaluation devices are difficult to institutionalize, since the fortunes of politicians depend on the electorate's approving their earlier actions. Although the circumstances which led those in power to act in a specific fashion may have changed, although too little time may have passed for the new interventions to become fully operative, and although the evidence is inconclusive, the opposition will not be constrained from seeking to persuade the electorate that a governmental program was faulty in conception, in execution, or both. Those in office who recognize their vulnerability will be more interested in keeping damaging data out of the hands of their opponents and the public than in encouraging an objective evaluation, since they know that the electorate will make a decision for or against them long before all the evidence is at hand and sifted. The importance of establishing and maintaining feedback mechanisms for the critical assessment of public policies and programs remains a major challenge to all democratic governments, particularly since officials may seek to rationalize the need for secrecy on the grounds of national security or on similar grounds.

The foregoing discussion has directed attention to the powerful value premises that underlie our conception of the role of government in a progressive society. An effective government has the responsibility to:

Achieve consensus in an environment that proscribes violence and that provides for the participation of all members of the society in different aspects of the decision-making process.

Prevent concentration of excessive power in the hands of any group and keep access to economic opportunity as open as possible, which will, among other benefits, inhibit the coercion of political dissidents.

Provide all political groups with reasonable access to the channels of communications to facilitate open and free discussion, the only true basis for meaningful citizen participation.

Experiment to strengthen feedback mechanisms so that policy and programmatic changes can be made in light of experience.

The value premises by which the functioning of the economic system is to be judged involve no fewer than six distinct criteria spanning a broad range from adequate employment opportunities to a lessened inequality in the distribution of rewards.

A society whose economy fails to provide employment opportunities for all who are able and willing to work falls short of meeting a basic precondition for justice and freedom, since underemployed and unemployed persons often lack sufficient income for sustenance without which no individual is truly free. Poverty, like racism, can restrict a person's freedom. The availability of work is a first requirement of a properly functioning economy, and as more women seek employment out of the home, a society must strive to make jobs available to all persons who need or desire to work.

Men cooperate in economic activities because they know that, through specialization and scale, they can enjoy more benefits with less effort. A primary challenge to every economy therefore is to develop organizations and mechanisms which will facilitate cooperation among individuals and groups and thus add to the effective use of human and physical resources. The more efficient production and distribution of goods and services remain a basic challenge to the economy.

Important as the criterion of efficiency is, however, it does not stand alone. To elicit the cooperation on which it depends, an economy must be responsive to the demand for equity. Otherwise, those who feel exploited will withhold part of their efforts and will be less productive than they might otherwise be. Analyses of equity are particularly complex in a society which values individual initiative and which approves personal accumulation, since there is no broad agreement about how best to apportion the profits which accrue from an enlarged output which results from the combined contributions of various groups, including workers, managers, and stockholders.

Although equity considerations are complex and do not permit a simple solution, the social scientist dare not ignore them. One of the limitations of economics is that issues of distribution have been neglected or treated in a banal manner. For instance, the dominant view is that every contributor to output is paid according to his marginal contribution, but proof of this generalization is adduced by arguing in a circle and inferring the value of the resource from the reward that it earns.

Another criterion is the ability of the economy to avoid wide fluctuations in activity, since such fluctuations result in the waste of human and physical resources. An important test of the performance of an economy is the size of the gap between its available resources and their effective use.

There are two additional demands which a well functioning economy should meet. The first is to provide opportunities for the continued growth of the skills and competences of the work force. At forty-five, people should be able to perform more effectively than they did at twenty. The extent to which an economy enables the members of the work force to broaden and deepen their skills and to make effective use of them is a critical measure of its performance.

The final measure of an economy is its effect on the lives of those who spend so many hours on the factory floor or in the office. To neglect the interaction between the worker and his work is to overlook a major segment of a person's life. At the end of every working day, a man's physical, emotional, intellectual, and even moral energies have been consumed, conserved, replenished, or eroded. At the end of every day, a worker has either grown or been diminished. Whether the workday is good or bad should be a matter of concern to the social investigator; its importance cannot be minimized with the comment that, after all, men must work if they are to eat, and work is not to be confused with play. As men escape from living at a precarious margin of subsistence, the question of how they spend their time, particularly their time at work, becomes a critical determinant of the quality of life they lead. A related facet of this new concern extends beyond the workplace to the role that the larger society must play in ensuring that, in increasing current output, the environment is not permanently damaged, for this would place unconscionable costs on later generations.

We have found that the demands on the economy are many and complex. They include:

The establishment of a sufficient number of jobs so that all who desire and are able to work, women as well as men, have the opportunity to do so.

Arrangements under which men cooperate in the pursuit of their economic goals which are conducive to efficiency.

The establishment of equitable rewards for the different contributors to output.

Freedom from severe fluctuations in the level of economic activity.

Work so structured that opportunities are available for people to add to their skills and competences.

Conditions of the workplace that add rather than detract from the quality of the worker's life.

The structuring of production and distribution so that social benefits are increased and social costs reduced.

Since the principal aim of this work is to delineate the manpower development system and to explicate its operation, only brief attention will be directed at this point to summarizing the value premises which underlie it.

The family is the cornerstone of the manpower development institutions. Unless parents are able and willing to put forth the effort required to nurture their offspring, their children will not be properly prepared for life and work. If esoteric experiments such as the kibbutz in Israel are put to one side, there is no alternative to leaving the onus on the family as the responsible unit for rearing children. However, there are important differences among societies in the assistance which they provide to the family in its rearing task.

Because families differ in their abilities to meet their responsibilities by virtue of differences in educational background, emotional stability, and economic resources, the developmental opportunities available to their children vary. It has been observed that if a child chooses the right parents, his future will take care of itself. Even in affluent societies many families are unable on their own to rear their young properly. Because of a variety of lacks—competence, health, income, emotional stability—many families need help in raising their children.

Societies with surplus disposable income must use part of it to provide support to parents who need assistance and, on rare occasions, to arrange for the transfer of children to foster homes. Without such help, many children, by accident of birth, will be unable to obtain access to opportunities available to other young people whose parents are able to meet their responsibilities.

Affluent societies must also provide access to educational and training opportunities so that every young person will be able to acquire the general and specific knowledge which is essential to enable him to participate effectively as an adult—as a citizen, a worker, and a parent. Since young people differ markedly in their interest in and ability to master different types of knowledge and in their ability to extract value from different developmental experiences, a responsive society will seek to provide a range of learning opportunities to help meet the needs of each new generation. To try to force all young people into a single mold will ensure that many will not reach adulthood prepared to cope effectively with their responsibilities.

No society to date has succeeded in providing a desirable range of learning opportunities. Each has encountered difficulties on one or more fronts: the provision of adequate facilities, staff, curricula, planning, and experimentation aimed at adapting resources to the needs of different groups of pupils, adequate articulation between school and employing institutions. To date, no society has met the test of fairness. Each child is entitled not to be arbitrarily cut off from access to opportunities, irrespective of the status and competence of his parents. In fact, children whose families are seriously deprived have a special claim for consideration.

Even if a society were to provide more support to disadvantaged families, many young people would complete their adolescence poorly prepared to assume their adult responsibilities. There are just too many places for slippage within the family, between family and school, between school and work, and between rebellious youngsters and the law enforcement authorities to enable all young people to make a smooth transition to adulthood. A responsive society must be concerned not only with the needs of adolescents but also with other groups in the process of transition from one sector to another, such as veterans, persons being released from prison, and patients discharged from long-term hospitals or other therapeutic environments such as drug rehabilitation centers. No society can eliminate failure, but a good society should attempt to provide a second chance for those who fail a first time.

Most people, with the help and guidance of family and friends, are able to negotiate the complex institutions that constitute a modern society. However, the effectiveness with which they do so is influenced by the presence or absence of facilitating mechanisms. Schools without competent guidance and counseling services, a labor market without an effective employment service, and a high-consumption economy without consumer protection agencies will fall short of performing at or close to their optimal levels. Consequently, a society which invests heavily in basic institutions aimed at the effective development and utilization of its human resources should be alert to the necessity of providing informational and related support services so that the public can make more effective use of these institutions. As a society becomes more specialized and the number of its special-purpose institutions increases, the role of informational services which can help link the individual to the ever larger complex of institutions becomes critical.

This summary consideration of the manpower development system stipulated the following:

> The family plays a critical role in rearing its children and in laying the foundations on which their performance in adulthood is based.
>
> The society must invest a significant part of its disposable income to

provide special support for families which are unable, on their own, to assure their children a reasonable start in life.

The society must underwrite a broadly diversified educational and training system so that it can engage the interests and develop the potential of all youngsters, thereby helping to ensure that they will acquire a range of skills and competences.

The basic preparatory system must be supplemented by other institutions so that young persons as well as adults who have encountered difficulties have a "second chance."

The society must collect and disseminate information about the operations of its principal developmental and employment structures, and it must provide counseling and related services so that individuals can better formulate and implement their plans.

Early in this chapter the proposition was advanced that the values which inform the approach of the social scientist determine the problems he selects, the methodology employed, and the conclusions for policy which are drawn from the findings. The purpose of this chapter has been to set forth one investigator's views of the values that should guide a dynamic democratic society which seeks to expand the freedom of its members while encouraging their fuller participation in its work and providing equitable rewards for their efforts.

Many social theorists hold values at variance with those just elaborated. Some deny the existence of a moral imperative or the collective competence of a society to enlarge the freedom of its members and to broaden the opportunities for those who are currently deprived. Others place a higher value on social stability or individual opportunity than on the redistribution of rewards and privilege. And many would deny that the social scientist should be concerned with advocacy and change.

However, differences in value premises are not the critical issue here. Rather the contention is advanced that every social investigator has an obligation to set forth his value premises so that his analytic structure and policy recommendations can be seen in context. This has been the aim here so that the reader will not have to ferret out for himself the assumptions that underlie this work.

To go one step further: the central concern of this book is the critical role of human resources in providing the motive power for the economy and the direction for the society. All institutional arrangements should be designed to further the well-being and welfare of the human beings who, living in association with each other, constitute the society. Of course, many societies, in fact most of them up to this point in time, have not been so oriented but have reflected instead the control of the many by the few. If, as has just been postulated, societies are to be measured by their contribution to improving the quality of life of their members, primary attention must be directed to how well their institutions serve the whole citizenry.

Accordingly, this book provides a framework for analyzing the alternative approaches that societies can follow in developing and utilizing the capacities and skills of their members. While human beings are the critical actors in the process of social development, it is their well-being and welfare which are the goals toward which all development is, or should be, directed.

A question that has been skirted until now should be at least briefly confronted. Does the value position put forward here hold only for the democratic-private enterprise economies of the West and Japan, or does it have applicability for nations with quite different social and economic systems? The simplest answer is that the principal criteria used here reflect primarily the experience of the Western world. While important differences attach to what they are seeking to achieve in the near and far term, most of the developing and developed nations alike confront comparable tasks of modifying and changing their governmental, economic, and manpower development systems in order to be better able to accomplish their priority goals. Therefore, the human resources approach has a wide reach.

Since the organization and functioning of the principal institutions which condition the development and utilization of human competence have not been the primary concern of earlier investigations, the present work is directed to structuring such a framework. Since such an effort, by definition, must be exploratory, certain consequences follow. The analytic structure cannot be developed beyond an initial stage. It will inevitably draw heavily on the investigator's knowledge and experience. There will be no opportunity to test the tentative formulations beyond assessing how well historical and comparative data confirm the findings. These are stringent limitations, but if scholarly inquiry is a cumulative process, then initial efforts are required before improved studies can be undertaken.

The final question bears on the potential of a theory of human resources to contribute to public policy. If the analytic framework hereinafter elaborated does in fact provide a new understanding of how skill is developed and utilized, then it should prove useful for policy. All societies, poor as well as rich, expend a significant proportion of their national income on human resources development. Their actions are guided by theory, although in most instances the theory is implicit. This chapter has insisted that social inquiry and social action should be in tandem. Improved theory

therefore should contribute to improved policy, although it is only one of the critical elements. To claim more would be naive; to claim less would be to misread the process of social change.

· 3 ·

The Manpower Development System

THIS CHAPTER WILL LAY THE FOUNDATION for the analysis that follows, which is directed to explicating how people, in different types of societies, accumulate skills and use them. In carrying out this task, the principal institutions that constitute the manpower development system and the principal functions they perform will be identified. Then, the relation of the manpower development system to the other principal societal systems—values, government, and the economy—will be sketched and their interdependence traced. No important social system can function alone; the multiple roles that men perform as they respond to the constraints that limit them and to the dreams that inspire them are rooted not in one system alone, but in all that shape their actions.

Before entering upon the delineation of the principal institutions that constitute the manpower development system, the centrality of the institutional approach which underlies this work will be set forth briefly. Institutions are social structures that have evolved in response to a people's experiences and which order and direct their behavior. The institutions that men have created are the hallmark of their civilizations. It is impossible even to conceptualize a society without institutions, and the core of social analysis is to understand how these institutions develop, function, and are transformed.

This emphasis on the importance of institutions does not preclude concern for the individual. The two are ineluctably linked. A society consists of a group of individuals who, through exposures to the same institutions, acquire many qualities and characteristics in common. Once we realize that the lives people lead are largely determined by the institutions to which they have been exposed, from their parental family to the national state, the imperative for social analysis to focus on institutions becomes clear.

Institutions are the vehicles through which men are able to carry out a wide range of functions, from caring for their young to transferring property after death. Their strength derives from the fact that they are the products of a people's shared experience and are the social repositories of lessons learned. Their survival attests to the fact that they continue to perform essential social functions.

Although their strength derives from their having been validated by history and reinforced by their social roles, institutions are not immune to the forces of change. They are often challenged from within, and they are always vulnerable to forces in the external environment.

The process of social change involves the transformation of institutions, that is, the adaptation of existing structures, the establishment of new ones, and the decline and disappearance of those that no longer discharge their functions effectively. In contrast to the ideologue who sees the core of social change in the transformation of ideas and beliefs that people cherish, the social realist recognizes that significant and lasting social change involves the restructuring of basic institutions in accordance with whatever new ideas men come to accept.

This parallelism between changes in ideas and institutions has intrigued students of revolutions, who have noted substantial continuities cheek by jowl with major reconstructions. Precommunist Russia was characterized by a deeply patriotic people, steeped in orthodoxy, ruled by an imperialistically oriented autocracy which looked with envy and suspicion on the outside world. Much has changed, but much has remained the same. The czar and his court have been replaced by the party and the politburo; communism has filled the role of the Greek Orthodox religion; Mother Russia continues to command the allegiance of the masses; the leadership is still expansionist; foreign ideas continue to evoke suspicion; the secret police remain the right arm of those in power; anti-Semitism has not been extirpated; tensions between White Russians and the other nationalities have not been resolved.

On the value front there are both striking continuities and important changes as a result of the Russian Revolution. Nationalism, orthodoxy, and absolutism provide strong links with the past. On the other hand, egalitarianism and materialism represent powerful new thrusts. Although a revolution implies major changes in the structure and functioning of a society, many critical elements have changed relatively little: power remains concentrated in the hands of a small group; political opposition is barred;

thought control is strictly enforced; the secret police stand above the law; terrorism against individuals and groups is still a weapon.

The leaders of the Chinese revolution have also demonstrated considerable skill in drawing strength from the continuities in their culture while fashioning new structures aimed at reshaping their goals and activities.

Now the principal tasks that have been set for this chapter may be undertaken—to outline the constituent elements of the manpower development system and to relate that system to the other principal social systems with which it interacts. The first task is to define the manpower development system, since its existence, functioning, and significance have not been previously recognized, surely not adequately delineated.

In outline, the manpower development system consists of a series of major institutions loosely linked to each other which together are responsible for teaching the skills and competences needed by a population; which provide the conditions under which people are able to use their skills and further develop them; and which assure those who are unable to support themselves, either because of their lack of skills or inability to put them to use, the goods and services essential for their survival.

In a traditional agricultural society, the manpower development system is coexistent with the extended family. What the child or young person needs to learn so that he can assume his responsibilities as an adult, both as a worker and as a member of the community, is taught to him by his elders. His family is not only his instructor but in many cases eventually also his employer. When a young person reaches an age when he can make a contribution to the running of the farm or the household, he joins the work group and receives increasingly important assignments geared to his age, skill, and competence.

An outstanding characteristic of advanced societies is the extent to which the several dimensions of the skill acquisition and utilization processes have been splintered among a group of independent institutions which are loosely linked to each other. The family, generally the nuclear family, continues to have primary responsibility for the nurturing and initial socialization of the child, but by the time a child reaches the age of three, surely the age of six, the school assumes a major complementary role, particularly in the development of the child's cognitive skills. Since even young children spend about half of their day in school, as members of a group under the control of a teacher, they are continuously learning how to conduct themselves in relation to their peers and elders. The social learning that accompanies their formal classroom instruction in basic cognitive skills becomes an important element in their later capacity to function effectively as workers and citizens.

The formal educational system is subdivided into several relatively freestanding parts—lower, intermediate, and higher—with further differentiation based on specialized curricula and particularized goals. The extent to which an individual is able to progress through the several echelons of the educational system depends, as will be made clear in Part II, on a complex set of interacting factors—personal, family, societal. Although there are connecting links between family and school, such as laws which require that all children be enrolled in school at a certain age and remain until their fifteenth or sixteenth year, the transition between school and work is less clearly defined, particularly in the United States, where the individual (and his family) have the primary responsibility to locate his initial job and to find another if he is dissatisfied with the first.

During periods when military conscription is in force, the armed services form another element of the manpower development system, at least for young men who are able to meet the physical and mental screening criteria. For varying periods of time, in the United States usually a period of two to four years, young men in uniform undergo a mixed regimen of instruction, duty assignments, and a highly specialized type of socialization. There are many parallels between military and civilian life (especially in the absence of combat), but there are also striking differences. A recruit selected for electronics training may pursue a combination of training and assignments in the military that would closely parallel his experiences in civilian life were he to pursue the same occupational path. Of course there is no such parallel for the infantryman or the submariner.

The next critical institution in the manpower development system is the array of employing organizations from the family-owned enterprise to the multinational corporation. Whether or not an individual who has acquired skills will have an opportunity to use them in the first instance and whether or not he will be able to add to his skills and competences depends on his success in finding a job opening and in being hired. His preparatory efforts will be rewarded by the type of job he attains and the career he pursues. A strong preparation does not assure a successful adjustment to work. If a society is steeped in prejudice, a well-trained member of a minority group may be unable to obtain a suitable position. And if the economy is seriously depressed, as was the economy of the United States in the 1930's even recently licensed physicians may be forced to accept temporary positions in other fields because they are unable to establish a practice.

As suggested above, the type of job an individual is able to obtain is important not only for the opportunities it provides for him to make use of his skills but, equally important, also for the opportunities that it may open up through on-the-job or formal training and through structured assignments to add to his competences. A critical aspect of the human resources system is the dependence of further skill development on learning opportunities in the work setting.

Every advanced nation has developed institutions whose principal functions are to provide training and employment for most of its citizens and income support for adults who experience difficulty in the world of work because of limited skills, physical or emotional disabilities, or other personal or social handicaps or because of a high level of unemployment in the economy. These institutions include employment exchanges and adult training institutions to help vulnerable individuals improve their employability, and social security and welfare systems to provide those still more vulnerable with essential income support.

Consider, in contrast, the absence of comparable institutions in most societies at an early stage of economic development. One of the striking differences between a traditional low-income society and an advanced industrial state is the condition of the individual who is unable to work or who cannot find a job. In a poor country such an individual has only two prospects. He must be cared for by members of his family, or he must seek alms. Only in the face of an overwhelming national calamity, such as famine or a war, will government step in to help. The manpower development system in a traditional agricultural society consists of the extended family, supplemented by a poorly functioning educational system, and a relatively small group of employers in the modern sector.

The differences in the breadth and depth of the skills and competences of the populations of developing and developed nations hold the clue to the substantial failure of most post-World War II programs of international aid aimed at speeding the economic growth of traditional societies. Many statesmen and scholars, in both the developing and developed nations, assumed that the key to speeding the development of the low-income nations was through the transfer of substantial amounts of capital to enable them to expand and deepen their infrastructure and otherwise add to their pool of productive resources.

But experience revealed that the weakness of the manpower development system was a major drag on the modernization process. In the three large Asian nations, India, Indonesia, and Pakistan, which before the establishment of Bangladesh in the early 1970s accounted for approximately 800 million people, or a quarter of the world's population, the pace of industrialization and modernization was slowed by the small numbers of managerial, technical, and skilled personnel.

There are many reasons that Asian farmers have encountered serious difficulties in taking advantage of the Green Revolution, but widespread illiteracy has severely compounded their problem of calculating whether the costs of additional inputs could be covered by additional sales at a profitable price.

The Dutch, during their centuries of rule in Indonesia, had deliberately blocked all natives from obtaining either managerial or professional skills, with the result that, after the country had achieved its independence, there were only a few trained people available to help operate the new government and rebuild the war-weakened economy. The military oligarchy that ruled Pakistan until its civil war had pursued a policy of minimal educational expenditures on the assumption that what really counted was an effective coalition between the military and economic elites.

In India, the planners pressed ahead with large capital investments in basic plants—steel, machine tools, fertilizer—often with American or Russian aid. The planners had no doubt that this was the path to economic independence and a rising standard of living. But the record revealed otherwise. The basic error of the planners was that they did not take account of the importance of entrepreneurial skill and the time required to build large organizations to the point where they could function effectively. The Indians further complicated their task by adhering to a political ideology which made them wary about trusting their own moneyed elite, which made it difficuilt for foreign companies to bring trained management into the country, and which mistakenly assumed that a member of the Indian Administrative Service who had a good record in a bureaucratic post could run a modern steel mill with 50,000 employees.

In retrospect, it is clear that even if the developed nations had been much more liberal with their grants and loans, most traditional societies would nevertheless have encountered major obstacles in their economic development because of the generally low skill levels of the population. Capital alone, even in greater amounts, could not have assured a rapid and continuing rate of economic development. It takes decades, even generations, to raise significantly the skill level of a population and to build substantial organizations capable of effectively deploying substantial economic resources.

The criticality of the manpower development system can be further illuminated by considering briefly the experience of Germany and Japan as they rebuilt their societies after their defeats in World War II.

At the end of World War II, West Germany was threatened with large-scale starvation. Much of her industrial structure had been damaged or destroyed and she had lost the flower of her young men. Moreover, she had to contend with the implacable hatred of her neighbors. Yet within a decade, Germany was well on the way to recovery, and before a second decade had passed, she had regained her position in the forefront of the industrial nations of the world.

Some believe that the wellspring of this phenomenal turnaround was in the conservative economic policies that Ludwig Erhard followed, whereby he avoided inflation and balance-of-payment deficits, while others cite the liberal assistance made available by the United States, particularly under the Marshall Plan. The more likely explanation, however, is in the competence and zeal of German management, workers, and bureaucrats. Although the denazification program forced many of the former leaders into retirement, the knowledge required to operate a modern state, a large corporation, the banking and insurance systems, and the other parts of the socioeconomic infrastructure was sufficiently diffused that, within a few years, the key institutions were once again back in operation. Imports of capital speeded the process of rehabilitation, but the know-how required to operate a sophisticated economy had survived the physical destruction that had been visited on Germany. With her human resources diminished but still highly competent, she was able to rebuild all that had been destroyed.

The recovery of Japan followed much the same script. The physical destruction suffered by Japan was even worse than that inflicted on Germany. What the bombs had failed to level, fire had burned to ashes. Here, too, thousands who had held high military or civilian office were barred from active participation in economic or political activities. But there were many well-trained people one or two echelons down from the top ready to assume responsibility. It was only a few years before much of the former infrastructure was back in place, and new organizations, skilled in production and marketing, were establishing a strong position in the domestic market, quickly followed by successful expansion overseas. Liberal aid from the United States government, reinforced by several thousand contracts with private American firms, which gave Japanese industry access to advanced technology, greatly facilitated the rate of rehabilitation and recovery. Once again, as in Germany, it was the large numbers of managerial, technical, and skilled personnel with a deep understanding of the dynamics of a modern society and economy which assured that the assistance that was provided was put to effective use.

Now that the manpower development system has been outlined and its importance for economic development illustrated in two contrasting instances, we are in a position to move on to the second half of this chapter's assignment, which is to sketch how this system relates to the other principal societal systems—the value structure, government, and the economy. The values of a society exercise a critical influence on the manner in which its human resources are developed and utilized. According to Maimonides, the leader of the Hispanic Jewish community in the twelfth century, the preferred division of a man's day was three hours of work and nine hours of study of the holy books. Survey data reveal that many American adults read only one book a year.

Unfriendly critics writing about Ireland in the eighteenth century, noted with amazement that the Irish had more holidays than workdays—an allocation of effort which they found hard to credit in light of the low level of material well-being of the Irish peasantry.

The traders from West European countries who sought to open markets in Africa, Asia, and Latin America during the nineteenth century were astounded by what they referred to as the lack of desire of the native populations for material possessions, a condition that has a counterpart in the present-day traditions of some agricultural societies. In the absence of a desire for a better life, there was little prospect of the traders' organizing the natives into a disciplined work force willing to exchange their labor for wages which could be used to purchase goods previously not available to them.

In contrast, Americans are so consumption-oriented that they carry a heavy burden of debt so that they can enjoy possessions before they can afford to own them outright; they commit a sizable proportion of their future working time and wages to paying for goods and services that they have already used.

These few illustrations indicate the extent to which societies differ in their values concerning work, material accumulation, and consumption. Economics has operated on the assumption that there is a Scotsman inside every man, in every country, past, present, and future. However, we know that societies attach different importance to four critical values—rationality, egalitarianism, materialism, and individualism—and these differences in turn play a critical role in the manner in which societies deal with their manpower resources. The following paragraphs suggest some of the important linkages between these potent values and the manner in which different societies approach and resolve the problem of developing and utilizing their human resources.

For most of recorded history, societies have been organized around a set of supernatural beliefs beyond the arena of demonstration or proof. Their faith gives meaning and direction to their lives. One consequence of this almost universal belief in the supernatural has been to place the authority and legitimacy of the leadership beyond the reach of discussion or action. The ordering of society was preordained: men had their roles to play. Many were destined to be hewers of wood or drawers of water; a few would serve as warriors or priests; and one would serve as ruler. In such ordered societies, in which it was believed that a man's place was assigned to him in heaven and determined at the moment of his birth, few men attempted to alter their conditions. In a society in which the relations among people and classes were fixed, there was little tolerance for man-directed change.

All this has been altered, however, with the commitment of Western nations to rationalism and scientism. These countries have become increasingly committed to the view that men can enrich their personal lives and strengthen their societies by pursuing knowledge. An openness to inquiry, through the use of trained intelligence, has resulted in a new perspective concerning the malleability of man. Instead of maintaining a fixed and rigid position toward the inherent qualities of people and their institutions, scholars have subjected to searching inquiry more and more aspects of human and social experience, and the results have led to radical changes in both thought and action. This revolution from belief in the supernatural to the rational, from authority to science, and from immutable order to potential change has been one of the transforming events of modern times, one which is indelibly altering the way in which human resources are perceived and treated.

A second critical value which plays a role in the way in which a society deals with its human resources is its view of elitism or egalitarianism. An elitist society sees talent and competence as gifts of the gods or the ascriptions of those who are born to high position. Such a society is a little concerned with the mass of the population and even less with broadening opportunities for them to become educated and trained. During the many centuries of its dominance, the Catholic church attempted to limit the knowledge of how to read and interpret the Holy Writ to a small number of leaders who could be relied upon to fend off unsettling ideas, often the precursors to social upheaval. One objective of an elitist leadership is to maintain control over the society by acting as gatekeepers to knowledge and opportunity.

The belief that all men are entitled to share in the good things of life, which first came to the fore at the end of the eighteenth century, has become widely diffused. Accordingly, all political leaders pay at least lip service to the doctrine that all men are entitled to have access to the opportunities and to share in the rewards the society provides. This doctrine does not deny that some men will continue to prosper more than others by virtue of their superior talent, wealth, or status. But the good society is one in which inequality is being rapidly and markedly reduced. At a minimum, every man should have the opportunity to develop his potential. When opportunity is made generally available, there is less concern about the fact that some men will earn more than others.

A third value orientation about which societies differ is the importance attached to the material aspects of life. In advanced societies, the accumulation of goods is a major objective to which people direct a great deal of their time and energies. Wealth accumulation is a central goal. In other societies, the dominant value system ascribes greater weight to what a person is and what he is striving to become. The emphasis is inward, contemplative, more directed to bringing men into closer harmony with nature and God.

The preference for the spiritual life over the material life is often less a matter of choice than necessity. People who live in straitened circumstances are not likely to develop a philosophy of materialism; instead, they seek to moderate the stark reality that bounds their existence by beliefs and practices which can help them ignore, at least for a time, their depressing circumstances.

In materialistically oriented societies, the economy is considered to be an engine of development capable of providing more consumer goods and services for all citizens. In nonmaterialistic societies, there is an underlying assumption that the poverty or near poverty which is their most conspicuous characteristic cannot be altered. In the first case, a concern with human resources is always present, since the society perceives that the progress of the economy is closely linked to raising the productivity of the work force. But a developing society has no way of accomplishing this result.

The fourth and most important difference in values relates to the role of individualism. Strong collectivist societies, such as Communist Russia or the People's Republic of China, are concerned with raising the competence of their people if only to speed the realization of their new goals. But these governments are selective about which skills they encourage; they develop only those which they consider essential. For example, the Soviet leadership encourages the training of engineers but has interdicted the training of psychoanalysts.

Although individualistically oriented societies have been committed to establishing freedom of occupational choice, they have fallen short, often seriously, in fulfilling this commitment by failing to remove the barriers to higher education that open the gates to preferred careers. In contrast, a communist society which is growing rapidly, such as the U.S.S.R., despite its preoccupation with matching skills to national goals, may provide many previously excluded groups with opportunities to enter preferred occupations. Here, as elsewhere, one must look behind the ideology to test the reality.

We have seen that societies differ in the emphasis they place on rationality, equality, materialism, and individualism. Each of these major value orientations is linked to the importance that different societies attach to the development and utilization of their human resources. A society which is rooted in a rigid caste structure or in the cultivation of the religious and aesthetic is less likely than a materialistic society to consider its human resources as a principal means for expanding the welfare of the individual as well as that of the group.

The second societal system with which the manpower development system interacts is that of government. From this vantage the following four dimensions must be explored: the extent to which government is representative of all the people or of a small group which has control of the levers of power; the effectiveness with which the governmental apparatus discharges its multiple functions which affect manpower development and utilization; the extent to which government can affect the level of employment; and the extent to which government is able and willing to alter the life chances of those who are disadvantaged as a result of personal, family, or other handicaps.

When a government is representative of the entire citizenry, where those who govern are chosen from among the body politic and lose their right to rule when they fall out of favor, the elected officials are under continuing pressure to adopt policies aimed at broadening opportunities for many groups in the society. This does not preclude the majority's seeking to deny a minority certain privileges and benefits, but the logic of participatory government is to broaden its reach to include all citizens. Its human resources policy is shaped accordingly.

When a small elite is in control of a government, those in power usually seek to restrict opportunity except when, as in Mandarin China, they open limited opportunities to those whose assistance they require.

A second consideration relates to the effectiveness of government. A government with the best intentions cannot contribute effectively to the development and utilization of the nation's human resources if it has limited revenues, incompetent officials, and poorly functioning institutions and mechanisms. These deficiencies explain why many developing nations have been unable to deliver on their promises to educate their citizenry, improve their health, and speed their economic well-being. If the terrain is large and the people over whom government exercises dominion belong to diverse groups, as in India, the government will find it difficult to provide effective services. It is one thing for a senior official in New Delhi to sign a paper establishing a fertilizer plant; it is another matter for the plant to be built and fertilizer produced and sold.

The governments of the older nation-states in the West are better positioned. Over the years they have developed considerable expertise in the provision of public services; they have large resources at their command; they have considerable freedom to innovate and maneuver. All Western governments are increasingly committed to strengthening their policies and programs aimed at enhancing the skills and competences of their people.

Two other factors bear on the impact of government on a nation's human resources. Some governments are in good position to determine the aggregate demand for labor. Communist Russia does this through central planning; the less-controlled industrial societies of the West (including Japan) rely on a composite of fiscal-monetary-budgetary and related economic measures to accomplish the same objective. The governments of all advanced economics are constantly experimenting with new ways of assuring that only small numbers of their people are unemployed.

In contrast, weak governments, characterized by a lack of resources, popular support, and expertise, can do little to speed the growth of their economies and less to raise the level of employment and income. A weak government is precluded from establishing an effective human resources policy.

While strong governments often fail to provide an adequate range and quality of services to facilitate the development and utilization of their people's skills and competences, most advanced societies have fashioned a large number of specialized institutions that contribute significantly to the more effective use of their human resources. Poorly organized and poorly financed governments can do little in this regard. Moreover, such investments as they are able to make to strengthen their manpower development institutions often have limited value because they address the wrong problems or use the wrong methods.

Four significant ways in which the governmental structure interacts with the nation's manpower development have been identified. The more representative and responsive the government, the more capable it is of assisting in developing the potential of the entire population. The more competent the bureaucracy, the more effective its manpower programming. The greater the capacity of government to influence the level and direction of economic activity, the more it will be able to provide employment opportunities for all who want to work. And, finally, the stronger the government, the better able it is to put into place a group of manpower institutions that provide direct and backup support for people who are seeking to develop and utilize their skills and competences.

Of all the major social systems the one which bears most directly on the development and utilization of human resources is the economy, which largely determines the employment opportunities, the productivity of labor, the resources available for skill development, the parameters of manpower utilization, and the alternatives to earned income. The easiest way to illustrate these linkages is to consider briefly a developed and a developing economy.

The characteristics of a developed economy include, as noted earlier, the maintenance of an employment level that provides job opportunities for most of the population who are able and willing to work. This means that, in good times, only a relatively small amount of potential labor is permitted to run to waste as a result of unemployment.

A second characteristic of an advanced economy is the high order of specialization and scale it has been able to develop which, together with the availability of capital, organization, and technical know-how, contribute to raising the level of productivity. Such a specialized economy also creates a demand for a large number of managers, specialists, and technicians.

A third characteristic of an advanced economy is the sizable resources at the disposal of families, business organizations, and government which can be devoted to education and training, which in turn develop the potentials of the currently employed as well as the next generation which is preparing for work and adulthood.

Finally, an advanced economy is able to devote considerable resources to the task of bringing men and jobs together and to providing alternative sources of income in the form of social insurance or welfare grants for those who are unable to earn their own livelihoods and who cannot be cared for by their families.

The interfacing of the economy and manpower development institutions in a less-developed economy based on traditional agriculture, small-scale trade, and handicrafts is different indeed. The first observation is that most agricultural societies have a shortfall in the opportunities available to people to earn their livelihood. Many farmers have too little land to absorb their labor and that of their families. A comparable type of under-employment, if not outright unemployment, is also characteristic of the trade and handicraft sectors.

The underdeveloped state of these economies leads to a further barrier to the effective use of the country's manpower. An inadequate infrastructure means that the countryside and the city are poorly linked. As a consequence there is limited specialization, and few enterprises enjoy the benefits of scale. This means that most self-employed farmers must operate as self-sufficient units, and the productivity of labor is further constrained.

Finally, most developing countries are unable to find the resources that can make a significant difference in the rate of skill development; moreover, they cannot expand employment opportunities without which the available skills cannot be put to use.

The interfacing between a developed nation's economy and its manpower development institutions indicates that the greater the extent of its specialization and the more surplus it generates, the easier it is for it to expand opportunities for the further development of the population's skills and competences and for utilizing these human assets. In less-developed countries, the stagnant economy seriously constrains the forces that can contribute to the more effective development and utilization of the human resources.

The manpower development system differs from the other three systems with which it interacts both with respect to its principal output and in terms of its underlying dynamic. The function of the manpower development institutions is the production of competence, which it accomplishes in large measure through the process of affiliation which underlies the child's relation to his family, the student's to the educational system, and the worker's to the employing organization.

The economic system is concerned primarily with increasing the goods and services available to the citizenry; in a market-oriented society, the critical dynamic is the transaction between buyer and seller.

The governmental system must assure that a large and diverse population, frequently scattered over a considerable area, is able to determine the goals which it desires to achieve collectively. Moreover, decision-making mechanisms must be available to permit a selection among competing objectives and goals and to assure that those that are chosen will be implemented. The principal dynamic for accomplishing these functions is the establishment of effective coalitions among the principal interest groups through a competent bureaucracy that sees its task as one of effective implementation.

The value structure is not fully congruent with the other three systems. Its principal function is to establish a set of norms and standards which help to order individual and group behavior by distinguishing between desirable and proscribed actions. The value structure does not produce a specific output, but establishes the framework for the outputs of the other three systems.

In this chapter, the characteristics of the manpower development system have been delineated, and the characteristics of the principal social systems with which it interacts have been described. The next step will be to illuminate some of the dynamic interrelations among the four principal societal systems. While it is easier to analyze one system at a time, the realities of individual and societal existence require that the interactional dimension be captured. No person, group, or nation operates within the confines of a single system.

· 4 ·

Human Resources and Social Change

EACH OF THE FOUR MAJOR SOCIETAL SYSTEMS that have been described is characterized by a tendency toward continuity, stability, and equilibrium. Within each are potent mechanisms operating to maintain the existing situation. This tendency to stabilization in each of the societal systems can be readily illustrated.

First, the value structure: the norms, standards, and beliefs that a society has evolved out of its experiences are carefully inculcated in the members of each generation in an effort to ensure that children will act and react much as their parents and grandparents did. All the principal institutions of the society—family, religion, ethnic group and state—ascribe great importance to the process of indoctrination and reinforcement, since they understand that their culture can best be strengthened and safeguarded through the transmission of the underlying value structure.

For this reason, each of the principal institutions resorts to repressive measures against the individual or group which challenges any of the society's basic norms in the realms of religion, family relations, and state-craft. From antiquity down to the twentieth century, the challenger not only had placed his life at risk but had also subjected the members of his family to seizure and punishment. The cruelty of the punishments visited upon the challengers of the status quo, which have included burning at the stake, stoning, and quartering, underscores the importance which societies attach to protecting their value structures.

Government also evinces the same strong tendency toward continuity and stability. Those who sit in the seats of power as well as most of the

46

citizenry understand that, in the absence of unbearable oppression and exploitation, it is better to accept the existing political structure than to seek to undermine and replace it. This cautionary, conservative stance toward the political status quo is usually the outgrowth of vicarious rather than direct experience. Most governments, no matter how arbitrary or inefficient, have been able to stay in power primarily because their leaders have such potent instruments under their control—the military, the police, the courts—with which to thwart their active opponents and to intimidate those who would be sympathetic to a change.

In addition to the naked power at the command of those who rule, the stability of governments is reinforced by the convictions of most citizens that the costs of political change are too high in terms of civil strife, which may be reflected in the potential loss of life, destruction of property, and the collapse of established institutions, to justify rebellion and revolution. These cautionary views of the body politic are reinforced by the lessons people have learned which suggest that when a corrupt government has finally been toppled at great cost, there is no guarantee and, in fact, little likelihood that its successor will be much better.

The economy also is so structured that it contributes to the maintenance of the existing system. A society's achievements are limited by the stage of its economic development, that is, by the output it is able to produce, including the amount of surplus it can devote to new investment. The amount and quality of the economy's output, in turn, is a function of the infrastructure it has developed and the skill level of its people. Since the infrastructure and the skill level are subject to alteration only over long periods of time, there is a strong element of continuity embedded in even dynamic economies because of the mutual determination and dependence among its level of performance, and the stage of development of its basic institutions and the skills and competence of its work force.

There are other potent mechanisms operating in favor of stability within the economic system. In market-oriented economies (to which even non-market-oriented countries must accommodate when they engage in international trade), the price mechanism helps to keep fluctuations in either demand or supply within limits. Movements in prices shift the forces of supply and demand, and through such mechanisms as substitution and the flow of capital and labor from one sector of the economy to another (as well as among the economies of different countries) a constant reshuffling of resources takes place which reinforces the tendency toward equilibrium. This tendency may not be as potent as the early economists assumed, since modern societies have seen fit to intervene in the operations of market mechanisms, but these interventions have not deprived these mechanisms of an important equilibrating role.

The manpower development institutions—the last of the four societal systems—likewise manifest a strong proclivity toward continuity and stability. The task of these institutions is to transmit previously acquired knowledge, skills, and techniques. To accomplish this task, the future staffs of these institutions are educated and trained so that they can successfully discharge this function. They are conditioned to recognize and respect intellectual achievement and technical competence. A large part of their indoctrination is directed to the fundamentals of their respective disciplines in the hope and expectation that, after mastering both their content and method, they will be able to transmit their accumulated pool of knowledge, skills, and competences to the next generation.

The other principal mechanisms on which the manpower development institutions rely, from curricula construction through student selection and promotion, to the granting of diplomas and degrees, all contribute to the maintenance of a basically stable developmental system, which in turn is directed to contributing to the stability of the society and economy with which it is so closely linked.

We find, therefore, that each of the principal societal systems is structured and operates in a manner that is conducive to maintaining its own stability. Further, to the extent that these systems are successful in achieving this end, they help to stabilize the society, provide continuity for it, and keep it in balance. The first lesson of an institutional analysis of society is the proclivity of all institutions to maintain themselves and to survive, which means that they are potent factors in assuring the stability and continuity of the society of which they are a part.

But the forces operating in favor of institutional and societal stability confront another set of potent forces which have the power to unsettle established situations and which explain why instability and change have been characteristic of all societies, particularly Western societies since the Renaissance.

Even traditional societies, whose basic beliefs and institutions are particularly geared to stability and continuity, are not immune to the forces of change. One set of forces which most disturbs the status quo grows out of natural calamities, especially those which threaten conventional sources of food supply. Most agricultural economies are able to produce enough to support their populations at or close to a level of basic subsistence, seldom more. Consequently, any radical diminution in the available food supply, especially if it continues for a period of years and people face starvation or death, is likely to create severe stresses and strains. Confronted by this ultimate calamity, even people deeply steeped in traditional ways will break out of their conservative mold.

A second source of disturbance in a stable society is man-made calamity, particularly war. If hostilities last for years, and if the numbers who die represent a significant proportion of all able-bodied men, it is inevitable that the foundations of the basic institutions—government, the economy, the family—will be eroded. The dynamic of war is such that unless it is annihilated, the defeated society will seek revenge after its wounds heal and it has replaced its losses, and this assures that any return to stability will be temporary rather than permanent.

A third cause of change is embedded in the instability in power relations that are part and parcel of every society, even one that is rigidly structured and tightly controlled. Despite appearances, power is never captured by any one goup, and certainly not by any one individual. Therefore, every society's political structure is inherently unstable, although some considerable period may pass without an overt challenge to the leadership.

Most of the forces of change that have impacted traditional societies have been concentrated in the governmental arena. The value structure, the economy, and the manpower development institutions have been only slightly disturbed. In most traditional societies, matters involving beliefs, work, and skill are transmitted from one generation to the next with little change.

The contours of the stability-change phenomenon underwent a major transformation with the emergence of the scientific approach which captured the Western world after the Renaissance. This transformation was reinforced by the erosion of religion and was strongly supported by the new doctrines of individual freedom and the perfectibility of man; it was further assisted by the forces unleashed by economic growth and by the growth of the manpower development institutions.

Each of these forces was potent by itself. Together they destroyed the old foundations and left Western societies with little choice but to accommodate to the dynamics of constant change. It is difficult to point to any phenomenon of the last half millennium, particularly the last two centuries, that has had a more pronounced influence on reshaping the life of men and nations than the unleashing of these potent forces for continuing change.

As will be demonstrated below, these forces undermined each of the principal societal systems in terms of both the premises on which they had been operating and the consequences that flowed therefrom. In the arena of values and beliefs, the exploratory, experimental approach of modern science to the search for the truth stands in basic contradiction to the dogmas and doctrines of Western religions, whose roots are deep in the miracle of revelation. The believers of a true religion accept on the basis of faith its doctrines as interpreted by its leaders. Although the wisest among the princes of the Catholic church and the leaders of the new science sought to avoid the collision course on which they were traveling, the less sophisticated spokesmen in each camp recognized the inevitable conflict between the guardians of revealed truth and those committed to search for it in accordance with the rules of logic and empirical evidence.

After the scientific approach became accepted, the foundation on which former beliefs rested became loosened and, in time, the foundation became unable to uphold them, as the citizenry learned that today's scientific truth will be tomorrow's scientific error. The old certainties, verities, and fundamentals which once served to direct men's actions could no longer provide guidance.

To this undermining of the system of values and beliefs must be added the consequences of the new ideas that came to the fore concerning the balance between the individual and the sovereign power of the state. For millennia, it was assumed by all who thought and taught about such matters that the ruler was to be respected and obeyed, no matter how oppressive his commands and orders. It was believed that if individuals were free to disobey, the very existence of an organized community would be destroyed. Only in matters of conscience—and not always then—was there support for challenging authority.

Soon new and strange doctrines, some with roots in ancient Greece, began to challenge the divine right of kings; by the end of the eighteenth century, in both the American colonies and France, a new philosophy of political democracy came to the fore. This doctrine held that the state has limited, not total, jurisdiction over the individual; moreover, the individual has a right to be consulted about laws which he will be required to obey. The multiple ramifications of this democratic ethos still remain to be resolved as men continue to experiment in the reshaping of their societies.

One impact, however, is beyond dispute. The assumption that it is desirable to maintain stability in the political structure and in the relations between those with power and those over whom power is exercised no longer exists. Citizens in a democracy, at least a significant proportion of them, give evidence by their actions that they favor continuing experimentation in the political arena with an aim of making government more responsive to their needs and desires.

The theory that every man has a right to participate in the running of his government was reinforced by the emergence of a related doctrine that looks upon current social evils as remediable. Men can be improved; in fact, they can be perfected if both leaders and followers study sufficiently the laws of nature and follow them. Democracy and the doctrine of the perfectibility of man were mutually reinforcing and supporting, and neither Thomas Malthus nor any other conservative thinker succeeded in extirpating the idea of progress.

Important as is the role of new ideas and new beliefs in influencing the behavior of men, even more potent are the changes they bring in their wake if the material foundations of the society are significantly transformed at the same time. That is exactly what happened during the past two centuries in Western Europe and the British dominions, and latterly in other societies as well, with the quickening pace of economic life under the influence of industrialization.

The substantial and continuous rise in the real standard of living of the populations of countries caught up in the process of economic development had several important effects. The growth process itself modified and altered many basic institutions. The pursuit of wealth usually wins out in direct confrontations with those parts of the social structure that stand in its way. Further, the substantial surpluses that many families and governments were able to command opened new vistas for further transforming the circumstances conditioning the lives of individuals and groups.

The increasing economic surplus laid the groundwork for a striking transformation in the manpower development institutions by creating the conditions that supported the establishment of a system of mass education, initially for children through the age of puberty and later up to and including college for a high proportion of the total age group. The proliferation of the formal educational system was merely the most spectacular of the social investments directed to developing the potential of all the people. There were parallel large-scale efforts in most of the affluent countries in health services, recreation, training, and income support aimed at providing all individuals with the opportunity to develop their latent capabilities.

The willingness to invest part of the growing surplus in strengthening the human resources system was reinforced by the increasing specialization of the occupational structure, which provided an earnings premium for those who succeeded in acquiring professional or technical skills. In turn, the growing competence and sophistication of the labor force resulted in an increased productivity of the economy, which led to further economic growth and still larger surpluses.

This abbreviated account indicates that, for better or worse, modern advanced societies live in an environment of constant change. One consequence of this is that advanced societies undergo continuing tensions because the principal institutions on which they rely are rooted in the past and find their strength in continuity. Their need for stability is threatened by their inability to escape from an environment that is characterized by change. Their success in moderating between these conflicting forces holds the clue to their survival and well-being. They must ensure that the transformation in one system does not proceed without corresponding adjustments in the other systems. No advanced nation which desires to take advantage of selective changes—be they in the realm of science, technology, the economy, defense, communications, or health—can expect to maintain its other institutions unchanged. The most it can do is to contain the disequilibrium that changes introduce among its principal systems.

The dynamics of change, disequilibrium, and institutional adjustments will be illustrated with three cases—transitional societies in the process of economic development, Western nations as they established the welfare state, and the U.S.S.R. as it seeks to speed its economic growth while maintaining rigid political control over its citizenry. In each instance, an attempt will be made to illuminate how the transformation of one societal system impacted on the other systems, the ensuing tensions that this created, and the outlook for moderating these tensions.

The dynamics of a society entering upon a period of economic growth can be illuminated by reference to the experiences of such countries as Brazil, Iran, and South Korea, each of which had undergone a substantial quickening of its economy since World War II. Without elaboration, it can be specified that accelerated economic growth in each of these countries reflected each country's ability to produce a larger surplus than earlier. From this vantage the following discussion will point up some of the impacts of accumulated change in the economic realm on the value system, the government, and the manpower development institutions of each of these countries.

In Brazil, many members of the Catholic hierarchy felt compelled to alter their conventional stance of avoiding such highly charged concerns as the distribution of income and became spokesmen for the impoverished masses, many of whom were left behind in the onrush of development. In some regions of the country, such as São Paulo and environs, the advances in industrialization led to major changes in the attitudes and behavior of the expanding factory work force, changes which affected not only their working habits but also their intrafamily relationships and their roles as citizens.

Much of Brazil's economic development has been correctly attributed to the success of the military junta in establishing a sufficiently tight control over its political opponents so that difficult governmental decisions could be taken and implemented. Relying on competent professionals, the government brought the runaway inflation within tolerable limits; encouraged large-scale foreign investment; made substantial investments in infrastructure, from expanding education to opening the lands of the Amazon; and at the same time contained the pressures exerted by the interest groups which opposed its plans and policies.

The combination of Brazil's substantial resource base, skillful economic policies, foreign investment, and large potential market both within its own borders and in neighboring countries provided the foundation for rapid growth in many, but by no means all, parts of its extended territories.

On the human resources front, rapid economic development created an environment for the talented and educated among the native population conducive to broadening their scope of activities; foreigners added to the available pool of competence, particularly in managerial and technical areas; and the government made substantial new investments in all levels of the educational system. In addition, rapid industrialization was possible only because factory managers assumed continuing responsibility for providing initial and upgrading training for their work force.

In Iran, the dominant figure has been the Shah, who for decades has been engaged in forcing the pace of modernization. Here, too, the value structure has been substantially modified by the rush to modernization, reinforced by the Shah's confrontation with the mullahs and the large landowners who fought to maintain the status quo characterized by a servile peasantry, uneducated, without property of its own, who look to their landlords and religious teachers for guidance.

Like the military junta in Brazil, the Shah was able to keep tight control of the political apparatus during the years of rapid change, and, again like the government in Brazil, he relied heavily on a small group of competent professionals. As did Brazil, Iran encouraged foreign companies to establish branch operations within its borders and in the process to bring managerial and technical staff from abroad which helped to supplement the modest pool of locally trained people.

While much of the economic expansion was initially centered in Teheran and a few other cities, the accelerated development program that followed upon the steep increase in oil revenues in the mid-1970s has begun to permeate a much wider area involving many more millions of Iranians.

Starting at two different points of the manpower development cycle, the Shah early sought to use conscription as a lever for attenuating illiteracy in the countryside; he made it possible for college students to discharge their military obligation by joining the teacher corps. At the upper end of the educational spectrum, the government initially sought a controlled expansion of its institutions of higher learning, moderated by the twin considerations of resource constraints and a cautionary attitude toward increasing the ranks of university students, potential troublemakers.

South Korea, without the support of a large resource base such as Brazil's or the advantages of large oil revenues that have been available to Iran, nevertheless has been able to speed its economic development during the past two decades. It has done this by a skillful redirection of its labor force from agriculture to export industries, making use of local and foreign enterprises to help in the process, in which even arch enemies such as the Japanese were welcomed if they were willing to assist. The economy was also helped by the continuing and substantial inflow of United States military and civilian aid.

As in the other countries in transition, rapid economic development in Seoul and other urban centers resulted in striking changes in the established value structure, particularly as it related to intrafamily relations among husband, wife, and children. The new urban environment, with married women and adolescent girls working out of the home and with young men no longer dependent on their fathers for their livelihood and future, has loosened the reciprocal relations among the generations that for so long were a source of continuity in South Korea.

The closest parallel among South Korea, Brazil, and Iran relates to the presence of a strong government in which the civil head has his power base in the military. Once again, there is a governmental apparatus with sufficient cohesion and control to be able to determine policy and to implement it, thereby helping to establish an environment conducive to investment.

South Korea, with a proliferation of educational institutions, was under less pressure than either Brazil or Iran to take special action to expand its educational infrastructure. However, the relatively large number of educated and trained personnel not only facilitated the push to modernization and industrialization but also resulted in considerable numbers of South Koreans emigrating abroad and sending home sizable sums from their overseas employment.

All three countries, then, are making substantial gains in considerable measure because of the ability of the political leadership to exercise effective control over resource allocation and related development measures. But we must also observe that the ruling group, in exercising its control, is keeping many who are pressing to participate in political decision making at bay and is pursuing repressive measures to do so. Consequently, the future outlook is less stable. There is no need to argue that if these transitional societies had to face the problem of succession in leadership, their economic progress would come to an end. But that might be the outcome if the question of succession precipitated a long struggle. As the classical economists understood, economic development flourishes best in an environment free of political disorders.

In the context of the present analysis, we find that continuing progress towards any interim set of objectives requires that the society's principal systems remain in acceptable balance with each other. While a strong autocratic government may be an asset in speeding development at one stage, it can become a liability at a later point if its repressive and exclusionary policies preclude activist groups from playing a significant part in political decision making. If a policy of exclusion is maintained for many years, it is almost inevitable that internal strife will ensue when the existing leadership is weakened or toppled. And such strife could bring to an end, at least for a time, the steady advances the society has been making to modernize and raise its standard of living.

The second case in this discussion of the dynamics of change relates to the difficulties that the Western nations, particularly Sweden, the United Kingdom and the United States, encountered as they sought to improve the life chances and circumstances of their people, especially those at the lower end of the income distribution. The affluent democracies came to realize that it is morally wrong to force every individual to rely solely on himself and his immediate relatives. Many exigencies of life are beyond his control—unemployment, ill health, accidents, old age, mental or emotional disabilities. They are certainly beyond the control of a child whose family is incapable of properly nurturing him.

The funds required to support a broad program of social legislation were easier to raise because of the substantial and steady increases in real income which made it possible to help the disadvantaged without seriously diminishing the resources at the disposal of the rest of the electorate. Moreover, the enthusiasm for the welfare state was reinforced by the growing belief that many of these income transfers were in the nature of a social investment: the unemployed man who was put to work, the emotionally disturbed child who was treated, and the widowed mother who was assisted in raising her children would add to the number of citizens capable of productive work and who would subsequently become taxpayers.

However, the advanced democracies encountered difficulties in implementing these social welfare programs. The premise on which the welfare

efforts were constructed—an expanded humanitarianism—came under challenge as governments sought to decrease inequalities in opportunities and
income. If protection against risk is defined as a right to which all persons
are eligible without reference to a means test—as in a socialized health system—the costs of the program can quickly reach levels that place a heavy
strain on the national budget. When benefits are geared to an income test,
government bureaucrats run into other problems. In a dynamic economy,
family incomes fluctuate from one year to the next, and many persons risk
losing valuable social benefits, such as subsidized housing, if their earnings
increase to a level just above the cutoff point.

The establishment of cutoff points itself is a cause of difficulty. Those
who are just above the income level which entitles them to participate in a
particular program resent the fact that they are excluded, while others, in
much the same situation as they, are able to enjoy valuable benefits.

Although modern governments had no difficulty in implementing social welfare programs which were limited to writing checks, they encountered considerable problems when it came to expanding and improving the
quality of services to low-income families, such as, in their attempts to increase the effectiveness of schools located in slum areas or to provide adequate medical services to the rural population.

Moreover, since the rate growth of the national income was not sufficiently rapid to cover all the additional costs of expensive transfer programs, taxpayer resistance began to mount. To tax the rich to help the poor
is a program that can elicit widespread support in an affluent democracy.
But to add to the tax burden of those in the middle of the income distribution in an effort to improve the circumstances of those at the bottom will
encounter growing opposition. And that is in fact what happened.

Time also disclosed that the theory of social investment which initially
rallied support to the welfare state was found wanting and that extensive
redistribution might lower the productivity of the economy by deflecting
too much of the surplus to consumption, leaving too little for new investment. In addition, a critical review of some of the new programs suggested
that they were probably dysfunctional because they provided income to
people under conditions which weakened rather than strengthened their
proclivities to work and to care for themselves.

Further uncertainty about the effectiveness of the income transfer program, particularly about its limits, derived from the growing recognition
that the elaborate structure of new taxes and new benefits was not altering
the underlying conditions which gave rise to the inequalities in the first
place. In light of the limited responsiveness of the government, the econ-

omy, and the manpower development institutions, this concern is leading to a reconsideration of the goals of the effort. All the welfare states are engaged in reassessing their prospects in the near and intermediate future of broadening opportunities and otherwise improving the conditions of life of the least advantaged among their citizens in light of their experiences. Since there remains a strong dynamic in all prosperous nations to narrow the inequalities among individuals and families, the open question is what new approaches will be designed that hold greater promise of realizing this societal imperative.

The present disenchantment with governmental interventions may reflect inflated ideas about the efficacy of such interventions. To ameliorate the conditions of the least advantaged members of a dynamic society does not imply that all inequalities will be erased, dependency will disappear, and social harmony will prevail. It may be that the welfare state has performed reasonably well and its touted failure reflects more excessive expectations than shortfalls in achievements.

The third case used to illustrate the dynamics of change explores the implications of the U.S.S.R.'s continuing to strive for a position of economic leadership among the nations of the world while the leaders of the Communist party are determined to maintain their hold on the levers of power. It was Lenin's conviction that the best prospect of Russia's catching up with and overtaking the more advanced European nations was through a massive educational effort which would speedily improve the skills and competences of the Russian people. After a half century, it is clear that the Communist leadership had paid heed to Lenin's advice and expanded the educational, research, and scientific base. This expansion led to correspondingly large increases in the number of qualified professional and technical personnel. But the Communist leadership continues to confront the question of how to assure the productive use of this ever-larger cadre of educated persons in an environment that discourages independent thought and action. There is an increasing disequilibrium between the government and the other societal systems.

One consequence of the vast increase in the size of the educated group has been the increase in the number of Russians who have become acquainted with the values and orientations of other peoples through reading, traveling, and personal relations. It has not been possible for the Communist regime to maintain the isolation of its citizens from foreign thought and values, a policy it pursued with considerable success in earlier decades. There is a growing intelligentsia that is pressing constantly for more individual freedom of thought and action.

Secondly, there is a contradiction in the leadership's seeking to speed the productivity of the economy at the same time that it insists that managers and technologists conform to directives issued by successive levels of the bureaucracy. Able people can make their optimal contribution only to the extent that they have both the responsibility and the authority to make decisions over a broad range of issues and are rewarded for their successes and are held to account for their failures. But the Communist leaders are reluctant to encourage this kind of discretion because they are afraid of losing effective control.

Finally, there is an increasing tension in the educational, training, and research institutions between the push toward the full development of talent and competence and the constraints that the political leadership feels obliged to maintain to assure respect for the prevailing ideology and to prevent the growth of nonconforming opinions. The regime correctly perceived that it is a relatively small step from freedom of thought to freedom of political action, and the latter is a threat that it cannot tolerate.

There appears, then, to be an irreconcilable conflict between the economic goals the Communist leaders are pursuing and their unwillingness to tolerate the basic adjustments in their other societal systems without which their economic goals cannot be realized. By improvising, the regime has been successful in buying off many members of the intelligentsia with career opportunities and rewards. But a growing number refuse to accept these emoluments, and the tensions grow. At some point in the future an accommodation must occur: either the political leadership will have to forgo the dream of economic and technological leadership, or it will have to allow greater freedom in the realms of values, the economy, and manpower development.

The three cases make a single point. They indicate that a significant transformation in any one societal system cannot yield continuing gains unless the other societal systems are modified. Without these modifications, the tensions between the old and the new will reach the breaking point. A society whose basic systems are in disequilibrium will be unable to function effectively.

This brings us to the concluding theme of this chapter: the mechanisms available to a dynamic society to help keep its basic societal system out of a state of disequilibrium. The first observation is that when the public (and its leaders) recognize that the institutions and societal systems are dysfunctional, they need not tolerate their malfunctioning. Through collective action, a decision can be made to modify the existing structures or to establish new ones that hold the promise of being more responsive to current and future needs. In societies in which experimentation is not acceptable, this kind of relief is largely precluded.

Secondly, the body politic can translate hitherto unmet needs and desires into new goals, policies, and programs which, when implemented, hold promise of widening the horizons of the society. This response also rests on the application of rational analysis reinforced by a tolerance for social experimentation.

The fact that a modern, complex society consists of a few basic systems and a larger number of critical institutions suggests that the process of change need not necessarily be directed solely on a systemwide basis. Often, important changes can be initiated and carried a considerable distance through limited interventions in particular institutions. This less-than-total approach has distinct advantages, including the fact that the resistance to experimentation will be lower and the costs of failure less.

The life of society, like that of an individual, is characterized by the potential for continued learning. There is no way for a people to know ahead of time whether a hitherto untried policy or program will prove successful and what costs must be met to assure success. While prior analysis can help to illuminate the advantages and dangers of a society's acting, or not acting, it can never provide definitive answers. They wait upon experience. Consequently, experience is a valuable asset for every society which seeks to improve its capacity to deal with change. The presence of feedback mechanisms which can capture the lessons of experience and introduce these lessons into the decision-making apparatus strengthens the base for future experimentation and augurs well for improved solutions.

One important mechanism that can facilitate a society's adjustment to change is its sense of timing and appropriateness of response. One of the dangers facing a dynamic society, especially one that has shed its inhibitions to experiment, is the tendency to venture too much, too quickly. There is also the opposite danger that it will move too slowly or with too little force when new departures are called for. If its statesmen are astute, the voting public sophisticated, and its researchers thorough, a society is less likely to err in its timing. Much goes awry in the lives of individuals and groups for which there is no remedy other than time itself, which may eventually ameliorate conditions which cannot be cured. It is important not to intervene when restraint is indicated. When intervention is called for and the society decides to act, there is the correlative issue of the resources it is able and willing to devote to the task. These must be adequate to the task at hand. If the resources are insufficient, the condition will not be remedied; if they are excessive, they will be wasted.

The burden of this analysis has been to highlight the tensions that inevitably exist in a society whose basic systems and institutions are structured primarily to favor stability but which exist in an environment in which the forces of change have been unleashed. Disequilibrium is the fate of all modern societies, and they must strive to keep the tensions among their institutions and systems within acceptable limits. Their success will depend in the first instance on how well their human resources system performs its basic mission of developing the potential of the citizenry and how well the ancillary systems are kept in balance so that their potential can be effectively utilized. Societies which meet this challenge are more likely to avoid the consequences of disequilibrium which are manifest in frustration, turmoil, and internecine conflict.

PART II

« « « · » » »

THE DEVELOPMENT
OF SKILL

*The difference between the most dissimilar characters, be-
tween a philosopher and a common street porter, for example, seems to arise not so much from nature, as from
habit, custom, and education. When they came into the
world, and for the first six or eight years of their existence,
they were, perhaps, very much alike, and neither their parents nor playfellows could perceive any remarkable difference. About that age, or soon after, they come to be employed in very different occupations. The difference of talents
comes then to be taken notice of, and widens by degrees, till
at last the vanity of the philosopher is willing to acknowledge
scarce any resemblance.*

—ADAM SMITH, *The Wealth of Nations*

· 5 ·

The Process of Skill Acquisition

THE ABILITY OF A SOCIETY to survive and to prosper depends first on its having institutions in place to provide the members of each generation with the values, knowledge, and skills that will enable them to meet the challenges they will encounter as they grow up and assume their adult roles as workers, parents, and citizens. An individual will not be able to recognize, much less meet, the range of challenges he will encounter unless he has been trained. All accomplishments, from earning a livelihood to protecting his life or his property, are predicated on prior learning. To earn a livelihood, to distinguish between friend and foe, and to recognize the difference between acceptable and unacceptable actions, a young person must be taught by his elders and peers. No individual can survive by relying solely on his instincts. The study of human resources, therefore, must start with an explication of the process of learning, since skill is the foundation of all human achievement.

This chapter and the following two chapters form a unit which focuses on the manner in which people acquire skills and competences. This chapter will delineate the principal institutions that play critical roles in the skill acquisition process, primarily in developed societies. The next will amplify the manner in which the process is affected first by the resources available to the primary institution, the family, and the contribution that families make to the development of their offspring by helping them to link into the secondary and tertiary institutions, the educational system and the world of work. The third chapter addresses the variations in the process which derive from the fact that every individual is unique and, irrespective of his family's

63

resources, can in some measure shape his career and his life by means of his personal endowment, motivation, and opportunity, especially if the environment is favorable.

This chapter will first describe the role that each of the principal institutions plays in the developmental process; it will then consider the manner in which the individual is formed and transformed by moving from one institutional setting to the next. When this analysis has been completed, it will be possible to identify the critical mechanisms which exercise a determining influence on the level of skill and competence acquired by individuals.

As we have noted, all societies, past and present, developing and developed, irrespective of their form of government, expect the family to play the dominant role in raising children. There has never been a substitute for the family as the nurturing institution, although different societies have different family structures. Anthropologists distinguish between the extended and the nuclear family, and in some societies today, families include individuals with no blood relationship.

One need only sketch the multiple developmental tasks the family performs to understand why it has been and remains the primary developmental institution. First, the family provides for the physical needs of the newborn and the child. If an infant is not fed, it will die. In fact, infanticide has long been used by some societies as a method of population control. We know that in many low-income societies, a child is particularly vulnerable when he is weaned. The number of years the child remains dependent on the family varies among different peoples and cultures, but it is rare, even in harsh economic environments, for children to fend for themselves before their teens.

A second responsibility that devolves on the family is to assist in the emotional development of the child. The interaction between infant and mother and between the young child and his parents and siblings was recognized long before Freud described the stages of the psychosexual process. The Jesuits have stated that if they can have a child up to the age of seven, they will be able to determine his character.

We know, of course, that building a healthy emotional base takes more than the concern, resources, and intelligence of the parents. Many parents who want the best for their children may be unable to build a child's psyche so that it is not excessively vulnerable to anxiety, aggression, and other crippling forces. The emotional development of the child is not the result of his parents' efforts alone. It is the result of the interaction among parents, siblings, and peers.

The third task of the family lies in the cognitive arena. Mother, father, and siblings can facilitate or retard the intellectual development of the infant or child by the time and effort they devote to stimulating his curiosity and to engaging in play, object identification, and language comprehension. Some experts in cognitive development believe that the key to adult competence lies in the exposures and experiences of the infant and young child (prior to the age of two); they believe that the basic structure for later learning is laid down by the time the child is four.

The fourth and final responsibility of the family is to assist in socializing the young child, in helping him to recognize the demands and bounds that society has established and to understand that he must accept and abide by them. Now we must take at least passing notice of the gross differences in the role of families in diverse societies. In traditional agricultural societies, which are characterized by the absence of both a broad educational system and a differentiated labor market, the family not only plays the key role in personality development but also serves, as we have noted, as educator and trainer and, eventually, as employer of the next generation. Even in nonliterate societies, there is an oral tradition which must be transmitted and which provides the young with a history, a system of beliefs, and heroes. Continuity in social experience is a function of a transfer of common experience from one generation to the next, and it is the responsibility of each family to contribute to the process.

In these traditional societies, the family has a further role as educator in the practical arena. The boy acquires the skills he needs to till the land and care for the cattle and perform other essential tasks from his father, uncles, and brothers, that is, from the members of his family. The same family structure assures that young girls acquire the range of competences they will need as adults, particularly those skills involving food preparation, caring for the young, and running the household. Here the girl's teachers are her mother, grandmother, and other older female members of the family.

Once the young person reaches working age, the family introduces him to the world of work by arranging age-relevant tasks in or around the house or in the fields, with older members of the household serving as teachers. In many settled agricultural societies where there is no additional land available, it is often necessary for a son to wait until his father dies—and he may be a mature man by the time that happens—before he can assume responsibility for managing the farm.

The family has been described as the almost exclusive developmental institution in traditional societies—as the rearer of the young, educator, and employer. While the centrality of the family in the developmental process in all traditional agricultural societies is beyond challenge, it should be noted that the family does not carry the entire responsibility for indoctrinating and preparing the young. In every traditional society there are religious institutions and communal arrangements involving the people of the village or the region which help to reinforce the dominant value structure and which assume leadership for particular aspects of community life. But the principal socializing agent remains the family.

If one seeks to generalize about the principal difference in child rearing practices among developed nations, the focus must be on the age when children are cared for by communal arrangements. In many of the Communist countries of Eastern Europe, particularly the U.S.S.R., Hungary, and Czechoslovakia, governments, seeking a rapid expansion of the urban labor force, established creches and nurseries so that women with infants could return to work within a few weeks or months after giving birth. While similar institutions exist in noncommunist countries, they are less pervasive, and children tend to be considerably older when they are first accepted in day-care centers. The increasing trend of married women in Western countries to return to work while their last child is still quite young has been a factor behind the push for the expansion of child care facilities under public auspices, suggesting once again that ideology and politics may be less potent than the desires of individuals or the imperatives of the economy.

This schematic approach to the role of the family in the process of skill acquisition can be summarized:

The family is responsible for the basic socializing of the child, which involves helping him to put a rein on his demands for the immediate gratification of his instinctual needs, to accept guidance and supervision from adults, to participate as a member of a group, to follow instructions, to apply himself to tasks commensurate with his competence, and to tolerate change.

These specific behavioral patterns can be learned more readily if the child feels secure and loved by his parents, who are his first teachers. The interactions between the child and his parents, his siblings, and others with whom he is in continuing contact help shape his personality, which in turn conditions his approach to all later tasks and relationships.

As we have seen, the family is also the child's first teacher of language, numbers, and concepts. Through speaking, reading, answering questions, and other interactions, parents can create or fail to create an environment which caters to the curiosity of the child and expands his interests and stimulates his intellectual development.

Even young children develop an initial appreciation of the importance their parents attach to knowledge, work, and accomplishment, as well as to money, creature comforts, and social approval. The areas of parental agreement and disagreement about what is important are subtly communicated to the young child, who uses these inputs as building blocks for his own personality.

The second principal institution of critical importance in the process of skill acquisition is the educational establishment, which, in most countries, is the specific responsibility of government. The basic educational structure consists of three levels—primary, secondary, and higher—but in affluent countries additional levels have been added, such as nursery schools and kindergartens and, at the upper end, courses for adults. The educational structure also includes the training institutions, some of which, such as vocational and technical schools, are an integral part of the formal educational system, while others are outside the system and are privately owned and operated. Additional skill-developing institutions include apprenticeship and military schools, as well as employing organizations which offer extended training. These last can either be treated under the present rubric of the educational-training establishment or be subsumed under the activities of employing institutions, which is the approach that will be followed here.

The development of a formal educational structure, which is increasingly characteristic of all countries and which has been in place for years in the developed world, reflects in the first instance the inability of the family to meet all the needs of its offspring under conditions where literacy has become a basic requirement for work and citizenship and where the advanced skills required for the effective operation of a complex technological society can be acquired only through a long period of specialized education and training. Not even a wealthy family can provide its children with a university or a professional course of study; nor can families with modest incomes cover the costs of ten or twelve years of schooling on their own. Consequently, governments have had to assume responsibility for the financing of education, a financial obligation that they were more inclined to undertake because of the contribution that an educated citizenry can make to the building of a nation.

It is not possible to describe all the variations in the educational systems of the developed and developing countries. But this kind of detail is not necessary for the task of delineating the role of the educational system in the skill acquisition process. Once again, one can resort to a degree of schematization without much loss.

When children reach the age of six—in some industrialized countries it is as early as three (nursery school)—formal responsibility for education is assumed by the school. In most countries school attendance becomes compulsory at the age of six or seven. The educational authorities are responsible for the curriculum, for the selection and retention of teachers, for the way in which classes are conducted, for the setting and grading of examinations, and in fact, for the structure and functioning of the entire process of schooling. In some countries, such as the United States, parents have a voice in the selection of the chief educational officer in their community who consults with them on matters of broad policy. But in most countries, the educational establishment, under broad directions from the political leadership, has wide discretion in determining how the schools discharge their societal functions.

Since educators are responsible not only for instructing the young but also for assuring the safety and proper conduct of children under their supervision, they rely on routines to oversee children during the hours they are in school. In a major metropolitan center, the educational authorities may have a million students under their control. With classes including from twenty-five to fifty children each, the teacher must maintain order, engage the students' interest, carry out a lesson plan, stimulate youngsters to do their homework, be alert to children with special problems, and perform a host of additional functions, such as supervising play activities or taking the class on an occasional visit to an airport or factory.

The child also faces a challenge as he makes the transition from being the center of attention in the nuclear family to assuming his new role as a quasi-anonymous occupant of a seat in the third row. If the child comes to school before he is emotionally ready to be separated from his mother, or if he finds it difficult to absorb the materials taught, or if he has a health problem that interferes with his complying with the myriad rules, the transition from family to school can be traumatic.

The sheer numbers in the educational channels help to explain why the individual student must accommodate to the system rather than the reverse. While most young children are able to meet the demands of the system, a minority experience varying degrees of difficulties, and if they do not receive special attention and support by the school and parents, they are likely to fall behind in their studies.

Under the best of circumstances, the school focuses on a few areas. Its emphasis is on language, numbers, and concept formation. It pays some attention to the arts, including music and drawing, but it concentrates on teaching the three R's. These are the skills required for advancement up the educational ladder. Other competences are minimized or ignored. Most children who are able to accept the authority of their parents and teachers and who win their approval are able to cope with school without much difficulty. Quick learners distinguish themselves and are rewarded by high marks. But even in the early years, some youngsters begin to lag behind. The more they fall behind, the more likely they are to become unsettled and disaffected and the less they are able to profit from their educational experience. Over time, more and more students fall off the track because of their earlier failure to master the fundamentals and because of a lack of interest, competitiveness, and achievement. The steady increase in the failure rate through the grades has been considered the inevitable concomitant of an educational system that seeks to be increasingly selective as students move through it.

While many large educational systems begin in the first grade to group students according to ability, the first major branching usually occurs at the end of the six years of elementary school. It is at this point that most systems provide alternative tracks. The tracking aims to select those who have the aptitude, desire, and family support to concentrate on academic studies which will lead to college and to distribute the remainder among programs which end earlier and have a vocational orientation. In low- and middle-income countries, the decision whether a student goes one route or the other rests largely with the educational authorities; in more affluent nations, parental and student choices are more often determining.

In the pre-World War II period, the educational systems of the countries of Western Europe employed a major triage usually when students reached the age of eleven or twelve. At that point, a small minority were selected to pursue an academic curriculum. At the end of their secondary schooling, all who passed the matriculation examination were admitted to the university. Others pursued an education with a vocational orientation until their fourteenth or sixteenth year. To a lesser extent, such differentiation also occurred in the United States, starting in the seventh grade, at the beginning of junior high school, and was reinforced in the tenth grade at the transition to senior high school. However, the American pattern was less rigid: more youngsters, if they desired, were permitted to remain on the academic track; many who found difficulty with a curriculum of foreign languages, science, and mathematics were permitted to take a watered-down version (general curriculum) of the academic track which led to a high school diploma. Only about one-quarter pursued a specifically vocational program. Moreover, in the post-World War II era, a growing proportion of those who earned a general or vocational diploma have been able to make the transition to a junior or senior college, although those on the academic track found it easier to do so.

In almost every advanced technological society, the post-World War II era has led to a restructuring of the traditional educational system with an aim of broadening access to the university for many who were previously excluded. The explanation for expanded college and university admissions reflects a congruence of several distinct trends, including the many more secondary school graduates enlarging the pool from which university students are chosen; the growing affluence that makes it easier for families to forgo the potential earnings of their older children; the growth of the democratic ethos which objects to a rigid class structure that separates those with higher education from the rest of the population; the willingness and ability of governments to appropriate large sums for higher education in the belief that more technically trained persons will speed a nation's economic growth, and, perhaps above all, the conviction held by many students seeking admission to colleges that they will be able to enter preferred careers by acquiring higher degrees.

The twentieth century has witnessed three parallel trends: the increased requirements of a modern society and economy for a larger number of professionals and specialists, the expansion of higher education to meet these needs, and the higher salaries and emoluments available to the better educated. The last provided the political leverage that forced open the gates of the universities. As long as only a select few were accepted, there was little equality of opportunity in the work arena. The democratization of higher education, particularly the broadened access for all academically qualified students, reflects a new egalitarianism that increasingly characterizes both capitalist and communist societies.

Although most countries can point to large increases in the proportion of the age group who continue their education after having received their diplomas from secondary school, the number of those who acquire a higher degree is still relatively small. Even in the United States, where about 80 percent of the age group completes high school and half continues with some form of postsecondary education or training, not more than 1 in 4 earns a college or first professional degree.

The elongated preparatory system makes three distinct contributions to the skill acquisition process. The longer a young person remains in the bureaucratized educational system, the more he will be conditioned to other large organizations, particularly the corporation, which increasingly dominates the work environment in advanced economies. Next, many years of exposure to didactic instruction in the classroom, supplemented by reading assignments on the outside, result in young people's acquiring a considerable stock of knowledge that helps inform their judgments about private and public issues on which they must act. The schools are not solely responsible for these horizon-stretching, comprehension-deepening efforts, for the media play important complementary roles. But the contribution of the formal educational system is primary.

The third contribution of the educational system is that it provides specific work skills for some young people, including those who do not remain in the educational channel long enough to acquire professional degrees. Several facts are beyond dispute. In most affluent countries, almost all school leavers and high school graduates sooner or later make the transition into the world of work. The economy has a place for most persons able and willing to work, even if the new worker can offer little beyond literacy. In modern economies, where goods-producing jobs represent less than half and sometimes as little as a third of the total, communications and mathematical skills, the by-products of a secondary school education, provide young people with the basic prerequisites for white-collar jobs.

The educational system is less responsive to the needs of the nonbookish students who find academic work boring and difficult. If their high school experience is to be constructive, they need orientation to and skill preparation for the world of work, but most educational systems have not been able to provide this kind of learning environment because of the high costs of vocational education and the difficulties of developing effective work-study programs. Consequently, many young people, especially men, drop out or complete high school ill-prepared for blue-collar or service jobs. Young women generally do better because they are able to acquire in school the basic clerical skills that facilitate their employment.

The failure of many secondary schools to provide their students with specific occupational skills helps to explain the expansion, at least in the United States and other affluent societies, of postsecondary educational and training institutions. Here there is an admixture of curricula that includes general courses as well as others that are occupation-specific. Since each country has its own pattern, it is not possible to generalize about the transitional paths for postsecondary school graduates into work. For some the path is direct: the young person who has acquired a certificate or associate degree attesting to competence in a technical field such as drafting, computer programming, or dental hygiene generally finds a position. But many others, such as those who pursue or complete a course of studies in the humanities, are handicapped in their job search because they lack job-specific skills. While the additional general education which they have acquired may prove to have some advantage, those with specific occupational skills are likely to make a smoother transition into work.

In addition to the vocational elements that are part and parcel of the formal educational systems of most advanced societies, including vocational curricula in comprehensive high schools, the vocational high school, and the technical institute, there are also a number of private, profit-making training establishments in these societies. The private establishments provide a wide range of courses aimed at preparing people for entrance into specific occupations, such as medical technician, office machine operator, and airplane mechanic. These private schools also prepare people for civil service examinations; often the successful competitors are able to have desirable jobs and careers in the public sector.

Another facet of the training structures in advanced technological societies is the proliferation of government-sponsored occupational training. It is characteristic of a dynamic economy that some workers have difficulties in finding or holding a job. Some of these workers live in areas where employment is being eroded; others find that their skills have become obsolescent as a result of technological changes; still others have lost their jobs because their companies went out of business. Almost every advanced economy now offers a range of training opportunities for disadvantaged workers such as these in the belief that unemployed and underemployed workers who receive help in acquiring new skills or refurbishing old ones will more quickly be able to support themselves and their dependents.

This schematic review suggests that the formal educational-training system contributes substantially to the skill acquisition process, first, by providing all students with a base of general knowledge and information; secondly, by offering initial skill training for those who pursue a vocational curriculum; and, thirdly, by enabling university students to become qualified for careers in professional and technical fields—from research to medicine and the law. However, the educational system does much more. It takes over from the family a large part of the socializing task; it strengthens certain types of behavior; it reinforces particular values; it performs a major sorting task by pointing some students toward the professions and others to intermediate technical occupations; and, by pushing still others off the educational track early in their development, it almost assures that they will be trapped in lowly occupations.

This brings us to the third principal institution involved in the skill acquisition process—the employing organization. Most large organizations prefer to hire young persons and train them to meet their assignments. The employer, knowing the jobs he has to fill and the skills and potentials of his work force, can provide the training to meet his specific needs. If he had to look to the labor market for individuals with the necessary competences, the likelihood is that he would find most prospective employees either overqualified or underqualified.

Large organizations are paying increasing attention to the training of their managerial personnel. An organization considers it important to broaden the outlook of those moving up the hierarchy by alerting them to the changing environment within which the organization operates. An organization also considers it important to refurbish the technical skills that middle management had acquired years earlier during their formal education and professional training and to expose middle management to particular orientations and values that the leadership believes can contribute to organizational harmony and morale.

In the United States and other advanced economies, there are many apprenticeship programs, controlled jointly by management and trade unions. The route from apprentice to journeyman provides the worker with a succession of increasingly difficult assignments under supervision together with an opportunity to master the underlying theory of his craft. This usually requires that he attend school for the equivalent of one day a week over a period of years.

Considerable training is provided by the Armed Forces, which, in both developed and developing countries, produce a high proportion of the specialists they require to operate and repair their complex weapons systems and support services. The increasing sophistication of the weapons systems, from supersonic aircraft to nuclear submarines, has forced the military into extensive classroom and on-the-job training. It has been estimated that, in the mid-1970s, the Department of Defense spends about $10 billion annually on all forms of training, a sum greatly in excess of the amount spent on formal training by industrial organizations. One reason for these exceptionally large training expenditures is that the military must offer both basic and advanced training to successive cohorts of servicemen, since many leave after their initial enlistment. However, men who earlier acquired skills in the military and who return to civilian life can add significantly to the pool of trained manpower available to the civilian economy. In developing countries, many truck drivers learned their skills in the military; in the United States, many civilian pilots were trained initially to fly combat or military transport planes.

Since large organizations move their employees into more demanding and rewarding jobs as they gain experience, the assignment and reassignment system—independent of formal training—contributes significantly to skill acquisition. If men remain in the same assignment for a long period after they have mastered their jobs, they are not likely to acquire additional skills. The mobility made possible by the assignment and promotional procedures followed by most large organizations is a major force in broadening the skills of workers.

There is a counterpart system operating in the external labor market where the key agent is the individual in search of advancement rather than the organization in search of a balanced work force. A dynamic economy is characterized by highly differentiated jobs with differentiated skill requirements and rewards. When the labor market is tight, workers, by changing their jobs and the organizations for which they work, can locate new job opportunities which enable them to add to their skills. If the economy remains buoyant for a number of years, many young workers, by changing jobs, can accumulate considerable skills. This is true for both blue-collar and white-collar workers. Even in countries where formal apprenticeships dominate, many workers eventually reach journeyman status without having negotiated the formal system. Rather, they succeed through job changes to "pick up" the skills and experiences they need to qualify as craftsmen. The same pattern is followed by many who succeed in moving rapidly up the managerial and administrative hierarchy. Here, too, young men and women in search of rapid advancement can broaden and deepen their skills and competences by making the right moves among work assignments, employers, industries, and sectors.

The last important work arena which contributes to skill acquisition is the home. Although the work that women perform in the home is not included in the national accounts, clearly they carry out a diversified group of functions from budgeting and controlling household expenditures to providing emotional support for their husbands and children. The accepted view is that the running of a household offers relatively little opportunity for women to master skills for which there is a market demand. It is said that cooking for a small family is quite different from cooking for a school or commercial restaurant; sewing an occasional dress does not prepare a woman for employment as a dress designer; nursing her husband or child does not qualify a woman for hospital duty as a practical nurse; furnishing an apartment or house is not the same as entering upon a career as an interior decorator. But this may overstate the nontransferability of skill. Married women in developed countries have a wide range of competences that can contribute to their transition from work in the home to paid employment. They have acquired considerable general and even specialized education that gives them ready access to a range of jobs. Moreover, many have developed wide-ranging interests, competences, and experiences from their diversified activities as homemakers and volunteers which can assist them when they are ready to enter or reenter the labor market.

The fact that in developed countries about two in every five workers are women and that more and more women spend an increasing proportion of their adult lives in paid employment underscores the need to pay close attention to the process of skill development and utilization, in relation to both their market and nonmarket activities. The fact that the national income accounts do not include the contribution that women make in running their households and raising their children does not diminish the size of their contribution as homemakers or paid workers.

Several important findings can be extracted from this summary review of the role of employing organizations in the process of skill acquisition. First, no matter how extensive the individual's preparatory training, the employer confronts the task of instructing him in the ways of the organization. Second, since many skills that the organization requires cannot be obtained in the marketplace, many employing organizations have no option but to enter upon elaborate training efforts to assure themselves the competences they need. Third, there is a critical feedback relation between the assignments a person receives and the range and level of skill that he or she is able to achieve. Competence requires exposure and experience. Only those who are challenged at work will be able to reach a high level of performance.

The principal characteristics of the process of skill acquisition can be reviewed from the vantage of the multiplicity of institutions that are involved, their distinctive goals and purposes, the linkages among them, and the consequences that flow from these interrelationships.

The first observation relates to the diversity of institutions that play a role in the process, from the nuclear family to the large employing organization. No one institution has the entire responsibility for providing the range of learning opportunities that people require to accumulate the skills to perform their multiple roles competently. Each of the principal institutions has a partial responsibility for providing skill training. After a child reaches the age of compulsory schooling, the family generally looks to government (the educational authorities) to assume the primary responsibility for preparing him for work and life. Government, in turn, supports a far-flung educational system for a series of interrelated purposes, only partially directed to assisting students to acquire work skills. Formal schooling is, in the first instance, directed to molding the child into a responsible citizen by teaching him cognitive skills and by indoctrinating him with the values of his society. Further, the school seeks to transmit the key elements of his culture as well as the history of major civilizations.

The employer is first and foremost concerned with the production of output for a profit; he is only indirectly concerned with training his work force. The personnel policies which the employer follows have a direct effect on the skill acquisition process, but his primary concern is to make effective use of the members of his work force; only incidentally is he concerned with training them.

The first generalization, then, is that the institutions primarily concerned with the process of skill acquisition—the family, government (through the educational system), and the employing organization—do not have a specific, and surely not an exclusive, training function. The contribution of these institutions to the acquisition of work skills is ancillary, not primary.

A second generalization relates to the multiplicity of institutions that play a role in the skill acquisition process. In addition to the principal three—the family, the educational system, and the employer— there are voluntary organizations, such as religious bodies and youth organizations; private training institutions; and the Armed Forces. They all contribute to skill acquisition, but here, too, as a by-product of their other missions.

We find, then, that the process of skill acquisition depends on a group of institutions which have only a secondary focus on training and the acquisition of competence. Moreover, no societal body has the responsibility of improving the articulation among these several independent institutions. Each has its own goals and interests and is free to pursue them. Finally, whether or not an individual succeeds in acquiring a desired level of competence depends on his success in negotiating his way through these several institutions. Therefore, the matter of access becomes crucial.

Access has several dimensions. One is that the learning acquired in one institution is frequently prerequisite for access to the next institution. A mentally deficient child may be rejected for admission to a public school on the ground that he is unable to profit from classroom instruction. If so, he may be permanently doomed to a peripheral existence. A pupil who drops out of school at an early grade may be rejected for military service because he cannot meet the minimum educational requirements, and he is thereby deprived of valuable training and experience. Many desirable jobs are closed to all who do not have the formal credentials, from the completion of an apprenticeship to a college degree.

With the exception of the family, each of the principal institutions engaged in the training of individuals is free to determine within wide margins the conditions under which it will accept applicants and the criteria it will use to assess their achievement. While there is pressure on the educational system and the military to accept most individuals who reach a stipulated age, both the school and the Armed Forces have some freedom to reject those who they judge will be unable to cope effectively with their programs. In addition, each institution has considerable freedom to design its own program. This means that the newcomer must meet the standards and conditions set by the organization. While requirements are set with an eye to the qualifications of potential applicants, it is usually the individual rather than the organization who must adjust. If an individual cannot meet the requirements, he drops out. The organization continues on its course.

There is a further consequence to this pattern of loose articulation among freestanding institutions involved in the training cycle. There are few transitional mechanisms to assist the child, young person, or adult as he moves from one institution to the next. The mother drops the newly enrolled pupil at the school's door and picks him up when the session is over. She cannot visit the classroom to reassure her youngster, who may be overwhelmed by the separation and the pressures to conform. He must adjust on his own or drop out. A similarly sharp transition must be made by the civilian who joins the Army. Once he is sworn in, sergeants and officers begin to bark orders at him, and their every move is calculated to break his ties with the past in order to speed his assimilation into an organization that relies on instant and complete obedience. Although this radical break in patterns of behavior is negotiated by most recruits without difficulty, a significant minority are overwhelmed by the abruptness of the transition, and some become ineffective because they receive little or no support. Much the same is true of the employment setting, in which many who have not worked before and who are uncertain about their ability to make the grade crumble under the strident demands of their foreman, who is often more concerned in establishing his authority than in facilitating the assimilation of new workers. Many voluntary "quits" occur in the first weeks of employment, which reflects the inability of many workers, particularly young workers, to make the transition to the new setting.

A critical aspect of the skill acquisition process in developed countries is its elongation. A young person is likely to be in his late teens or early twenties before he moves out of the education-training cycle into employment, and for many the training cycle continues during their period on the job. As the following two chapters seek to illustrate, individuals differ in their willingness and ability to undertake long periods of training because of the direct costs of training as well as having to forgo an income, because of the ease or difficulty that they find in completing a long course of training, and because of the alternative opportunities for the use of time. Other considerations include the pressures exerted on them by their peers, the estimate they make about whether they are likely to profit from the skills they are acquiring, and the extent to which their families are supportive.

These time- and money-conditioned aspects of training bring us back into the domain of economics, where the dominant viewpoint treats skill acquisition as an investment decision. The economic analysts contend that individuals, employers, and society invest in training because of the returns that attach to higher orders of skill and competence in the form of increased earnings, profits, and economic well-being. While the investment approach has some explanatory value, the critical question is, how much? In this connection it is well to recall the principal elements in the foregoing structure. Each of the major institutions involved in the process of skill acquisition—the family, the school, and the employer—is not primarily and surely not solely concerned with facilitating the accumulation of competence and know-how. For the most part, what these institutions contribute to the process of skill acquisition is ancillary to their primary mission of child rearing, cognitive education, or making goods and money. Secondly, no one of these institutions by itself can provide the range of experiences that a person requires for the mastery of skills and the acquisition of competence. Thirdly, the process involves the successful transition of individuals from one insituation to the next, while each institution can determine the conditions of entrance and the criteria of successful performance.

The foregoing can be summarized by considering the skill acquisition process in terms of a developmental path. To broaden their knowledge, skills, and competence, young people must be able to cope with each successive stage within approximately stipulated time periods. Their past accomplishments largely determine their future options. The dominant elements of the process, then, are sequence, cumulation, and timing. The control of these three elements over the outcomes is a function of the extent to which a society establishes alternatives for those who are forced or who opt to get off the developmental path and who later decide that they would like to return.

No objective observer would contend that our society, or any other, is providing optimal opportunities for skill acquisition. A more cautious preliminary assessment would be that a wide range of opportunities exists for different individuals and groups to acquire skills and competences that redound to their own and to their society's benefit. Since training involves both costs and benefits, the question remains how access to these opportunities is distributed and the extent to which different individuals and groups are able and willing to avail themselves of them. These are the concerns of the two chapters that follow.

· 6 ·

Access to Opportunity

THE DESCRIPTION PRESENTED in the preceding chapter of the principal institutions involved in the process of skill acquisition specified that mastery of competence by the individual entails a long period of training, both formal and informal, that starts shortly after birth and continues throughout life. The analysis called attention to the critical role of the family in laying the foundations on which all later learning is predicated.

Next it was stipulated that, in developed societies, the training role of the family is taken over by the school and the employer. In advanced societies, the young person is likely to remain on a developmental path for the first two decades of his life, and sometimes longer; even when he has completed the transition from school to work he continues to develop his skills and competences. Thus, the process of skill acquisition involves the developmental path which individuals traverse, particularly during the formative period of their lives.

The third point is the importance of affiliation: the status of the family into which a child is born determines the resources which will be available for his survival and development. If the youngster is to profit from his education, participation in a youth group, a tour of duty in the military, or the training provided by an employer, he must utilize his early opportunities. Unless a young person is admitted to and remains in school; unless he is able to join the neighborhood Boy Scout troop or is accepted by the local youth center; unless he meets the standards for enlistment into the Armed Forces; unless he obtains a job with an employer who provides a range of training opportunities—that is, unless the individual becomes affiliated with these institutions, he cannot easily build a solid base for skill acquisition and competence. Without the range of exposures, experiences, and learning that are tied to these and similar affiliations, the young person will not be able to recognize his preferences and assets; he will not have the critical information about the options open to him and the relative advantages of pursuing one or another goal. Successful affiliation therefore has a twofold significance: it alone provides the individual with access to environments where he can add to his stock of knowledge and develop his abilities; equally important, affiliation permits him to explore the options that are, or may be, open to him.

The elements involved in the acquisition of skills and competence therefore involve two critical dimensions: the opportunity for formal and informal learning, and the ability of the individual to get and stay on a path which provides access to environments where he can learn more about the options open to him and to make a selection that is congruent with his emerging interests, competences, and values.

Two words stand in a contrapuntal relationship: access and skill. Without access to the range of opportunities provided in every society by such basic institutions as the family, the school, and the employer, the skill and competence that an individual or group is able to acquire will be limited. This chapter will explore the ways in which different societies provide developmental opportunities and the consequences for different groups of the manner in which their access to the critical institutions is facilitated or impeded.

The present effort to deal with social class as a key determinant of skill and competence differs in several respects from earlier approaches. The classical economists developed an analysis of class structure in terms of economic specialization: different groups perform different economic functions and accordingly belong to the landowning, merchant and manufacturing, or laboring classes. The economists were concerned with providing a rationale for the economic returns that each of these principal orders of society received for their contribution to the national output. While they recognized that an occasional person may move from one to another class, they viewed the social structure as more or less fixed and permanent.

Karl Marx and his followers used an even more simplified model which consisted of only two classes, owners of property and the proletariat, distinguished by its lack of property. But Marx did not see the class structure as permanent. In fact the focus of his analysis was directed to uncovering the factors that were operating to undermine the existing relations between the two classes. He prognosticated the collapse of capitalism when unemployed workers would no longer be able to buy the products that capitalists had to sell. In developing his class dynamics, Marx was sensitive to the secondary consequences of poverty that prevented most children of the working poor from access to the developmental opportunities which would enable them to acquire competence and skill.

Modern sociologists working with a schema comprising between six and ten classes based on a composite index of education, occupation, and income have developed statistical measures of intra- and inter-generational social mobility. Their results have been in terms of averages and probabilities.

The aim of this chapter is to assess the way in which social class, which is defined here as being determined primarily by parental income, affects the opportunities of young people to acquire skill and competence. The approach that will be used is, first, intergenerational. Secondly, this chapter will seek to specify, more than is customarily done, the manner in which various institutions play a role in broadening or narrowing the opportunities open to children from different social classes to acquire skill and competence. The concern here is not with statistical averages but with illuminating the dynamic role of social class in the process of skill acquisition.

Since once again it is not practical to pursue the analysis of access to opportunity in different cultures except in a schematic fashion, the following presentation will be restricted to three principal cases: a traditional agricultural society; the United States as the prototype of an affluent economy with a record of expanding career opportunities; and the U.S.S.R., which has attempted to achieve both a buildup of its skill base and increased opportunities for many citizens formerly excluded from higher education and preferred careers.

One conspicuous characteristic of traditional agricultural societies is the element of continuity from one generation to the next, predicated on the stability of the economy, technology, social relations, and political arrangements. A second conspicuous factor is the organization of traditional societies around the extended family and the village, which is made up of a number of extended families. While contacts beyond the village are necessary for trade, selection of a spouse, and occasionally seasonal employment, local self-sufficiency is the dominant pattern.

A third characteristic, more readily recognizable when the traditional village is contrasted with a modern industrial community, is the absence of basic developmental institutions other than the extended family. This fact helps to emphasize the multiple responsibilities of the family in preparing young people for their adult roles, and, equally important, it helps to explain the overriding social and economic impact of the family on the lives and fortunes of its offspring. In most traditional societies, the disparity in income and status among families is even greater than in most advanced societies.

The amount of arable land (as well as other income-producing assets, such as cattle) that a rural family owns is the most important factor in determining the opportunities it can make available to its offspring. Whether a child survives, and particularly the condition of his health in adulthood are functions primarily of how well he was fed and otherwise nurtured during his formative years. High mortality and premature death are closely tied to the low economic position of a family. In many low-income societies, as many as a fifth, sometimes a third, occasionally as many as one-half, of all children die before they reach working age, and of those who survive, a high proportion carry throughout their lives the scars of inadequate diet in childhood, compounded by the sequelae of malnutrition.

In most traditional societies, there are sharp differences among groups based upon such factors as religion, ethnic background, and politics. Families which belong to a clearly disadvantaged minority, which is restricted in where it may live, the work it can engage in, and the extent to which it is permitted to participate in communal activities, are handicapped in preparing their children for adulthood. Family status and family income and wealth are the compelling forces affecting the allocation of opportunities in traditional societies.

The fourth critical element affecting traditional societies is location. The distance people live from centers of population concentration determines whether and to what extent they are likely to be affected by the dynamic factors impinging on their society. Proximity to urban centers usually implies broadened opportunities for education, work, and income.

A second advantage attaches to those who are city-based or who live within the shadow of the city. Even traditional societies, which provide only a limited number of public services, particularly education and health, provide them primarily for the urban population. For example, a new hospital or a secondary school is usually erected in the capital or in another important urban center.

The first consequence of low income, discrimination, and isolation is easily described. Children who grow up in families which do not have enough to eat or whose diet is unbalanced are unlikely to profit from school exposure, even if they attend. Educators have recently become aware that even in developed societies some children in the first grades of school are apathetic and have difficulty in following the lessons. Upon investigation, it was learned that this apathy appears to be related to their poor nutrition. Many children come to school hungry, and a hungry child is not able to concentrate or to learn.

Low family income reduces the prospects of a child's profiting from school experiences in still other ways. Although most agricultural societies have more people than opportunities for productive employment, there are periods of the year when every person is needed to work. Then, the low-income family is likely to need its children's assistance. As with malnutrition, absenteeism diminishes a child's ability to profit from school.

Young people from low-income families are further handicapped because of the difficulties they have in making the transition from the local elementary school to the intermediate or secondary school, which frequently is located beyond commuting distance from their homes. Since governments of most developing countries have been able to establish intermediate and secondary schools only in large cities, the child in a rural area can continue his education only if he lives away from home. Even if relatives cooperate, such an arrangement usually involves some financial outlay for his parents. The longer the young person remains in the educational process, the greater the drain on family finances. Since low-income families in low-income countries operate on very narrow margins, most find it impossible to keep their children long in the educational system.

The limited occupational differentiation characteristic of most traditional societies facilitates the transfer of skill from father to son. This in turn implies that outsiders have little or no chance to break into a preferred occupation. The situation is compounded for members of a minority held in low esteem, particularly in rural areas where the social structure is rigid.

Geographic isolation also takes a heavy toll. In the capital and other large cities, a small modern sector usually creates new opportunities in transportation, construction, tourism, the operation of public utilities, certain occupations in the commercial sector, and government employment. Those growing up far from these nodules of economic development will not have access to such new opportunities and may not even be aware of them. They are handicapped by both their limited vision and their constricted environment. It does not follow that the masses who are urban-based or those who migrate from the countryside to an urban center will necessarily be better off than those who remain in the rural backwater. The numbers seeking to improve their circumstances are always in excess of the opportunities available. But if there is any quickening of city life, and there usually is, those at or close to the bottom of the urban society are not as completely trapped as are those in an isolated village, where the absence of change reinforces rigid class and family differences.

We find, in the less-developed countries, then, an educational system and an employment structure that tend to allocate developmental opportunities in favor of families higher on the social and economic scale. The children of such families come to school in better health; they are better nourished, and they are less likely to be absent because of the family's need for their labor. Consequently, they are more likely to profit from their educational experiences. Some remain in school long enough to qualify for admission to the university. If they complete their course of study and earn a degree, they are in a relatively good position because of their family connections to get a job, even one with prospects. Young people from affluent families who balk at extended schooling often are helped to get a start in farming or business through their family's intervention.

Those at the lower end of the socioeconomic scale are correspondingly handicapped in all these regards: they are likely to grow up with impaired health, to have less schooling, and to be under pressure to accept any kind of work they can get. If they are rural-based and, worse, if they belong to a disadvantaged minority, their job problems will be even more difficult since they may have to earn their livelihood at demeaning and the most low-paying work.

We have seen that the relatively stagnant rural economy and the slow growth of the modern sector in most developing countries assure that those most likely to find satisfactory employment and income-earning opportunities are the children of well-positioned families which have land to transfer to them, a shop to pass on, or good connections that will enable their sons to get positions in a large private or public enterprise. Without family support and connections, there is little prospect that young people growing up in a rural community will do better than their fathers; many do worse. In the city, with its more dynamic economy, the number of opportunities is greater, but so is the number of aspirants, since, as we have seen, the city draws many from the countryside who believe that they have nothing to lose by leaving home. In sum, economic backwardness, rurality, and social stratification provide an environment of limited opportunities, most of which are preempted by the families at the middle and upper ends of the socioeconomic hierarchy.

Before considering the conditions governing access to opportunities in advanced societies, democratic or communist, it would be well to summarize the principal differences in the structures of a traditional society and an advanced technological nation that affect the issue of opportunity.

In an advanced economy the occupational structure is much more diversified and subject to more rapid change; consequently, it is more difficult for fathers to transfer their occupational status directly to their sons.

The ownership of property plays a much smaller role than wage employment in the determination of personal income. About three-fourths of all personal income in the United States is earned via wages and salaries. Unless he is wealthy, a father cannot transfer sufficient property to assure his offspring a high standard of living. The best way to help a child acquire preferred occupational status and income is by assisting him in obtaining a superior education, the open sesame to a good career.

Most parents in developed countries are able to provide their children with a satisfactory start in life. While inadequate diet, lack of ready access to health services, and other deterrents to optimal development afflict a significant minority of families, the proportion who live at or near the poverty level is much smaller than in less-developed countries. In the mid-1970s, the median income of United States families was in excess of $12,000!

In developed countries, a high proportion of the total population lives in urban centers, and the rural areas are linked to the cities by superior communications systems, from automobiles to television. Therefore, the extreme isolation and backwardness characteristic of the rural population in less-developed countries have no parallel in advanced societies. In affluent countries, the gap between life in the city and life on the farm, including differences in opportunities for development, is relatively much smaller.

One important consequence of a high level of economic development is the larger proportion of the national income at the disposal of government for investment in a range of services, many of which relate directly to expanding developmental opportunities for the citizenry. These expenditures are of two kinds: major sums are directed to broadening access to education, particularly at the collegiate and university levels, for students who qualify; the second involves a broad sweep of social welfare programs aimed at assisting families which are unable to provide adequately for themselves.

One additional difference should be noted. In less-developed countries, a small number of families exercise a disproportionate influence on the control and management of important organizations in both the private and public sectors. As a consequence, ties of kinship play a dominant role in the allocation of career opportunities. While pull and connections are also present and potent in advanced societies, family ties are less important in determining who is hired and who is promoted.

A series of interacting factors contributes to the wider access to opportunity in developed societies than in developing societies, including the importance of wage versus property income, the larger role of public investment in critical services, and the narrower gap between countryside and city. This does not mean, however, that in an affluent society access to opportunity is shared equally by all groups. It is not.

The nurturing that parents are able to provide their offspring depends not only on their total income, important as that factor is, but also on the number of children among whom it must be divided. If a middle-income family has three times as much income as a family living at the poverty level, the ratio of their relative expenditures per child will not be 3 to 1 but more like 5 to 1, because low-income families tend to have more children.

Children born into well-to-do families have many advantages. They are more likely to have educated parents. In the United States, both the father and the mother may have attended college. This means that their children spend their earliest years in an environment where they are daily exposed to words, ideas, abstract concepts, books, and general cultural experiences. Many are ready for school before they enter, and this transition poses no special problem, since their lives at home have prepared them for the classroom. The youngster whose parents dropped out of high school, whose parents are not readers and cannot deal with abstractions, begins his own educational cycle under different circumstances. He does not start at the same point as the youngster from the affluent, better-educated family.

The inequalities reflected in family conditions are reinforced by inequalities in the schools which the well-to-do and poor children attend. Poor families tend to live in poor neighborhoods, rich families in affluent suburbs. In the United States, since school financing comes largely from local taxes, the facilities, staff, curriculum, and supplemental services are likely to be much better in high-income areas. The crux of the difference lies less in the physical environment and more in the learning milieu. Upper-income children go to school knowing that they must adjust. They may find much of the teaching dull, even boring, but they have been conditioned at home to adjust to school. Not so, youngsters from low-income homes. Boys, in particular, resent the physical constraint under which they are kept. And both these boys and girls encounter teachers who consider them and treat them as inferior, since their manners and behavior patterns differ from those of the middle class. Many of these disadvantaged youngsters have difficulty in mastering the classroom materials, with the consequence that they early become antagonistic toward the school, which in turn labels them as ineffective or failures. In a few years, many youngsters begin acting up, and the teaching staff must then spend more and more of its time and energies in keeping order. This further estranges the hostile youngsters and further retards their ability to learn.

The adjustment of a child to school is conditioned not only by what transpires in the classroom and by the support he receives at home but also by his out-of-school activities—how he spends his free time. The child of affluent parents is likely to visit museums, go to theaters, attend concerts, spend summers at camp, and travel during the winter. Vacation experiences make it easier for him to understand what goes on in school at the same time that they reinforce his growing perception that a good education is prerequisite for a good life.

Perhaps the most critical difference is in the self-image and the goals that children develop. Those from upper-income homes, whose parents are educated and whose fathers—and increasingly whose mothers also—hold good jobs, assume that they, too, will be able to obtain desirable positions if they follow parental guidance and attend to their studies. In contrast are the youngsters from low-income homes whose parents have unskilled jobs, suffer intermittent spells of unemployment, and are in a continuing struggle to keep their families afloat. These adverse conditions frame the lives of most families in a low-income neighborhood. The more successful relocate. The youngster in a poor family early recognizes that the odds are heavily stacked against him, and his views of himself and his plans for the future are shaped accordingly.

Since access to opportunity in an advanced economy is closely linked to the successful negotiation of higher education, we will consider the ways in which the school system affects differentially the futures of children from affluent homes and from poor homes. We will consider the impact of the following conventional practices and procedures: testing, tracking, guidance, admission policies, and fees. With respect to each, the child from a low-income home is at a disadvantage, frequently a serious disadvantage.

Most schools use intelligence tests to assess the learning potential of pupils, and these tests provide the basis on which the schools make decisions about admissions, assignments, and promotions. While experts differ, there is a growing consensus that these tests are skewed in favor of youngsters from middle-class families and against youngsters from low-income families where there is greater dissonance between their styles of life and the dominant culture. As a consequence, the test results are often misread: the middle-class children are assumed to be brighter than they are; those from low-income homes are considered more handicapped than they are.

Since they must deal with large numbers of children and young people over a considerable span of years, the educational authorities in all technologically advanced societies have resorted to tracking, that is, to assigning different groups of students to different educational tracks where they are exposed to different curricula which lead to different career outcomes. While the preferences of parents and children play some part in the decision making, the assignments often reflect the preconceptions of the educational establishment. A relatively high proportion of children from low-income homes is arbitrarily or subtly deflected from pursuing an academic course of studies, the best path into higher education and the prestigious occupations. Most schools would hesitate, however, to advise a youngster from an affluent family, even a student with consistently low marks, to shift to a course that would substantially reduce his prospects of being admitted to college.

As the educational and occupational structures become more varied, parents find it increasingly difficult to provide their children with the advice and counsel they need to negotiate the highly differentiated preparatory systems. During the last decades, therefore, there has been a proliferation of guidance services aimed at providing professional advice. However, school counselors are part of the educational hierarchy; they share with principals and teachers certain preconceptions and prejudices, and their advice frequently reflects their biases. Moreover, often poorly informed about the critical changes that are taking place in the educational and employment sectors, they often mislead the young people they counsel. School counselors who have not kept abreast of the changing economy cannot alert youngsters to opportunities which are opening up for the first time or which are being expanded.

Each higher level of the educational system makes use of selection devices. No society has yet been able or willing to invest sufficient resources in the educational-training system to obviate the need for selection. In graduate or professional education, where unit costs are high, selection procedures are often stringent, since the number of applicants is often far in excess of capacity. Most university admissions procedures place heavy weight on prior academic performance, often making use of national norms. Since most young people from affluent homes have attended better schools, their chances for admission to college and graduate or professional schools are much better than those of young people from low-income families. Often, the advantaged youngster has also profited from special tutoring, attendance at summer sessions, and guidance from siblings and friends about how to cope with the hurdles of the admissions process.

Finally, reference must be made to the economic costs of pursuing higher education. Even when tuition and fees are low by virtue of state financing, that is not the whole of the matter. A young person who attends school full time and pursues his studies seriously is not able to hold a full-time job. He must therefore obtain all or some of the funds he needs to cover his schooling and living expenses. If his parents are barely able to make ends meet, it is unlikely that they will be able to provide him with more than modest help. If he lives at home while he attends a tuition-free institution, he will probably be able to earn sufficient money to cover his incidental expenses. But if he attends a college or university in another city, especially if he must also pay for all or part of his tuition, the lack of money presents a major hurdle. If he converts most of his free hours into paid employment, his academic performance is likely to be mediocre, and if he is enrolled in a demanding curriculum such as engineering, law, or medicine, he will be under great strain if he attempts to study and support himself at the same time.

While modern societies have gone a long way to reduce the financial barriers facing students pursuing higher education, only the exceptional student from a low-income family in the United States receives sufficient financial support so that he does not have to spend at least part of his time and energy on income-earning activities.

Despite the enlarged public expenditures for higher education that have removed many barriers in the path of young people from low-income families, the foregoing review emphasizes the marked competitive advantages that remain with the more affluent in their pursuit of educational credentials.

This brings us to the third arena, employment, where the reach of family background also operates. It is not only the jobs at the top of the occupational hierarchy, professional and managerial, that require advanced education. Many desirable jobs in the middle range of administrative, sales, and craft occupations have educational and training prerequisites. Since four out of five young people complete high school in the United States, most opening positions with built-in promotional opportunities, that is—apprenticeship, civil service, and positions in large organizations—are often closed to the one in five who has not acquired a high school diploma. The 20 percent who fail to complete high school are not randomly distributed among the population. They include a disproportionate number of young people with the following characteristics: they come from low-income families; their parents have a low level of educational achievement; they have grown up in a low-income area where a higher-than-average number of youngsters drop out of school before earning a diploma.

In addition to having a bias in favor of those with higher educational achievement, the operations of the labor market also favor young people from affluent families. There is the simple but important matter of information. In most advanced economies, employers use their work force for recruiting. The assumption is that a long-time worker, familiar with the needs of the establishment, is in a good position to recommend an applicant for a job opening. Consequently, young people whose parents and relatives are well positioned to learn about desirable job openings have an advantage. The offspring of the poor, on the other hand, are handicapped by virtue of the fact that their relatives and friends, holding the least desirable jobs, seldom learn about good openings.

Long-time employees frequently exercise a strong influence on who is hired. For instance, apprentices are accepted on the recommendation of journeymen, subject to their meeting certain formal requirements which traditionally have favored sons and relatives of union members. Large corporations seek to fill their openings for junior executives from among the graduates of a limited number of leading colleges and business schools. The justices of the U.S. Supreme Court pick their clerks from among the top students in the top-ranking law schools. The best students from leading medical schools have the first choice of desirable residencies.

There are other factors that give a young person from an established family the edge in the job market. He is not under pressure to accept the first offer. He can be more selective because he can afford to wait. Moreover, he is more likely to marry a young woman from an affluent family whose father may be able and willing to give his son-in-law an assist.

The discussion to this point has focused on how family income and status operate as major differentiators of opportunity through their influence on early development within the home, on educational preparation, and on employment. Two additional factors, referred to in our discussion of developing countries, should be briefly noted here. They are discrimination and rurality. Although industrialization, urbanization, and political democracy have helped to reduce the role of prejudice in the distribution of opportunity, discrimination is present in varying degrees in every modern society.

The adverse consequences of discrimination are manifest in the special difficulties that members of minority groups encounter in seeking admission into preferred educational programs and in obtaining desirable jobs. Furthermore, discrimination undermines the self-esteem and distorts the expectations of those who grow up in an environment characterized by prejudice and hostility. Moreover, many members of minority groups, because of earlier discriminatory practices on the part of the dominant majority, tend to have less education, hold less attractive jobs, earn less income, live in less desirable neighborhoods, and generally enjoy less of the material goods available to others.

Rurality also has an adverse influence on access to opportunity. Although in most advanced economies a relatively small number of people are engaged in agriculture—often as few as 1 in 10 or even 1 in 20—many among the rural population face the following conditions: low family income, access to only poor public services, a narrow occupational structure, and a paucity of cultural activities. As a consequence, young people growing up in rural areas have fewer developmental opportunities than their urban peers, and many rural youths who are unable to find suitable employment in their immediate environs sooner or later migrate to the city.

The foregoing account of the manner in which access to developmental opportunities is structured in advanced societies used the United States as the prototype. We will now consider briefly whether an advanced communist society, the U.S.S.R., parallels or differs substantially from the United States model in order to determine the importance of egalitarian goals in the structuring of opportunity.

A few preliminary observations: we noted earlier that the U.S.S.R. relies to a greater degree than the United States on creches and nurseries to facilitate the employment of married women. Closely related was the early loosening of occupational barriers based on sex. Women in the U.S.S.R. have had easier access to a wide range of professions including medicine, engineering, science, management, and politics, although the top positions in most of these fields have not been as open to women as to men.

Another aspect of the role of discrimination in the opportunity structure of the U.S.S.R. was expressed in the policy, especially in earlier decades, of preventing the sons and daughters of the aristocracy and bourgeoisie from entering educational and other channels that led to positions of power and prestige. In addition, the regime set tight quotas on the number of Jews accepted by universities and excluded them from institutions which train young people for diplomatic careers.

Although discrimination based on sex, class background, religion, and ethnic origin has persisted in varying degrees in the U.S.S.R., a more pervasive barrier to equality of developmental opportunity results from the persistent wide differentials between urban and rural life and the consequences that flow therefrom. The locational factor, if not determining, is important in opening or closing opportunities to both young people and adults. The odds strongly favor the city resident, especially if he grows up in the national, or an important regional, capital. To the extent that development is facilitated by cultural stimulation and good schools, the advantages which accrue to the urban dweller are indeed substantial.

Since the military represents one of the important power centers and provides attractive careers, note should be taken of the special schools which admit a limited number of children at the age of six or so; the children receive a carefully tailored educational experience aimed at qualifying them for careers as military officers. There is nothing directly comparable to such a carefully controlled developmental experience in other developed nations.

The principal path to a preferred career, however, even in Soviet Russia, is through higher education. Although the U.S.S.R. has made great efforts to expand secondary and higher education opportunities, the numbers seeking entrance into the university system far exceed the number of available places, particularly in the preferred specialties, with the result that the competition has been, and continues to be, keen.

Secondary school teachers direct much of their efforts to helping their better pupils pass the qualifying examinations with marks high enough to assure their admission to a university. Next, parents in a position to do so obtain special tutoring for their children. There is scattered evidence that points to the importance in the admissions process of "political connections," both parental and political (the latter via service in various youth organizations). For a time, Khrushchev sought to reduce the pressure on university admissions by establishing the requirement that applicants had to demonstrate their diligence and interest by two years of regular employment before they were eligible to enter upon a course of higher studies, but this requirement was later eased.

Once a student is accepted at the university, he receives basic support from the state so that he is able to devote most of his time to his studies. This is in keeping with the European tradition, which frowns on students' combining work and university studies.

It appears that access to opportunity in the U.S.S.R. is not very different from that in the United States and other developed nations. Since there are no private institutions, the young person in pursuit of a professional career must be admitted to the university primarily on the basis of his grades. These, in turn, are influenced, much as in the United States, by the quality of his previous schooling, which, in the U.S.S.R., clearly favors those whose families live in large cities. Discrimination on grounds other than location exists, but it is difficult to assess its pervasiveness.

Perhaps the overriding difference between the United States and the U.S.S.R. with regard to access to developmental opportunities is the greater public investment made by the United States in higher education, which makes it less necessary for American institutions to ration admission. Another important facet is the range of opportunities available in each country to those without higher education. It may well be that the differences, here as elsewhere, are less than one might at first assume. We know that there are substantial wage differentials in Russian industry which are related to differentials in skill or which reflect the superior productivity of particular enterprises and workers. We also know that those with superior skills have often had the advantage of special employment-related training and experience. There are, then, many points of similarity between the United States and the U.S.S.R. with respect to skill differentials and rewards.

What generalizations can be distilled from this schematic analysis of access to opportunity in these different social systems? First and foremost is the predominant role of the family that does so much to shape the young child and in the process provides him with a better or worse start in life. In a traditional society there are few other developmental institutions. If the family is unable to provide the child with the essentials he needs, the deficiencies will not be remedied and the adverse consequences are likely to be permanent. Since the number of opportunities for skill acquisition are seriously limited and since the number of desirable employment prospects are even more limited, those who can look to continuing family support are likely to fare best. Without such support it is very difficult, and often impossible, for a young person to break out of the constraining environment into which he was born and brought up. The poverty of his parents will follow him all the days of his life.

In developed economies, both capitalist and communist, opportunities are less restricted for a variety of reasons, including the following: the average level of family income is sufficient so that, with the limitation of family size, most parents can provide their offspring with a reasonable start in life; the state has assumed the principal or sole responsibility for providing educational and training opportunities for all young people; progression through the educational system reflects to a considerable degree the differential capacity of students to master the material and their differential interests; acquisition of a higher degree provides access to preferred jobs and careers.

In both types of societies, parents with more than average amounts of property or power or both are able to facilitate the development of their offspring, but they are not able to assure a favorable outcome. The reason is that every man's (and increasingly every woman's) economic and social position reflects the level of his or her personal accomplishment in the world of work. Families make their principal contribution by helping their children obtain a superior education and by offering them a helping hand when they first enter regular employment. From there on, each new generation is increasingly on its own.

Finally, in both capitalist and communist countries, the developmental process has become increasingly elongated, and those young people who can stay the educational course are more likely to obtain good jobs. Moreover, the clue to each individual's future is the success he has in making the transitions from one critical affiliation to the next—from family to school, from one level of the educational system to the next, from school to the military, and from the military to civilian employment. Those who are able to make these successive transitions smoothly start their careers from a preferred vantage.

Even in a developed society, a child who is born into a family on the upper end of the income distribution has a distinct advantage. However, access to opportunity is much less dependent here than in traditional societies on the social class of the parental family. One of the important by-products of greater economic affluence which leads to greater social investment in the developmental system has been the substantial broadening of access to opportunity. Nevertheless, the offspring of the poor and the otherwise disadvantaged still have restricted access to opportunities; this remains an important item on the agendas of all societies which are committed to the reduction of inequality.

· 7 ·

Social Mobility

THE ANALYSIS SO FAR has indicated that the career opportunities available to adults are largely determined by the families into which they are born, moderated by the public services, particularly the educational system, to which they have had access. Even in a highly dynamic society, there is substantial continuity in socioeconomic position from one generation to the next as a consequence of the determining influence of the position of the family on the prospects of its offspring. When a society is characterized by relatively little change, as is a traditional agricultural economy, status stability from one generation to the next is pronounced.

Before exploring the factors, individual and societal, that can influence whether the status a person eventually achieves is significantly different from that of his parents, we will consider why the issue of social mobility is significant in the context of a human resources approach. There are many reasons. First, regardless of the stage of economic and social development, the extent to which people are willing to put forth effort in their work—and in their preparation for work—depends on their perception of the rewards and satisfactions they may be able to achieve. Consequently, the fuller development and utilization of their skills and competences is closely linked to their estimate of their prospects of personal gain from increased efforts.

Secondly, people who live in absolute or relative poverty and who have little or no status are not free, regardless of their political rights as citizens. If a man must struggle every day, from sunup to sundown, to support himself and his dependents, he does not have the time, energy, or resources to enjoy the good things of life. He is free only to keep fighting to stay alive.

However, the prospect of altering one's position through one's own efforts is a major source of hope. Men may be handicapped by birth and background, but as long as their society offers them some prospect of improving their circumstances, they can look forward to turning the promise of freedom into a reality at some time in the future. The hope may not be realized, but it is important that it exists. Men who can look forward to being free are more able to endure the burdens of their constraints.

Thirdly, the attitude of men toward themselves, their neighbors, and the larger society to which they belong is directly linked to their perception of the reasonableness with which the good things of life are distributed. This has been particularly so since the American and French Revolutions, which gave credence to the doctrine of equality, although they failed to spell out its specific meaning and limits. Two centuries later, the inheritors of these revolutionary legacies look to the principle of equity to govern the way in which rewards are distributed. There may be no better way of arranging the affairs of men than to have fate determine that some children are born to rich parents and some to poor. But it would be intolerable if the accident of birth were to determine all later outcomes. The prospect that, as a result of personal attributes, luck, or other circumstances, men may be able to alter their position on the socioeconomic ladder is an essential precondition for a society which seeks to hold the allegiance of its members. Men who see no possibility of altering their share of the world's goods and who have no prospect of improving their conditions or skills are not likely to feel committed to their society.

An affluent society which generates considerable surplus has a strong incentive to invest part of it in expanding the developmental opportunities for those whose families are poorly situated to assist them. These investments can contribute to the social mobility of the children of workers who are trapped in poor jobs and fall at the lower end of the income distribution. By expanding the opportunities for the children of families in the lower social classes, a society provides concrete evidence of its concern with reducing the power of property to determine the fate of the next generation. In addition, it will reap gains from the fuller development of the potential of these youngsters, much of which would run to waste unless the society intervenes.

The thrust of this chapter is to review the factors that operate to modify the marked influence of social class on career outcomes, primarily in developed societies. The analysis will deal sequentially with the following five constellations of forces which are sufficiently potent to modify the influence of social class on the career outcomes of the next generation: the unique qualities of individuals, the value systems of families and small groups which have special impact on the behavior of their offspring, the supportive institutional arrangements which a society has established for the explicit purpose of assisting youngsters who have limited family support, favorable developments in the labor market, and societal transformations. This multiplicity of transforming agencies suggests that potent as social class is in determining future outcomes, its power is far from absolute.

Even in a preindustrialized society, a few persons are able to escape the confinement of low status. For example, an exceptional man, even with minute initial capital, may manifest such financial acumen that he is able to multiply small sums into larger sums until he eventually breaks into a level of business operations involving trade, moneylending, real estate, and commodity speculation; he may continue to accumulate wealth until his lowly origins are obliterated by his outstanding success.

A few are able to use their ability in the performing or representational arts to reach a position that commands attention and acclaim. Building on his or her talent and spurred by a strong drive to perfect his or her art, a man or woman may, after years of apprenticeship and hard work, rise to be the star of a dance troupe. Another may become a recognized painter. If the base of patrons able and willing to support the arts is small, the possibility that individuals from lowly origins can make such a breakthrough is correspondingly small. But even in low-income countries, a few do succeed.

Entrance into powerful bureaucratic organizations, such as a religious order or the military, provides another avenue of advancement for the lowborn. While the more prestigious and powerful positions in such organizations are usually reserved for the wellborn and the well-connected, the dedicated, talented man with strong leadership potential may overcome the many obstacles in his path and make his mark. When new organizations are created in the urbanized sector of a traditional society, a man without family wealth or connections may be able to catapult himself forward by the strength of his personality and his political acumen. Although the leadership of newly organized political parties and trade unions is usually preempted by those who have had the advantage of formal education, including study leading to graduation from the university, occasionally a man with limited educational achievement is able to move toward the top.

Another way for a person to break out of the confines of an environment of poverty and ignorance is to operate outside the law. The penalties for being caught are severe, but an occasional person is willing to run the risk in the hope that he may be one of those lucky enough to evade the authorities until he can buy his way back into society.

These illustrations remind us that even in a traditional society an occasional person is able to overcome the constraints of having been born into a poor family. Despite the potency of social class in determining career and life outcomes, those few among the poor who develop unusual skill in moneymaking, leadership, or the arts have a chance to break out of their confining backgrounds. The important point in each of these illustrations, however, is that the spring which might lead to a change in one's socio-economic status is embedded in some unique personal quality. In each instance, it is not the society's institutional arrangements to facilitate social mobility, if any, which are crucial, nor need one look to significant changes on the economic and social fronts. What counts is personal charisma, determination, or talent.

The situation is noticeably different in modern, technologically advanced societies. We will again begin with the individual, since, in the final analysis, all career outcomes are determined by the individual's strengths and weaknesses. Parents can do much or little to pave a child's way, but no man completely controls another's fate. The chronicles of many peoples tell of a powerful king who leaves his land at peace and prosperous, only to be succeeded by a son who, through arrogance, avarice, or incompetence, loses his inheritance and often his life. Even Solomon, the wisest of men and the builder of the Temple, could not leave a legacy which would prevent the splintering of his kingdom after his death. The American folklore which relates the saga of a family which goes from rags to riches to rags in three generations implies that a wastrel son can lose as much as his successful father and grandfather were able to accumulate—and more quickly. It is not possible to remove the individual from the career stage. He alone speaks the lines.

Each individual has a unique genetic constitution which, through interaction with the environment, makes him distinct from all other persons. Some genetic qualities manifest themselves early, others later. Some are assets, others liabilities. A child with perfect pitch may eventually build a career around his special endowment, or he may ignore it, but the youngster with a hearing defect will probably be handicapped in whatever career he pursues.

The development of certain characteristics, such as height, is relatively easier to assess in a genetic-environmental context. The study of human genetics has clarified the extent to which height is determined by heredity and can be modified by environmental influences, particularly by nutrition and by the sequelae of diseases of infancy or childhood. Moreover, height is easy to measure. Other characteristics are complicated. Traits such as intelligence, creativity, and temperament presumably play a large role in career outcomes. Little is known about their genetic roots and still less about the complex ways in which inherited characteristics interact with the environment to shape these qualities. There is no agreement among the experts as to the constituent elements of intelligence, creativity, or temperament. Disagreements persist among the experts about which criteria should be used to assess outcomes and about the chain of reasoning to support inferences. Disagreements persist even about the validity of the measuring instruments.

We can highlight some of these difficulties by considering the exceptional person—Keats, Beethoven, Einstein. No one any longer holds with the behaviorists of an earlier generation that a favorable environment can alone explain these highly creative persons. Today, it is presumed that endowment played a major role. But having postulated this, we still do not know how to explain the unique contributions of these highly creative persons. Moreover, we do not know how many children are born with a high potential for significant artistic or scientific accomplishment yet stagnate because the environment in which they grow up stultifies their interests and atrophies their potentials. We are not much further ahead in our understanding of the creative function than the ancients who looked upon the genius as a biologic sport, a gift from the gods.

Ours, however, is an easier task. We need not explain the dynamics of genius; we need only consider the extent to which the special strengths of some individuals enable them to transcend their backgrounds in their career progression. A good place to begin is with individuals who make their mark through sports.

Outstanding accomplishment in sports, particularly in the United States, has for many years provided an important pathway for upward mobility for a significant number of men and a few women from socially deprived families. Since the opportunities for demonstrating potential are generally available—in a sandlot or a local gymnasium—and since specialized training is not essential to attract attention initially, many young people from low-income families, both white and black, have made their mark via boxing, baseball, football, basketball, and other competitive sports.

Several factors are involved. Professional baseball teams were the first to search systematically for talent by sending scouts to observe local teams at play in the hope of spotting promising players. Once recruited, a young man had broadened opportunities for access to the training and experience essential for his further development. As he progressed, he was kept under close supervision by trainers and managers who assessed how far he was likely to go and what further opportunities he needed to reach his full development.

Since American high schools and colleges have emphasized competitive sports, another channel has been provided for the good athlete from a disadvantaged background. The high school athlete, especially if he showed promise of being a good football player, was avidly sought by college scouts who offered scholarships, spending money, and the promise of a good job after graduation. The recruiters assured him further that if he needed help with his college studies, that too would be available.

The reason that competitive sports offer such an important avenue for occupational mobility grows out of the psychological reinforcement that occurs when a poor boy without other claims to distinction brings credit to himself, his team, and his institution. The attention and acclaim he elicits and receives encourage him to put forth the special efforts to undergo the long and exhausting training which is required if he is to excel.

For girls, pulchritude and attractiveness have been the counterparts of sports. The roots of the Cinderella story are found in the oldest folklore. In addition to attracting successful men and improving their status through marriage, beautiful young women from modest circumstances have sought to make their way in fields where their special assets are highly valued: theater, movies, modeling. Since attractiveness is never a factor of features alone but involves speech, carriage, and emotions, a pretty face and a good figure represent potential, nothing more. The movie industry in its heyday operated a scouting system that closely resembled that of professional baseball. Scouts searched high school and college dramatic clubs for the future starlet. Once she was identified and recruited, Hollywood provided the coaching and exposure required for judging whether the promising youngster had the making of a star. Not even a multimillionaire producer could force the American public to accept his favorite.

Musical ability is another type of endowment out of which some young people from deprived backgrounds have been able to develop successful careers. Some have been able to rise to the very top of the artistic hierarchy, while others have settled for a career several notches lower. The young person with a good voice or with aptitude for the piano or the violin can usually attract the attention he needs to obtain access to professional training. Once he reaches the arena which the experts control, his progress depends in large measure on the depth of his talent and his ability to meet the arduous demands of long, hard years of further training.

As we have noted, even in societies where access to wealth is tightly controlled and where the barriers against outsiders are high, some few people have a penchant for moneymaking. In dynamic economies, with their much larger number of moneymaking opportunities, many more individuals are able, with little or no help from their families, to use their wits, their sense of timing, and their eye for a bargain and eventually succeed in accumulating considerable wealth.

Successful speculators are a special ilk. They have great confidence in their own judgment and look on their fellowmen as inferior creatures who, like sheep, follow the group. Whatever their personality amalgam—quick intelligence, self-confidence, a flair for seizing the main opportunity, and above all consuming interest in accumulation—the nature of their talent remains obscure, and we know next to nothing about its component parts beyond the fact that many offspring of highly successful men show none of the qualities that distinguished their progenitors.

In advanced economies where the large corporation dominates, there is another route to the top which is sometimes scaled by a person from a handicapped background who has not had the advantages of a higher education, the usual qualification for a managerial career. Here, too, it is difficult to specify the amalgam of qualities that leads to success. Clearly, an ability to attract and hold the attention and respect of those who wield power without threatening them is one prerequisite; a problem-solving ability is another; the capacity to elicit loyalty and support from one's subordinates—all these are suggestive. But patience, a touch of ruthlessness, and the ability to mask one's feelings are also useful. Another factor is a determination to stay the course. Business schools can go only part of the way in preparing students for corporate life. They can introduce them to theories and methods that will facilitate their being employed and promoted. But as men move up the hierarchy, their progress will be less and less determined by their specialized competences and will reflect increasingly their organizational know-how and skills. The accumulation of organizational skills is an art which some acquire but which none can teach.

A few men succeed in breaking out of their confining backgrounds by building a new organization from scratch or by taking over a small enterprise and expanding it. The more specialized the society, the greater are the opportunities for such entrepreneurial activities. In the contemporary United States, an occasional man from a poor background succeeds in putting together a successful business enterprise, labor organization, ethnic society, gambling syndicate, or health movement. Through charisma or acumen, he is able to attract the resources and talent that a new or embryonic organization requires if it is to make its mark.

This brings us to that aspect of personality—intelligence—which geneticists, psychologists, and social scientists believe to be the dominant factor in career development and performance. Their studies have addressed such questions as the relation between intelligence and school achievement, the extent to which intelligence differentiates high performers from low performers in the occupational arena, and the differences in intelligence among subgroups in the population.

For seven decades psychologists have been giving "intelligence tests," primarily to children, and have used the results to assign children to different educational tracks, to guide them into different careers, and to judge the extent to which the status and accomplishments of groups appear to be rooted in differences in their average levels of intelligence. Most experts agree that intelligence is heavily influenced by genetic endowment; that a favorable environment can contribute to its fuller development, but only within a relatively narrow range; that the children of parents with high intelligence tend to regress toward the mean (that is, they will generally score below their parents); that high scorers are more likely to do well in school and remain longer; and that certain occupational fields—especially those requiring high powers of abstraction (mathematics, physics, logic)—can be successfully pursued only by individuals who rank at the upper end of the IQ distribution. Further, the experts point out that persons with high scores on intelligence tests are more likely to be found among those near the top of the occupational and income hierarchies.

The foregoing discussion outlines the arena of broad agreement among the experts, but sharp conflicts rage with regard to interpretations and even more about policy recommendations. The conflicts center around the nature of group differences, such as differences between the average scores of rich and poor children, black and white children, and males and females. The more cautious among the experts believe that since intelligence scores reflect the interaction of endowment and environment, no valid conclusions can be drawn about the genetic endowment of any group in light of the variability of environmental opportunities to which different groups are exposed. Moreover, many experts are disturbed about the quality of the instruments used to measure intelligence, since they realize that they tend to be culture-bound and that the scores reflect an admixture of environmental exposure and native endowment. But the strongest disagreements lie in the policy arena. The environmentalists argue in favor of equalizing developmental opportunities; they are convinced that the present shortfall in the average test scores of certain groups reflects their social deprivation, nothing more and nothing less. Others hold that equalizing efforts will certainly fail, since they believe that low-scoring groups have an inferior genetic endowment, a condition that cannot be alleviated by social intervention.

Within the context of the present analysis, which is directed at illuminating the personal characteristics that enable some individuals to break out of the confines of their social class and achieve a higher occupational status, it is necessary only to acknowledge that superior intelligence can provide the motive power for social mobility, although it can seldom do so on its own. The common expressions that a person is too smart for his own good, that he is not as smart as he thinks he is, or that smart though he be he is insufferable, point to the other dimensions of personality that must be present if a person is to utilize fully his superior intelligence. The one finding that stands up is that highly intelligent offspring of families low on the educational, economic, and social scales often obtain access to opportunities that enable them to pursue successful careers.

We have identified a series of traits—superior physique, pulchritude, artistic ability, skills in interpersonal relationships, intelligence—which provide the specially endowed person from a limited background with a means of escaping from the restrictions and constraints of the social class in which he was born and brought up.

Per contra, when offspring of parents in the privileged classes are deficient physically, intellectually, or emotionally, they may be unable to take advantage of the opportunities their families provide. As a consequence, they may be unable to prepare for or hold positions comparable to those of their fathers and may therefore slip one or more notches down the socioeconomic hierarchy.

A second source of variability in career outcomes results from family and group dynamics. The children of low-income families are twice handicapped, since, as we have seen, there is insufficient money, and it usually must be divided among a large number of claimants. But occasionally a low-income family has an only child, in which case it is better able to give him a reasonable start in life.

Although most poor families also have poor relatives, occasionally a rich or powerful relative is able to smooth the way for a nephew or niece. When a tradition of mutual aid exists among members of a group, some children in low-income families are able to obtain significant assistance from relatives in their career preparation.

To these family circumstances which occasionally help to broaden access to opportunity for the lowborn we must add intrafamilial forces. For instance, certain groups, such as the Jews, Mormons, and overseas Chinese, at every level of family income, attach high value to education and to economic independence. Children who grow up in these families are urged to set high goals and to strive to achieve them even in the face of limited family resources.

In addition, the emotional dynamics of intense parent-child relationships sometimes leave an indelible mark on a youngster. While the values and behavior patterns of all children are molded by their interactions with their parents, certain young people develop a life plan that is emotionally overcharged. Literature is replete with fictional and factual accounts of young men whose mothers spurred them to aim high and to invest every ounce of strength in realizing specific career goals. The same sources tell of sons who were determined to outdistance their fathers, if they did nothing else.

On occasion, these charged relationships lead to negative outcomes. Many sons of successful men go through life denigrating by word and action everything their successful fathers respect—hard work, productive accomplishment, and social acclaim. Less is known about the subtleties of family interactions on young women because the world of paid work has only recently been opened to them. Knowledge of the psychodynamic development of young women leads us to believe, however, that they, like their brothers, often shape and direct their lives and careers in exaggerated response to unresolved conflicts with their parents.

As a result of their emotional development, some young men and women are able to marshal their energies to accomplish high career goals which others, less strongly motivated, cannot formulate or realize in the face of the objective obstacles they encounter in their environments. Strong motivation, the result of special factors within the family or small groups, must be recognized as a distinct and potent source of variability in social mobility.

A third source of variability is the societal arrangements that have been put in place to enhance the developmental opportunities of children from low-income and otherwise disadvantaged families. Initial attention must be directed to the education and training system which controls the sluice gates into many prestigious occupations and careers. We have noted that although the transition from home to school is difficult for many youngsters from low-income and minority families, some disadvantaged youngsters respond positively to their educational experiences, enjoy and do well in their studies, and invest ego and energy in these pursuits. For these students, the school becomes a refuge from the drabness of their lives. They like their teachers, their studies, and their books, and the fact that they do well reinforces their initial positive responses. Since the educational system operates as a selection device, it singles out good students and often helps them on their way through special placement, guidance, financial aid, and other forms of assistance.

In addition to helping the talented student, there are other ways in which the educational-training system can broaden opportunities for those who come from disadvantaged backgrounds. In recent years, especially since the end of World War II, policy makers in both the United States and Western Europe have become increasingly aware of the fact that the traditional school system is dysfunctional for most children from low-income families, and they have sought to remedy the situation. In earlier periods, the school hastened the departure of many youngsters with handicapping backgrounds. Now it seeks to hold them. The Folk School in Scandinavia and open admissions to college in the United States are two adaptations aimed at facilitating both the personal development and the career development of disadvantaged youths. These and other mechanisms, including government financed manpower training programs, are opening new opportunities for many who previously, because of straitened family circumstances, were unable or unwilling to remain in the educational-training system.

At least passing reference must also be made to the panoply of family assistance, training, and manpower-support services which characterizes most advanced societies and which contributes directly or indirectly to broadening the developmental opportunities of young people from disadvantaged backgrounds. A few illustrations drawn from the American experience will make these linkages explicit. In certain localities, the welfare regulations provide that payments in behalf of adolescent children will continue if they are enrolled in college. Since the mid-1960s, the federal government has provided work assignments for students from low-income homes who are enrolled in high school or college. These assignments provide these students with money for their incidental expenses so that, it is hoped, they will be encouraged to remain in school and improve their preparation for adulthood.

For those who have left school with little useful knowledge or skill and without many of the essentials for successful socialization, the federal government has been operating a large number of residential and nonresidential Job Corps centers which represent second-chance opportunities. Some young men and women who stay the course are able to make the transition into a job with good career opportunities.

A further source of variability in career outcomes is introduced by developments in the labor market which help moderate the multiple advantages which always operate in favor of the offspring of the well-connected and the well-located. Even in a world that has erected high barriers against accepting permanent immigrants, Canada, the United States, various countries in Latin America, Australia, and South Africa do accept a limited number, most of whom are likely to improve their jobs and incomes as a result of relocating. In addition, there is growing evidence that the richest nations in the world will not get their "dirty work" done unless they grant at least temporary work permits to men and women from low-income countries who seek opportunities to better themselves.

Substantial internal migration, from farm to city and from declining regions to areas of expansion, has been a major track for poor people to follow to better their circumstances. The rapid economic growth of many West European countries since the end of World War II broadened this track, and, in turn, the large numbers of rural people who relocated in the expanding sectors of the economy helped to fuel the expansion by providing the additional labor force.

Large-scale internal migration has also been typical of the United States, where large numbers of rural whites and blacks relocated to urban centers primarily in the North and West. Through relocating, many low-income families greatly improve their prospects and those of their children. A man has a better chance to find regular full-time employment at a reasonable wage; his wife has more opportunities to find either part-time or full-time employment; his children have access to improved public services, including more and better schooling.

Although most young people from disadvantaged groups have difficulty in locating jobs which offer steady progress as they acquire experience and seniority—that is, jobs in large corporations, in craft unions, and in the civil service—a considerable number succeed. If the labor market is tight and remains tight, more men and women from disadvantaged groups will locate the interstices that lead to improved opportunities.

While the labor market tends to allocate the better jobs to those who are better educated, trained, and connected, there are many occasions when persons from low-income families can obtain employment with built-in mobility if they are in the right place at the right time. Once hired, they have a good chance to move up several levels as they acquire training, experience, and seniority.

The last principal source of career variability, and on occasion the most pervasive, is linked to major societal transformations such as those which occur in times of war, social reform, or political revolution. These societal upheavals loosen the institutional structures which had previously determined the allocation of opportunities among different groups.

When a modern country mobilizes for war, there is a great churning of jobs and people in both the military and civilian sectors, and this is repeated at the end of hostilities. While the key positions in the expanded military organization go primarily to career professionals or to individuals who had earlier achieved high status in civilian life or who are on their way to high positions, the demands are so great and the time pressures so severe that many persons with modest backgrounds encounter new opportunities. During World War II, a number of enlisted men in the regular Army of the United States rose to the rank of lieutenant colonel or colonel. Many civilians who earlier had had only poor jobs because of the depressed state of the American economy during the 1930s suddenly found themselves in important positions in charge of critical programs. For every man to whom the war represented a setback in career development or the loss of limb or even life, many more found broadened opportunities to mature, to test themselves, and to acquire valuable skills and experience which made them ready to enter a new and more promising career at the end of hostilities.

The withdrawal of prime male manpower from the civilian labor market during the war created opportunities for groups which previously had been ignored. Employers had to look to new sources of workers and had to modify their preconceptions and preferences in order to attract the labor they needed. Persons disadvantaged because of race, sex, or physical handicap, who had earlier been able to find jobs only at the bottom of the ladder, were hired into better jobs and were promoted as they acquired experience and skill.

The return to peace, especially in the United States, was accompanied by new governmental programs which provided liberal financial support for veterans willing to pursue additional education or training. While many young men did not avail themselves of the opportunity or frittered it away, millions used it wisely. Although the full story is yet to be written, the GI Bill of rights resulted in the largest reshuffling of career opportunities in the history of the United States. Literally millions of young men were able to reconsider their occupational choices and set and pursue new goals because of the liberal governmental benefits available to them.

Although World War II led to the first cracks in the discriminatory patterns governing the employment of blacks and women, it was not until a quarter of a century later, in the mid-1960s, that employers, under threat of the law and community pressure, began to seek out employees from minority groups. Once employers adopted affirmative action programs aimed at increasing the proportion of minority group employees on their payrolls, certain minority-group members were singled out for preferential treatment. Of course, not all black workers were shown preference; this was reserved for a minority who, because of specialized skills and competences, were ready to move into higher-level positions. In addition, employers were willing for the first time to hire as management trainees recent black college graduates.

After a lag of several years, that is, in the early 1970s, the combined influence of law and public opinion in the United States began to lower the barriers against the employment of women and the promotion of qualified women into desirable positions. Once again, as with qualified blacks, some qualified women were able to move into desirable openings, as employers sought to demonstrate compliance with the law and popular consensus.

These two illustrations of radical changes in social attitudes and behavior with respect to labor market practices show how some members of groups which had earlier suffered from discrimination can suddenly experience expanded career opportunities.

The other outstanding instance of large-scale reshuffling of career opportunities occurs in tandem with political revolutions that undermine the established class structure. The Russian Revolution, which led over time to the total liquidation of the bourgeoisie, is the leading example in this century. Other class upheavals incident to the rise of fascism and nazism in the 1920s and 1930s, the post-World War II Communist victories in Eastern Europe, the Chinese Revolution, the withdrawal of the colonial powers from Asia and Africa, the Cuban revolution, and other cases fit under this same rubric. In varying degrees, members of the upper classes, who had long enjoyed preferred access to opportunity with respect to both education and careers, were stripped of their property, power, and privileges. If they did not emigrate, they and their children were relegated to the bottom of the social and occupational hierarchy.

The leadership of a revolution can help to solidify its power by moving energetically to broaden opportunities for a large segment of the population which theretofore had been denied entrance to higher education and preferred occupations. If the leadership succeeds in accomplishing this goal, as it did in Russia, the beneficiaries are likely to tolerate many shortcomings and failures on the part of the regime. Many will measure the success of the revolution by the extent to which their sons—and the sons of their friends and neighbors—are able to move into the higher levels of the new society. If opportunity is now open for those who previously found the doors tightly shut, that is presumptive proof that the promises of the revolution to improve the conditions of the common man are being fulfilled. The tragedy that stalks every revolution is the emergence of a new dominant class which before long establishes a new monopoly over opportunity. An alert leadership can slow this development, although the forces leading to the solidification of a new class structure are powerful and are not easily deflected.

This chapter has called attention to five constellations of forces in developed societies which tend to moderate the compelling influence of social class on career outcomes. We noted the role of personal qualities which can help an individual from a depressed family background break out of confining circumstances. These include an array of special attributes: athletic prowess, pulchritude, artistic ability, aptitude for moneymaking, high intelligence, organizational and political skill, and other traits on which successful careers can be built.

Next, we noted the consequences that grow out of special family or small-group experiences, traditions, and values which stimulate and assist young people in setting and pursuing high occupational goals.

The next constellation considered was the institutional arrangements that a society has put into place to broaden access to the educational-training structure for all young people, including those from disadvantaged backgrounds, and also the special supports directed at those whose families cannot help them.

The final sources of variability that were addressed are grounded in the opportunities that are opened by a rapidly expanding economy in search of new workers and by a society that has undergone large-scale political changes which served to reduce the privileges of the establishment and open significant new opportunities for groups which were formerly excluded from entering the higher ranks.

With the exception of major social upheavals, each source of career variability outlined above affects relatively small numbers. But the multiple sources of variability suggest that the total number of persons able to surmount the handicaps of a deprived background is considerable. While social class remains the major allocator of opportunity, its influence, especially in developed societies, is moderated.

PART III

«« «« «« · »» »» »»

MANPOWER
UTILIZATION

*Whatever be the actual state of the skill, dexterity, and judg-
ment with which labour is applied in any nation, the abun-
dance or scantiness of its annual supply must depend, during
the continuance of that state, upon the proportion between
the number of those who are annually employed in useful labour, and that of those who are not so employed.*

—ADAM SMITH, *The Wealth of Nations*

· 8 ·

Employment Opportunities

NOW THAT THE PROCESSES of skill development have been delineated our focus shifts to the processes of manpower utilization. Specifically, this chapter and the next two chapters will address the following issues: the factors that determine the level of employment and income-earning opportunities which a society provides for its members and the forces that control changes in these opportunities; the employment structure with its range of jobs from good to poor and the distribution of jobs among different groups; and finally, the types of manpower imbalances that arise as the consequences of the employment structure and as a result of changes in the society. The principal aim of Part III will be to illuminate the extent to which employment and manpower utilization, based in the first instance on the capabilities of the economy, are also influenced by the other societal systems—the value structure, government and manpower development institutions.

Skill development and skill utilization are closely linked. The ties that bind them reflect the following assumption: investments in work preparation presume the existence of opportunities to utilize the preparation at a later time; few would embark upon extended training without a prospect of later benefits.

Secondly, a suitable employment arrangement is essential to carry initial training to a higher level. This is possible only when workers have a work environment which contributes to their further accumulation of skills.

Thirdly, the level at which an economy operates with efficiency and effectiveness reflects in large measure the competence of its labor force. This in turn depends on the quality of the earlier preparation of the work force.

The final linkage reflects the connections among the skills of the work force, the performance of the economy, and the surplus which the economy is able to generate. An enhanced skill level leads to a more effective performance which, in turn, generates a larger surplus. With a larger surplus, a society can make larger investments in its human and physical resources, which will provide a stronger basis for additional growth.

The symbiotic relations between skill development and manpower utilization can be dramatically illustrated by contrasting conditions in an advanced economy, such as the United States, where a neurosurgeon may receive $2,000 for a craniotomy which may take four or five hours to perform, with conditions in an LDC, where $2,000 represents the annual earnings of about ten adults.

In general, the stage of economic development that a nation has reached reflects the level to which its human resources have been developed and the manner in which they are utilized. The prevailing view holds that the level of employment is determined by the aggregate demand for goods and services. People will be able to sell their labor or the products of their labor according to the ability of other members of the society (and foreigners) to employ them or buy their products. An employer can hire people and keep them on his payroll only if he can sell at a profit the output his work force produces, or if he has command over income from other sources (inheritance, earnings, savings) which enables him to pay for a time the wages of those he hires.

It is not surprising, therefore, that the analysis of employment is considered an integral part of the broader analysis of output and income. Except for people whose labor is directed primarily to producing essential items for their own consumption, the level of employment opportunities depends on the level of activity of the economy.

Nevertheless, employment opportunities are not solely a derivative of the economy's performance, important as that is. The economy operates in tandem with the other societal systems, whose institutional structures facilitate or retard the effectiveness with which its manpower resources are utilized. These intervening structures must be included in any assessment of the employment situation. The impact of these related systems on employment in both developing and developed societies is sketched below.

We can note the way in which the value system impacts on employment in traditional agricultural societies by calling attention to those countries where large numbers of monks and priests are supported by alms, where there is an interdependence between systems of land tenure and the output of the farm population, where there is poor alignment between the educational system and the skill needs of a largely rural population, and where government has a tendency to use the limited resources that it is able to squeeze out of the population for purposes that contribute relatively little to the expansion of employment and income.

The employment outlook in developed nations also is affected by the societal systems that reinforce or detract from the influences generated by the economy. For example, changes in value orientations have led to a vast increase in the total pool of labor since women have started to participate more fully and effectively in paid employment; modern governments have become increasingly concerned with improving their policies aimed at keeping the level of employment as close to the optimum as possible; and appropriations for human resources development aimed at broadening the nation's pool of skills have increased.

This encapsulated consideration of the manner in which the principal societal systems impinge on the employment situation in both developing and developed nations was presented to ensure that the framework of the analysis makes room not only for the economy but also for the other three major societal systems. The presumption is that the level of employment opportunities will reflect the interaction of all the systems.

The remainder of this chapter will consider employment opportunities in both developing and developed nations, as well as the conditions that are likely to restrict or increase the number of opportunities available. One useful schema involves the conditions that determine the numbers who are productively employed in farming, in various types of self-employment from fishing to retailing, as wage or salary earners in the profit-making sector, and on the government's payroll. The relative importance of these four areas of employment varies among nations at different stages of economic development and to a lesser extent among nations at the same stage of development.

In some parts of the world, including the two most populous countries, China and India, farming and farm-related occupations employ not less than three out of four workers. In these countries, then, the key to employment and income is embedded in the patterns of agricultural life.

In predominantly agricultural societies, whether a man can make productive use of his labor depends in the first instance on the amount and quality of the land he owns or rents and, if he rents, on the conditions under which he shares the produce with the owner. The amount of arable land in most societies is limited, and little or no additional land is available, especially in populated areas. To oversimplify: in most agricultural societies a relatively small number of wealthy families own a disproportionate amount of the total arable land. A second group owns sufficient land that the crops it raises provide an adequate livelihood for its families. But a sizable proportion of the rural population, often one-third to one-half, has no land, or such small parcels that it is impossible for the people to earn enough to meet the minimum needs of their families. Those without land must hire out as laborers to landowners who cannot meet their peak labor requirements from within their own families. Sometimes poor farm families are able to supplement their earnings through the production and sale of handicrafts or through public employment on road-building jobs. In some areas, they are permitted to collect wood which they can use or sell.

The life of the landless as well as that of the family with little land is precarious. These families live so close to the margin of subsistence that any adverse circumstance, such as drought, blight, or flood, can have devastating results. If he is a tenant, not an owner, a farmer may be further discouraged from putting forth efforts to use his free time productively. Many rental arrangements are so drawn that all the benefits from improvements accrue to the owner; occasionally, a tenant may run the risk of having his rent raised because of the very improvements he himself adds. In traditional societies, in which the outlying areas have little or no linkage to urban places, or where the distances are so great or the terrain so adverse that the transportation of bulky products is precluded, even the farmer with relatively large land holdings may come to realize that it is impossible to sell or trade his surplus.

In the absence of a market in which he can sell for either domestic or foreign use the surplus he is able to produce, the farmer is locked into a continuing low level of productivity because he cannot finance, or there is no point to his trying to do so, the additional inputs of water, seed, fertilizer, pesticides, livestock, or farm machinery which would enhance his output. Even if he could work most of the year, as some are able to do in areas where two and even three crops can be raised within a twelve-month period, the farmer is chained to his preexisting level of productivity. Unless he can generate some surplus or borrow some capital, he will be unable to increase his output.

It is not surprising, therefore, that most farm families in traditional agricultural societies live at or close to the margin of subsistence. Many must eke out a livelihood from too little land that often carries a high rent; they are often unable to sell any surplus they can produce; they have little prospect of finding alternative employment opportunities during the slack months of the year.

The self-employed workers in nonagricultural pursuits, who account for the second largest component of the labor force in a traditional society, face comparable problems. If a self-employed worker earns his livelihood in trade, the odds are overwhelming that his scale of activities is constrained by his limited stock on the one hand and by the limited demand for his wares on the other. The small trader may attempt to obtain additional stock on credit, and if he can turn it over several times during the course of the year, he may be able to earn enough to support his family, but this prospect is diminished by the many traders who are trying to do the same.

While the shortage of capital is one explanation of the limited amount of business and the small earnings of most traders, the low level of disposable income among the consuming public is a second constraint. Poor people make cash purchases only when they must. They buy as little as possible. They haggle over the price. In rural areas where family income is usually low, a large inventory would not be justified. The market demand is weak, and there may be no way for the trader to increase the number of customers. Even in large urban centers, most shops are characterized by a small number of customers and the smaller numbers who make a purchase. Consequently shopkeepers spend most of the day sitting and waiting, as do the members of their families who are at hand ready to assist but whose help is rarely needed. A great amount of potential labor runs to waste because the number of shopkeepers is far in excess of the number required to serve the few customers.

Much the same pattern prevails among self-employed workers in manual and service occupations. Here, too, the sellers of labor are handicapped by their limited skills and by the limited demand for their services; most of them have only intermittent work. The local shoemaker works with poor tools, as do most other craftsmen. Again, the low level of disposable income means that most families try to do as much as possible for themselves to avoid making cash outlays. They will pay an outsider only when they have no alternative.

As for the underemployed farmer, so for the underemployed craftsman or laborer: the absence of regular employment opportunities dominates the worker's life. Many self-employed workers have many free hours which they are unable to put to profitable use. The labor market is simply not capable of providing employment opportunities for the large numbers who need and want to work or work more.

Against this background of inadequate employment opportunities which dominates both the agricultural and nonagricultural sectors of most traditional societies, people attempt to get onto a regular payroll either in the private sector or, better, the public sector. The job may be modest, the work may be hard, and the pay may be low, but security of employment and regular wages are assured. In most traditional societies, once a person is added to a regular payroll he cannot be dismissed unless he becomes unable to carry out his assignment or is caught stealing or otherwise breaks the code. There is great social and political pressure on all employers in developing countries to hire the largest possible number of workers and to retain them even if they do not need them because of the difficulties that families encounter if their principal breadwinner loses his job. The widespread practice in India, where construction workers have the right to be the first hired for jobs in the factories they have erected, attests to the importance that workers attach to job security.

The chronic shortage of employment and income-earning opportunities characteristic of most traditional societies is rooted in a series of interlocking weaknesses. In brief recapitulation, we should recall that a significant number of farm families simply do not own or cannot rent sufficient acreage to enable them to raise sufficient food for themselves plus the little extra they need to sell in order to pay their taxes and to buy the essentials they cannot produce.

Since so many live at or close to the margin of subsistence in both the countryside and the city, the traditional society produces a relatively small surplus, a large part of which accrues to the wealthy, who use some of it for sterile investment. Relatively little becomes available for investments aimed at stimulating the growth of the economy and expanding jobs and incomes for the mass of the population.

The small annual surplus also helps to explain the absence of an infrastructure which would link the countryside and the city and which could help expand the demand for the labor and products of each; moreover, the small surplus explains the limited investment the society is able to make in improving the education and skills of the population. Without training and educational institutions, the labor force is condemned to continue working at a low level of productivity.

Behind these explanations of the inadequate number of employment opportunities in traditional societies is the fact that, as Malthus warned, the numbers of people who are born and survive tend to approximate the numbers who can be supported by the available resources. Although many persons in traditional societies do not have opportunities to be fully and productively employed during many months of the year, the fact is that, except in years when the crops fail, the traditional economy enables the population to survive, although sizable numbers live at or below the margin of subsistence and suffer from malnutrition and disease. Although it is unable to provide adequate employment opportunities, the traditional society can meet the subsistence needs of its people most of the time.

A society that has reached an advanced stage of economic development has several marked advantages. In the first place its accumulated capital, elaborate infrastructure, and sophisticated education and training institutions provide the precondition for its labor force to be productively employed.

An advanced economy also has the capacity to produce a substantial surplus, much of which becomes available for investment in new employment-creating opportunities. In addition, these annual increments to the surplus make it possible for individuals, employers, and government to increase the opportunities available to the population to improve its skills and competences, which in turn will add to its future productivity.

Among the important advantages that an advanced society has with respect to the level and growth of employment opportunities is the relatively minor role of agriculture in the economy. The quantity of arable land is not a significant determinant of the continued growth of employment. The cutting edge is corporate enterprise, which is able to quasi-automatically generate large sums which, when reinvested, expand the number of useful jobs. The substantial surplus permits additional business investments in plant and equipment, which provide a foundation for raising productivity and continuing the cycle of expansion. The level of family income is sufficiently high that most consumers are able to purchase items other than necessities, thereby creating a potential market for new enterprises and new products. Finally, the linkages within and among advanced economies are constantly strengthened, and this facilitates further specialization and growth.

Another factor that contributes to employment expansion in a developed economy is a sustained period of business activity which eventually results in a tightening of the labor market. In a tight labor market, employers, concerned about their ability to hire workers when they need them, look to their personnel policies and procedures in the hope of being able to introduce improvements. They are likely to reassess their hiring, training, and assignment policies with an aim of developing more elasticity in meeting their manpower requirements.

Rapid economic growth contributes to improved manpower development and utilization in still another way. When organizations are expanding and many new jobs are being added to the economy, new occupational opportunities open up at the entrance level as well as at the middle and higher levels. This means that many able persons who otherwise would have to wait for five to ten years before advancing to a better, more responsible and more demanding position can move up more quickly and, as a result, make greater use of their potential and add to their skills and experience.

Economic growth also strengthens a nation's manpower resources by creating a favorable environment for many people in which to reassess their options. A continued satisfactory level of economic activity increases their willingness to undergo short-term costs for potential long-term gains. Many more young people are willing to extend their years of preparation for work if they believe that they will be able to get better jobs and enter more attractive careers. Others will be more willing to relocate in an expanding area if the long-term prospects are propitious. Many women will decide to combine marriage and a career if they see changes under way in the larger society that will broaden the opportunities open to them.

The foregoing paragraphs point to a series of potential adjustments to a period of sustained growth which both institutions and individuals can make which will contribute to speeding the expansion of employment. We have not noted so far, however, the fact that advanced economies, despite their better ability to meet the employment and income needs of their people, nonetheless confront the problem of the underutilization of a significant part of their potential and active labor force. A major source of strength of developed societies is the presence of potential workers who can be drawn into the industrial labor force as the economy expands. But if the rate of economic expansion lags and those on the periphery accumulate, it can be said that the society has an insufficiency of employment opportunities.

A first source of additional workers for an expanding economy is the partially employed farm population; many farm workers want to make a locational and occupational shift so that they can get full-time paid employment. The second major group on which advanced economies have been able to draw to increase their work force has been married women, primarily those living in metropolitan communities and therefore close to expanding jobs. Since most advanced societies invest sizable sums in the education of all young people, many of these potential workers have the basic preparation that makes their absorption into the regular labor force relatively easy. This obtains more generally for urban-educated women than for the rural in-migrant.

Many observers believe that a sustained period of growth of an advanced economy is likely to founder because of a shortage of workers with skills. At that point wages encroach on profits, labor productivity declines, production schedules are delayed because critical work is not being performed in time, labor discipline slackens. Although these and related adverse manpower developments are likely to accompany a long period of economic expansion, the conventional interpretation has not been proved. As we have just seen, no economy, no matter how advanced, can constantly operate at a level at which there is work for all who want to work, and certainly no economy has yet provided employment opportunities that make full use of the potential and skills of the entire work force. The conventional interpretation of the exhaustion of a boom speaks to manpower shortages and increases in labor costs. Alternatively, emphasis could be placed on the inertia inherent in the principal institutional structures—the slowness with which organizations are able and willing to alter their established patterns of manpower utilization; the lack of flexibility in the educational and training establishment; the failure of labor market mechanisms to respond to boom conditions. The knowledge that booms will later slacken is ingrained in the principal actors, and they are consequently wary about overresponding to a tight labor market.

The preceding analysis of employment in both developing and developed nations has been pursued without reference to major structural changes in both types of societies from forces they did not anticipate and cannot readily control. A better understanding of the difficulties of avoiding the underutilization of manpower requires at least a brief consideration of the problems of adjustment to unanticipated dynamic changes.

Rapid population growth presents one such case. The recent increase in the number of labor force entrants in most developing nations is a delayed response to the diffusion of death-restricting technology from the West after World War II in the form of DDT, antibiotics, and immunizations. The facts are unequivocal. The infants and children in the developing world who survived because of the diffusion of this health technology are now adults looking for work. While many developing countries have sought to introduce family planning methods to reduce their birthrates, the record to date is disappointing. No large preindustrial nation, with the possible exception of China, has yet had much success in its efforts to reduce its birthrate. Most of the developing world has little or no prospect of avoiding a steeply increasing number of job seekers until the twenty-first century.

The developing nations have made three principal adjustments to this overwhelming reality. Many farms have absorbed additional workers, as families have sought to provide their sons, daughters, and in-laws with an opportunity to work and support their dependents. The enlarged work force has produced a larger total output, but the additional workers have seldom been able to contribute, even modestly, to the surplus.

The second adjustment has been the absorption of some of the new work force on lands only recently opened for settlement. Although most large-scale, multipurpose irrigation plans are long-term, high-cost undertakings, several governments found the resources, primarily through grants and loans from abroad, to help finance these plans.

Another adjustment mechanism has been the accelerated flow of persons out of the rural areas and into the cities, which, in most developing countries, experienced substantial growth. Many left the countryside in the hope of bettering themselves in the urban environment where the economy was quickening and more opportunities for self-employment or regular jobs were opening up.

None of these three adjustments, however, was truly responsive. The absorption of additional labor on existing farms proved difficult, since the previously existing agricultural work force was already underemployed during much of the year. The cost of bringing new land under cultivation was high, and governments understandably hesitated to put much of their limited resources into expanding agricultural output, since they had concluded that the only hope for rapid growth was through industrial development.

The growth of cities in the developing world reflected the expansion of employment in government, industry, and commerce, reinforced by the growth of service employment which resulted from the expanding incomes in the modern sector. But each in-migrant who makes it in the city attracts others who often have greater difficulty in gaining a toehold in the urban economy, which also must provide jobs for the offspring of the residents of the city.

The growth of employment opportunities in traditional societies in transition has been hobbled because much of the modest surplus that the society accumulates each year is not readily available for investment. The primitive state of the financial market has prevented the pooling of the small savings of many individuals which, if it were possible, could be made available at reasonable rates of interest to potential borrowers. Since many traditional societies in transition are caught up in political dissension, some large savers send their surplus overseas as a hedge against the time when they may have to leave their country in the event that their political opponents come to power. Much of the remaining surplus is used by the wealthy to support retainers and to purchase imports, from automobiles to refrigerators and stereos, to sustain a Western style of life.

Another determinant of the rate of employment expansion is the effectiveness of government in raising funds for investment and using them wisely. In many developing countries, the government's record is undistinguished on both fronts. Even strongly entrenched politicians think twice before raising taxes, and most politicians in the developing world have only a tenuous hold on the levers of power. Moreover, the search for resources abroad, in the form of grants or loans, is beset with difficulties. As a result, the planned investment program usually requires more than the funds available. The political leadership, either through faulty analysis or a desire to maximize its popularity, invests in more projects than it can bring to fruition within the stipulated time, with the consequence that much of the new capital remains unproductive, and there is a serious shortfall in the anticipated additional employment.

The tendency of many government bureaucrats to avoid making decisions and to seek personal benefit from the decisions they do make further slows the rate of economic expansion and the growth of employment. In a society at an early stage of development, a businessman can do little without the approval of government, and when the bureaucracy is slow-moving, unimaginative, and venal, the limited forces operating in favor of expansion are often aborted.

This brief consideration of traditional societies in transition has emphasized that their rapidly increasing population and labor force has made it difficult to expand sufficiently their employment and output. Limitations of land, capital, infrastructure, managerial skills, and political consensus retard the growth of new jobs, while the number seeking employment continues to grow rapidly.

Several developed nations have also confronted a range of challenges, including demographic changes, which have made it difficult for them to meet and resolve their employment problems. The United States is a case in point. In the first decade after World War II, its birthrate skyrocketed, reversing a long-term downward trend. As a consequence, the number of teen-agers seeking part-time or full-time employment in the middle and late 1960s reached a new high. Despite the strong and continued expansion of the economy, the new entrants into the labor force raised the teenage unemployment rate to a disturbingly high level.

A more widespread phenomenon has been the accelerated entrance of married women into the labor force as a consequence of changes in their values and life styles, which reflect their increased education, urbanization, and the trend toward smaller families, reinforced by the expansion of white-collar and service jobs into which they can easily be absorbed. Despite the growth of employment opportunities for women in most developed countries, the numbers who would like to work have outpaced the supply of jobs, especially good jobs with good career prospects.

Although the developed economies outside the communist orbit continue to be defined as market-oriented, the fact is that, in the United States and in most of Western Europe, governments now play ever larger roles in determining the pattern of new investment, in shaping the demand for goods and services, and, consequently, in influencing the employment situation. A good example of such employment-creating, employment-stimulating, and employment-maintaining roles is in the area of defense and defense-related expenditures in the United States, which during most of the 1950s and 1960s accounted for about 10 percent of the GNP. For two decades, these expenditures served as a reinforcement for the employment in and well-being of critical occupations, industries, and regions.

The willingness of the U.S. Congress to appropriate such large sums for defense over an extended period unquestionably contributed to keeping the economy at a high level of output and employment by helping to stabilize a large sector of the total demand. However, the pattern carried at least two hidden risks: much of the nation's savings was directed toward ends that did not directly add to the productivity of the civilian economy, and when national priorities shifted in the late 1960s, the economic underpinnings of the defense-related sectors were eroded.

In Great Britain, both Conservative and Labour governments have used sizable public resources to maintain companies and industries which had lost their competitive edge, primarily because the political leadership could not tolerate being involved in precipitating the mass unemployment that would follow the collapse of these enterprises. In addition, when the Labour party was in power, it saw merit in pushing for the nationalization of many basic industries. However, widespread governmental support and take-overs have had negative intermediate and long-term consequences for the total growth of employment and income. On more than one occasion, the British government had to stop its rescue operations when it realized that the shrinkage or collapse of the enterprise or industry could be prevented only at a prohibitive cost in subsidies. Moreover, the dissipation each year of a large amount of the national surplus among a group of weak enterprises made it harder to bring about the multiple adjustments a dynamic economy requires if it is to expand employment and output in fields where it presently has or might obtain a competitive edge.

In varying degrees, all developed economies have encountered problems in attempting to maintain a satisfactory equilibrium between workers and jobs. The long-term adjustment mechanism in capitalist countries has been for "surplus" rural workers to remain on the farm until opportunities become available in the urban sector, at which point they relocate to find employment in manufacturing or services. While this classic process continued to operate in most developed countries after World War II, it occasionally encountered difficulty. In some countries, considerable numbers were left behind in outlying areas which had lost their economic viability; the in-migration to the cities was hampered by housing shortages; migrants from the rural areas who belong to a minority group—for example, blacks and Chicanos in the United States—were often discriminated against by their new neighbors. Lacking the education and skill that urban employers required, the in-migrant's search for regular employment was difficult.

Several of the developed nations have had employment problems in their manufacturing sectors as a result of a combination of adverse forces: a failure to keep their technology up to date, continuing labor troubles that raised costs to noncompetitive levels, and the flexibility of multinational companies in relocating their manufacturing operations to friendlier countries. Together, these forces can lead to a substantial loss of jobs and income.

All developed nations have attempted to design new types of entrepreneurial structures to facilitate the expansion of services in areas such as education, health, recreation, and transportation which cannot readily be provided by profit-seeking enterprises. When the relative and sometimes the absolute number of manufacturing jobs levels off, the ability of a high-income economy to continue expanding depends in part on the creation of new entrepreneurial structures that can facilitate the growth of the service sector, including public services.

We have called attention to three important roles of government that impinge directly on the employment level in developed economies: as direct purchaser of goods and services, especially in defense and defense-related activities; as redistributor of part of the national surplus to subsidize vulnerable sectors where workers are threatened with the loss of their jobs or to speed nationalization on ideological grounds; as innovator of new forms of entrepreneurship in a pluralistic economy.

In addition, modern governments have the responsibility of designing and implementing fiscal, monetary, and budgetary policies to keep their economies operating at or close to the full utilization of their resources, including their manpower resources. But they frequently find that the several economic goals which they must pursue, in addition to maintaining a high level of employment, may conflict. Under these circumstances, they may have to forgo, at least for a time, attempting to realize their employment goals. For these reasons, many governments have had to tolerate undesirable levels of unemployment in the post-World War II era.

The record suggests that although the developed economies have come a long way since World War II in meeting the critical challenge of providing work for all their members—and, in many West European countries, for many foreigners as well—the employment issue remains at the fore. Difficulties have arisen as a result of demographic and structural changes resulting in large surges in job applicants, the necessity to absorb substantial numbers of workers who had been forced to relocate, and the inflationary concomitants of national economic policies aimed at the maintenance of a high level of employment. Nonetheless, using the historical record as a criterion, we must conclude that since World War II most of the developed economies have done well in meeting the broad challenge of providing work for their citizens.

In each of three regards, the developed nations have been more fortunate than the developing nations: their rate of population growth has not pressed on their resources base; they have been able to generate large annual surpluses which have become available for private and public investment, thereby adding to job creation and productivity gains; their governments have demonstrated skill in steering their economies to prevent prolonged declines in employment.

While the developed nations are in a preferred position relative to the developing nations by virtue of the higher productivity of their economies, their larger surpluses available for investment, and their relative freedom from excessive population pressures, they too face problems on the employment front.

First, they have ignored the needs of large numbers of underemployed people waiting on the farms and in rural areas for an opportunity to get regular jobs. Next, they have not been responsive to many others who are outside the labor force—married women, older persons, youth, the handicapped—and who would welcome the opportunity to work. And they have not succeeded in operating their economies in such a way as to keep the disemployment consequences of rapid change within tolerable limits.

A strong and growing economy assures the continuing expansion of employment opportunities. But there is no guarantee that the number of jobs will match the number of job seekers. Whether a developed economy can reduce the underutilization of its manpower resources depends on more than the effectiveness with which the economy operates. It depends also on changes in the value system which raise the employment issue toward the top of the national agenda, on improvements in the governmental structure which will facilitate the formulation and implementation of policies aimed at full employment, and on the enhanced articulation between the manpower development system and the economy to improve the matching of job applicants and jobs.

Since a modern society and economy are in constant flux, and since they must respond to forces both within and outside, no policies designed to achieve a better solution of the employment issue can be viewed as permanent. If a nation attaches importance to finding effective answers to the challenge of employment for all its citizens, it must continue to address the problem, which, in a dynamic environment, will undergo continuing transformations.

· 9 ·

Job Structures

WE HAVE SEEN THAT the availability of employment opportunities is a critical factor in manpower utilization; another is the segmentation of the labor market. In every society, there is a hierarchy of jobs, from the most desirable in terms of pay and other perquisites at the top to the least desirable employment opportunities at the bottom.

What accounts for the universality of job segmentation, and how do the patterns differ among societies at different stages of development? Which groups have access to the preferred jobs, and to what extent can the life styles of families affect the outcomes? How does the dynamism of a modern society impinge on segmentation, and what are the consequences of persistent segmentation on manpower utilization?

Two pervasive factors underpin the segmentation that characterizes the job structures of different societies—a surplus of applicants seeking jobs and the desire of employers, especially large employers, to screen the available pool for those most likely to fit into their organizations. This chapter addresses the consequences of structure and segmentation on manpower utilization. Except for a cursory discussion of the theme in developing societies, the analysis will focus on developed countries with a highly differentiated occupational structure.

Since Adam Smith set forth his incisive analysis of wage differentials, economists have explained segmentation in the job market in terms of a society's willingness to reward more liberally those who, by endowment and training, have skills and competence that are relatively scarce. In addition to this basic explanation of significant differentials in rewards, they have followed Smith's reasoning that special rewards must attach to jobs which are particularly unpleasant, carry a risk of personal injury, require people to work at night or on holidays, offer only irregular employment, and necessitate a man's working beyond commuting distance from his home. Since jobs differ in terms of both the demands they make on workers and the contribution that workers make to the desired output of goods and services, both equity and efficiency call for some degree of differentiation.

Segmentation rests on economic rationality. Those who contribute more receive more. The analysis here accepts this interpretation, but it makes room for the other factors which strengthen segmentation, including the ability of various institutions and groups to influence the job structure to their own advantage. A review of the patterns of job segmentation in developing and developed nations, which include both market and state-controlled economies, will help to broaden our perspective of the role of factors from outside the economy that reinforce and strengthen the segmented job structure.

Observers of the efforts of developing nations to modernize and speed their economic growth have noted that, despite the outpouring of new teachers from the expanding teacher-training institutions and colleges, the salaries of teachers have remained relatively high. Here, as with other jobs in the modern sector of these societies, the market is not working or is working imperfectly. In fact, the market sector is so small in many of these developing nations that even if the leadership wanted to be guided by it, that would not be possible. For a considerable period, wages would have to be set by a combination of tradition, government revenues, the power of competing interest groups, and similar institutional forces.

There is further suggestive evidence from the experience of developing nations that points to the existence of strong segmentation in their job structures. To note an example in the modern sector: The characteristic wage rates for unskilled and semiskilled work are usually considerably above what new in-migrants or unemployed urban residents would accept. In fact many employed workers would welcome the opportunity to transfer to jobs with firms in the modern sector. Many of these larger firms have long waiting lists. We may ask why they pay more than they have to—for that is the implication of the foregoing. They believe that they can attract and retain a better group of workers by paying high wages; a reduction in the wage bill would have only a minor effect on their total profitability; they take pride in having a high wage structure; they believe that the superior wages they pay will provide insurance against militancy on the part of their work force; they may be under subtle, or direct, pressure from the political leadership to be pacesetters. These leading firms have considerable degrees of freedom to set a wage policy that pays only incidental attention to the signals of the market.

The small number of skilled workers in most traditional societies at their present stage of modernization creates another type of segmentation. If a foreign enterprise decides to open a modern hotel in a city that has had little contact with modern technology, the management will gladly pay double or triple the going wage for a local electrician who has the competence to install, maintain, and repair various types of electrical equipment. Its only alternative would be to bring from overseas a qualified worker, and this would involve an annual expenditure many times greater, as well as an ongoing struggle with the government bureaucracy which issues work permits.

The special efforts that modern-sector enterprises must make to train cadres of skilled workers, supervisors, and managers, particularly for airlines, telecommunications, electric power utilities, and railroads, also lead to segmentation, since these enterprises must put together a special package of pay, training opportunities, housing, and other emoluments, together with assurances of promotion and pensions, all of which far exceed the remuneration of other workers. The rates that these companies charge consumers are set at a level that will enable them to cover their wage costs, which obviously are considerable.

To shift our concern to developed nations with a market orientation: Are they also characterized by a significant segmentation in their job structures? The answer is an unequivocal yes. The simplest test of segmentation is whether jobs with comparable requirements provide differential rewards. If we put aside for the moment the top positions in the professions and in the ranks of management, we can distinguish the following major types of labor force attachment for the noncollege population in a country such as the United States. First is employment with a large organization in the business, governmental, or nonprofit sector, that is, with a large corporation, the civil service or the military, or a medical center or museum. An alternative employment pattern is that provided by journeyman's status, achieved through apprenticeship or other means; the jobs available and the wages paid result primarily from the recurrent negotiations between the trade union and the contractors' association. A third pattern is that of jobs with small or medium-size firms which provide both regular and intermittent employment for large numbers of workers. In addition, there are a considerable number of self-employment opportunities in all market economies.

The differences among these several types of work attachment can help to clarify the role of segmentation in the labor markets of modern competitive societies. In bureaucratic organizations, there are several constituent elements. First there is initial employment, after a qualifying period, with an unwritten expectation of long-term job security, that is, until a stipulated retirement age. Second, there are training and promotional opportunities on the basis of seniority; the average worker will usually be able to advance to a level where his wages and other benefits will be two to three times his initial earnings. In addition, most bureaucratic organizations concerned with maintaining a career force tend to offer different types of fringe benefits, particularly deferred benefits, usually in the form of liberal pensions, which deter employees from leaving.

Small and medium-size firms are seldom in a position to match these conditions. They often provide little or no formal training; they cannot offer much upward mobility, since they frequently employ a large number of semiskilled workers and only a few supervisors; they are less able to provide year-round employment; their profits can seldom support costly fringe and deferred benefits.

As for journeymen, such as those in the construction trades, their unions may have been strong enough to have bargained for a sufficiently high wage level to compensate for the time in the year when they will be without work. They may also have convinced the employer to participate in a good health and welfare program with benefits that may equal or even exceed those of large corporations or government. There are limited prospects for upward mobility within the craft, but many journeymen, after they have acquired experience and accumulated some savings, move on to become contractors. Some move back and forth according to the business cycle; they work for themselves in good times and for others when business is slack. But the more successful make a clean break and become independent businessmen.

Self-employment has been a declining sector in all advanced economies, but it continues to provide the basis for the labor force attachment of a sizable group of workers. Its liabilities are conspicuous: no employer-sponsored training, no quasi-automatic promotions, no subsidized health plans or other types of insurance, and no pensions. Furthermore, the availability of work and income is dependent on the vagaries of the market. However, in many advanced societies opportunities are provided for the self-employed to buy into various types of social insurance and pension arrangements.

A brief word about segmentation in communist economies. In the U.S.S.R., the employment opportunities provided in urban places are more attractive than those on the farm. The differentials have been so substantial in recent years that the officialdom has had to resort to strict controls over the movement of workers to hold them "down on the farm." Since the wage fund that an industry and its several plants have available for distribution depends in part on how well they meet their production quotas, those that meet or exceed their quotas often have additional wages or other benefits to distribute. Special wage premiums are also used as incentives and rewards for plants whose output is critical for meeting priority programs in defense or space or which can earn large amounts of foreign exchange. And some firms are in the fortunate position of being able to provide their work force with valuable emoluments, such as when they have new housing to allocate.

But the principal source of segmentation in the communist economies, as in the market economies, reflects the substantial differentials in total earnings—wages plus other emoluments—that have come to be attached to different sectors of the economy. Despite the ideological concern of communist countries with achieving a higher degree of equality in distribution, they have not been able to rationalize their wage structures. However, the fact that most social welfare benefits are available, not on a plant or industry basis, but to all workers, means that the communist states have substantially reduced one of the principal sources of gain to those who cornered the best jobs.

We must now explore the forces that lie back of the segmentation of job structures in these quite disparate societies. One explanation would be to point out that the market, with its strong propulsion toward equilibrium, simply does not operate effectively—surely not in developing nations whose market structures are embryonic, nor in communist societies where the central planning agency allocates scarce resources and sets the level of rewards. Even in market economies, many of the good jobs are located in sectors that do not operate under the harsh winds of competition. And an increasing proportion of the labor force in developed societies depends for its employment not on the sale of commodities and services in the marketplace but on government dollars derived from tax revenues and, to a minor degree, on philanthropic funds.

Another factor contributing to segmentation is the power possessed by large organizations by virtue of their strategic position in the economy. If they are able to price their products at a level that yields them extra revenue above their costs, which may be possible because of their favored position vis-à-vis other producers, then the management is in a position, especially if goaded by an aggressive union, to agree to a high wage scale.

In the developing nations, this is the typical situation in the national airlines and sometimes in the ports (especially if the latter are well organized). In the advanced market economies, the large oligopolistic firms, especially those with heavy capital investments—in steel, automobiles, or petroleum—tend to have a total compensation package far above that characteristic of firms which are exposed to the forces of the competitive market, such as those producing consumer goods. Well organized trade unions, especially those in fields such as construction, newspapers, municipal government, and urban transportation, where the employer is not free to relocate, are frequently able to obtain a rate of pay and other compensations considerably above those prevailing for comparable types of work. There is nothing in the operation of a modern market economy that points to an early dissolution of such shelters. Particular groups of workers are likely to hold on to their differentially higher rewards for considerable periods of time without jeopardizing the economic well-being of the organizations which employ them. Of course, the record tells of cases where workers in such positions of power pressed so hard that the employing organizations were forced to go out of business, decreased their operations, or relocated.

Up to this point the analysis has emphasized that the powers of government, corporations, and trade unions, individually and collectively, are responsible for much of the segmentation that exists in modern societies. But segmentation is not solely, or even primarily, a function of the power of these critical institutions to escape from the rigors of the competitive market. The differentially higher wages and other benefits that are attached to certain jobs reflect a mutual accommodation between these favored members of the work force and their employing organizations. There is a congruence, as we shall see in detail in Chapter 13, between the underlying interests of workers who seek high wages, greater job security, and valuable deferred benefits and the advantages that accrue to the employing organization which seeks workers who will stay, accept positions in new locations, and avoid confrontation and conflict.

We find then that, in quite different economies, jobs with comparable requirements carry different rewards. The equalization that the market theory implies is often illusory. The dominant pattern is one of a highly segmented job structure with marked differences in opportunities reflected in differences in basic earnings, regularity of employment, fringe benefits, perquisites, and job security. It is not surprising, especially in light of the market theory, that most of these dimensions of compensation are positively correlated; that is, jobs which pay the best tend to have the best supplementary benefits.

Having established the pervasiveness of segmentation in the labor market, we are now in a position to take a closer look at the groups in different societies which have the inside track to the preferred jobs. In a traditional society, especially one on the threshold of development, the sluice gates to opportunity are indeed narrow. Belonging to an affluent family is the best means to later advancement into a good job and a good income. Those lucky enough to inherit land or whose family owns a profitable enterprise will eventually be in a preferred economic position. Some may lose or squander their inheritance, but others will protect and increase theirs.

An affluent family can smooth a young man's path in other ways. Well-to-do families are in a good position to obtain an attractive opportunity for their offspring in a successful business enterprise or in the government bureaucracy. In addition, a prestigious family will probably enhance a young person's prospects of promotion, since his supervisor is likely to see profit for himself if he can find favor with the young man's family.

Another source of economic preferment based on family ties grows out of patterns of marriage: a young man usually marries a woman from a family on the same social and economic level as his own. Consequently, a young man from a well-to-do family is likely to find his employment prospects improved as a result of marriage, particularly if his wife's family has no sons and is looking to its sons-in-law to take over the family's enterprise.

The obverse of the wellborn and well-connected, of course, are the children in families with low income, low occupational status, and few connections. The vast majority of the lowborn will be precluded from gaining access to any of the better employment and income-earning opportunities on the land, in trade, in the bureaucracy, in industry, or in the professions.

If the societal arrangements are rigid, family income and status are more important in determining the employment and income prospects of the next generation. But, as we have seen, even a traditional agricultural society experiences some change and growth, if only in or near its principal urban centers. The question then becomes to what extent are factors other than family resources likely to come into play and provide at least some persons from disadvantaged backgrounds with an opportunity to obtain desirable employment and higher earnings? Since few from low-income families can stay the long course through higher education into a professional or managerial position, our concern here is with alternative routes into desirable employment for disadvantaged youngsters. Those who live on farms close to an urban area which is expanding may encounter new opportunities. First, they may be able to obtain a job in the city, thereby providing the members of their family with funds that will enable them to increase their farm output, which they can readily sell to the expanding urban population. If the city expands in their direction, they may be able to sell their land for a good price and thereby obtain the capital to enter a new field. These examples suggest that a few low-income families may escape the fate of most of the farm population.

Even a traditional economy in the early stages of development has some organizations which require a considerable number of persons with technical and administrative competence. As noted earlier, such organizations train their own staffs and rely largely on promotions from within for supervisors, at least up to the level of foreman or plant superintendent. Consequently, young people from low-income homes who are able to pass the screening test for initial employment, which often requires no more than six to eight years of schooling, and who demonstrate aptitude for and interest in their work are likely to move up in the organization as a result of training and experience. If an enterprise is expanding, a talented young person may move quite rapidly into a preferred position.

A comparable situation exists when an able young man is employed by a small enterprise in the private sector which expands because it has good management and a good product. If the young employee demonstrates a willingness to work hard and shows aptitude, the owner, struggling with the challenges of expansion, is likely to increase the young man's scope of responsibilities.

It is important to retain perspective. A low-income economy which is just beginning to develop a modern sector has relatively few good jobs, most of which the established families are able to obtain for their offspring, although even a modest quickening of the economy will expand openings for small numbers who earlier had little if any prospect of improving their circumstances.

In developed societies, the family remains a potent determinant of occupational outcomes, although less than in traditional societies because of the easier access of young people to higher education, the greater importance of wage employment, and the role of professional management in most large organizations.

To oversimplify: for a variety of reasons, young people who grow up in low-income homes are likely to be less educated; know less about the occupational opportunities available to them and how to pursue them; be blocked from enrolling in apprenticeship programs; know little about job openings with large employers or, when they do learn of them be unable to pass their screening tests; and face a multitude of other obstacles and barriers in seeking a firm footing in the economy. For instance, their families cannot give them the modest sums they need to obtain a franchise or cover a down payment on an investment, either of which might lead to an income-producing opportunity. These disabilities which young people from low-income families face in seeking desirable jobs are increased if they were born and grew up in a rural area or if they belong to a racial or ethnic minority.

In contrast are the large numbers of families who are able to encourage and support their children so that they finish high school or junior college and who, when their children are ready to look for a job, can smooth their way by referring them to their own place of employment or by calling their attention to desirable openings which they learned about from relatives or friends. They may be able to elicit the help of someone in political life who may be able to open doors. Finally, such a family may stake a young person to a modest amount of capital so he can take advantage of an opportunity which he has identified.

The burden of the foregoing is that the youngsters of families which stand high on the occupational, income, and social scales have preferred access to the good jobs. Up to this point a good job and a good income have been treated as an entity, but, as suggested below, the life style of a family, particularly in a developed society, can loosen this association so that the families of men who hold modest jobs can come to enjoy an above-average income.

When both husband and wife hold jobs, it is possible for the family to enjoy a satisfactory, even a good, income, although neither the husband nor his wife holds a good job. Their combined income, however, may place them considerably above the average on the income scale. One characteristic of most developed economies is the steadily growing proportion of married women who work for wages or salaries, thereby adding to total family money income. Although most women work less than fulltime, full-year, and are heavily concentrated in relatively low-wage occupations, a working wife is likely to raise her family's income considerably. If she works fulltime, her contribution is likely to increase family income by more than half. A first question about the family's life-style therefore is whether the wife works, and how much. The more she works, the more likely it is that the family will have an above-average income.

A second differentiating factor is the ability and willingness of the head of household to increase the family's income by working an extended day or week. By turning their leisure hours into income-earning activities, some skilled and service workers are able to accumulate the capital they need to change their occupational status from employee to entrepreneur. Many workers who want to go into business for themselves have no way of accumulating the minimum capital they need to buy a taxicab, open a small restaurant, or obtain a franchise for a gasoline station other than by turning their free time into extra earnings. Many who go this route succeed in moving into a higher income class, and some become successful. Others, of course, lose their life savings by entering the wrong business or discovering too late that they lack entrepreneurial skills.

Another route that some follow to improve their economic position is to engage in illicit or illegal activities which enable them to earn more than they could command through employment in the regular economy. The gamut of these income-producing opportunities is quite wide: the government official taking a kickback, the model letting her friend pay her rent, the truck driver earning extra dollars by transporting stolen goods. The extent to which such illicit and illegal work represents a significant opportunity for many to increase their incomes is suggested by the estimate that in the United States income from these activities may equal as much as 5 to 10 percent of total annual income.

Another way in which persons with modest endowment and limited training are able to improve their incomes, if not their occupational status, is to enter a second career after completing an earlier one which carries a valuable pension. A man who becomes regularly employed at eighteen and retires with a three-quarter pension after twenty or twenty-five years can enter a new line of work, the earnings from which, together with his pension, will put him at least one or two rungs above the average.

To some extent then the families which have special advantages because the primary wage earner has a preferred job are balanced in developed societies by other families which have multiple wage earners or whose principal earner is willing to extend the hours he devotes to work.

There are other important factors in a dynamic society that moderate the influence of the family in determining access to preferred jobs in the present and the future. The principal factors operating to shake up the segmentation structures are trends in general employment; in regional and subregional employment; in occupational, industrial and company employment; and in demography and discrimination. Each has an impact on the opportunities for different groups to compete successfully for the better-paying, more prestigious jobs.

Contrast the prospects of a young college graduate who entered the labor market in the United States in 1931 with the prospects of one who entered in 1951. In the earlier period the young man was likely to be unemployed, certainly underemployed for several years, since he was looking for a job at a time when many companies were letting experienced men go because of the Depression. Even if he were lucky enough to find a regular job, the odds were strong that he would have little opportunity to move up because his employer's work force was static, and it was difficult to make a lateral move. The persistence of a weak labor market for an entire decade acted as a depressant on the career mobility of many members of the work force, particularly those who were first getting established and those who, having lost their jobs, were attempting to make new attachments.

The young person starting off in 1951 entered an economy which, although not free of unemployment, was characterized by continuing increases in total job opportunities. Under these conditions, it was considerably easier for a man to get started, and with some competence and luck, he had a good chance to move ahead. Just as profitmaking is easier in a period of business expansion, so is it easier for people to move into better jobs when employers are adding to their work force. The quarter century since the end of World War II was a favorable period, particularly in the United States, for young people, especially those with college degrees, who were starting their careers; it was the longest sustained period of economic expansion in the country, unmarred by severe unemployment.

While the general trend of employment is an important parameter of the opportunity matrix, regional and subregional factors also play a part. Regions, and smaller areas within large regions, experience different employment conditions. Some areas suffer a net loss of jobs while the national total is increasing. Whether a person obtains employment in an advancing or in a declining area is an important determinant of his career prospects. In a labor-short area such as California during most of the quarter century following the outbreak of World War II, it was relatively easy for a man to move ahead. Employers were avidly seeking workers, and a man who had some skill and who was willing to work hard was usually able to improve his circumstances. The opposite obtained in the rural areas of the Southeastern states where the long-established cotton culture was no longer profitable. The only way that most tenant farmers or agricultural laborers could look forward to supporting their families was to pull up stakes and relocate. Many did just that and in the process improved their circumstances. However, migrants who seek to improve their earnings and their standard of living must compete with established workers in the communities to which they relocate. Native or long-term residents usually have the edge in securing the better jobs. Many are better educated; they know the labor market better, and they have more experience and more connections. Newcomers, almost without exception, are at a disadvantage. We can conclude, therefore, that the accident of location is an important factor in career outcomes; whether the region in which a worker begins to work undergoes expansion or contraction will materially affect his prospects.

There is also a close relation between geographic trends which affect the broad demand for labor in a region and specific industry-occupational trends. In an area where one economic activity predominates, such as coalmining, lumbering, or agriculture, the employment pattern is directly linked to the fortunes of that industry. If the mine in which workers have been employed for a decade or more is shut down, or if mining operations in the area are being phased out because of a loss in competitive position, the man who had a good job as well as one who is just starting out face economic misfortune. The first man has no option but to write off his skill and experience, and, together with the second man, he must start elsewhere close to or at the bottom of the job ladder.

In contrast, important career advantages accrue to those who got an early start in such diverse industries as automotive repair, commercial aviation, insurance, refrigeration, television, and computers for which there has been a rapidly expanding demand. Although not every worker who became employed some years ago in one of these expanding industries has been able to move into and hold onto a good job, most of the early starters have had a clear advantage because of the burgeoning of their industry.

While attachment to the right industry can certainly help a man move up in the occupational and income hierarchy, an even more important consideration is the experience of the specific company in which he obtains employment. When a company is a leader in its field and sets the pace, the members of its work force are in a preferred position to advance. As noted in our earlier analysis of developing countries, companies undergoing rapid expansion look first to members of their own work force when seeking personnel for higher level positions. When good jobs open up, those on the inside have the advantage.

Another factor which warrants attention is demography. It was noted in an earlier discussion of the challenges facing developing societies that a flood of new entrants into the labor force greatly compounds the difficulties of these economies in their efforts to provide even minimum opportunities for employment and income. Per contra, a relatively small inflow of new workers is an advantage to those seeking initial jobs as well as those competing for better jobs. Young males of prime working age, that is, from twenty-five to thirty-four, were in conspicuously short supply in the United States in the 1950s and early 1960s as a result of the depressed birthrates of a generation earlier. The trend in starting wages and salaries for the educated and skilled reflected the advantages that accrued to young men who started work in years characterized by a relatively small number of young male workers.

A related effect of the depressed birthrates of the 1930s was the relatively small number of men in the late 1960s in the next higher age group, many of whom customarily fill supervisory posts. With the economy booming, employers had no option in filling their supervisory and managerial positions but to promote young men into responsible positions as soon as they had demonstrated capacity.

The last factor affecting the distribution of good jobs is changes in the patterns of discrimination in the labor market. The post-World War II experience of the United States speaks directly to this theme. Employment discrimination had earlier been based on religion, national origin, and age, but these patterns were substantially eroded by the continuing tightness in the labor market. Remaining discriminatory practices were heavily centered on race and sex where entrenched prejudice had been translated into rigid policies and practices. However, the manpower stringencies during and after World War II, the political influence of Northern blacks on presidential elections, the decisions of the Supreme Court, and the higher educational levels of the young reinforced each other, and the framework of segregation and discrimination began to crack. The number of blacks who were hired for or promoted into staff, supervisory, and middle-management positions increased substantially when the law and public opinion began to reinforce each other in the 1960s. Discrimination based on sex is more equivocal. Promotional opportunities have been expanded for women, and more women are moving into desirable positions, but since their challenge came later, since they have been concentrated for years within a limited number of occupations, and since the number of educated white and black male competitors is steadily increasing, only small numbers of women have so far moved into the higher ranks. In the present context, we can aver that, in general, a reduction or reversal of long established patterns of discrimination will increase the opportunities for many who previously were blocked from competing for good jobs and high incomes.

Although job segmentation continues to be a dominant characteristic of developed as well as developing societies, the burden of the foregoing is to point out that the many dynamic forces to which modern economies are exposed reduce the hold of past segmentation on future developments. Because of these unstabilizing factors, there is a likelihood that some individuals who would otherwise have access to preferred jobs may fail to secure them, while others who would normally be blocked from obtaining a desirable employment relationship will eventually secure a preferred job and income.

The last question we will address in this chapter is the effect of job segmentation on manpower utilization. As so frequently happens when social arrangements are analyzed, the evidence is mixed. Segmentation has both a positive and a negative effect on utilization.

Since one of the dominant characteristics of many, though not all, preferred jobs is that they provide year-round employment, those who have preferred jobs are less likely to experience spells of unemployment. Another characteristic of preferred jobs is that they provide a long-term affiliation. Preferred jobs are also likely to offer their incumbents an opportunity for overtime work at premium pay. Probably the most positive contribution of preferred jobs to improved manpower utilization derives from the opportunities that most of these jobs provide the incumbents for continuing training and for expanded assignments. In each of these respects preferred jobs have a positive impact on manpower utilization for those who hold them.

The most important of the drawbacks is that workers in preferred jobs tend to get "locked in." Having accumulated considerable seniority and claims on valuable deferred benefits, they are reluctant to look for alternative employment, even when they realize that they have reached the end of the promotional cycle. They believe that they cannot afford to leave, even if they find their jobs unchallenging. One need not argue that all workers seek novelty and challenge or that if some workers were to leave their jobs they would be successful in their search for better positions, but the importance of job security does inhibit the continued growth of many workers.

There are drawbacks to employer-sponsored training. For reasons of cost and because of the fear that a worker who has acquired additional skill will leave because he is unable to advance, management has geared in-service training to the needs of the employing organization and often stops short of the optimal level to which workers are capable of being trained.

We see, then, that while the jobs that offer employment continuity, training, and promotional opportunities contribute considerably to the improved development and utilization of those who enjoy them, the resulting pattern is far from optimal, even for those fortunate workers, because the structure tends to make workers play it safe and avoid making job changes despite compelling reasons. Although there are drawbacks for workers employed in preferred jobs, those in nonpreferred jobs are much more likely to suffer from the segmentation of the structure, particularly from lack of opportunity for regular employment and further skill development.

This chapter has drawn attention to the causes and consequences of job segmentation that are characteristic of both developing and developed societies, and it has illuminated some of the linkages between segmentation and manpower utilization. In the following chapter, we will consider from a broader perspective the manpower imbalances that occur as a concomitant of the dynamism of a modern society characterized by job segmentation.

Up to this point we have taken note of some of the dysfunctional aspects of segmentation with regard to the manpower utilization of those who are fortunate enough to have preferred jobs. But a valid social accounting would have to include a consideration of the impact of segmentation on those who have less attractive jobs.

· 10 ·

Manpower Imbalances

ONE CRITICAL FINDING that emerged from the preceding two chapters was evidence of shortfalls in the effective utilization of manpower resources which resulted from an inadequate number of employment opportunities and, to a lesser degree, from the job segmentation that is characteristic of both developing and developed societies. The thrust of this chapter will be to explore the difficulties that stand in the way of a society's adjusting its basic institutions so that they can better respond to and reduce the gap between the numbers seeking work and the availability of suitable jobs. We will therefore inquire into the congruence between the changes in the economy, which is the principal determinant of what happens on the employment front, and the transformations that take place in the other principal societal systems—the value structure, government, and the manpower development institutions.

Conventional theory, concentrating as it does on the forces which contribute to the equilibrium between demand and supply, pays little attention to the many different types of manpower imbalances characteristic of both developed and developing economies. Several dimensions of imbalance can be distinguished along the following axes.

If the dominant value system is altered to acknowledge the claims of certain groups to suitable jobs, when previously they had been ignored, as were women and members of minority groups, a manpower imbalance is recognized for the first time, and attempts may be made to correct it. Imbalances are also recognized when governments assume responsibility for assuring a high level of employment, as have those of all developed nations, and then aim to discharge it. In earlier generations, it was accepted as part of the normal operations of a market economy that if men lost their jobs as a result of changes in international trade, new technology, the shifts of populations, or the exhaustion of resources—or for one of a thousand other reasons—it was up to each man himself to find another job, even if it meant uprooting his family and relocating a hundred or a thousand miles away. But once government assumes responsibility for a full-employment economy, imbalances arising from changes such as those cited above will be in the foreground of public concern.

A third source of imbalance, particularly in a developed society in which individuals remain for long periods in the preparatory system, is faulty articulation between the educational-training institutions and the economy's requirements for skill and competences. Slippage between the two is likely to result not only in the faulty investment of large public and private funds in the educational process but also in personal disappointment and frustration for those whose career objectives are frustrated.

Imbalances are also likely to arise as the principal factors within the employment system—management and labor—become locked in combat as management seeks to protect, and if possible increase, its prerogatives and scope for decision making and the leaders of labor attempt to restrict these prerogatives so that workers can secure greater control over their jobs and are better able to extract higher wages and improved benefits.

Before exploring each of these causes of manpower imbalance in developed societies, it may be illuminating to consider briefly the conditions which contribute to manpower waste in developing countries. The crux of manpower imbalances in developing countries is the large number of persons in rural areas who are unable to make productive use of their time and energies throughout the year because they do not own or control enough land or other capital and because of the inadequate demand from the owners of capital for their labor. The shortfall of employment opportunities is the root cause of manpower imbalances confronting developing countries, and the specific manifestations treated below are without exception derivatives of this underlying reality.

A number of developing countries have undertaken experimental programs aimed at absorbing at least part of their surplus labor. Their principal approaches have been to provide incentives to labor-surplus villages to undertake useful public works, such as building a road or a school; to encourage, through low-cost capital and other special devices, the growth of handicraft industries to broaden the income-earning potential of rural families; and to organize work groups of surplus laborers for employment in nearby areas that can use additional workers.

The record of these interventions has been uneven; failures outnumber successes. As noted earlier, one characteristic of less-developed countries is their primary reliance on the family as the principal institution for accomplishing a wide range of social and economic functions. Although communal and governmental structures exist and are useful, especially when the local economy requires cooperative action, such as in operating an irrigation system, these suprafamily agencies are the exception. Since village life is often characterized by conflicts between the wealthy and the poor or the moderates and the conservatives, local leaders have difficulty in organizing the community to accomplish common goals, even if the national or state government is willing to extend a helping hand. The fact that men have free time during several months of the year does not mean that they will readily contribute their labor to a community project unless they can see that it will directly benefit themselves. If the benefits are problematic, it is difficult to elicit their voluntary effort.

The stimulation of handicrafts to expand employment and income in labor-surplus regions also encounters formidable hurdles. Unless government guarantees a market for the output and provides additional assistance, such as reduced prices for raw materials, many village industries will not be able to compete with machine-made output produced at home or imported from abroad. Even with governmental assistance, handicrafters may find it difficult to compete because of shifts in consumer tastes, a lack of modern designs, or an absence of adequate market linkages. Although many rural families are able to earn a little extra income through work performed at home, mostly by women and children, governments have had limited success in using this route to reduce excessive underemployment and poverty in rural areas.

The same holds true for the third device—organizing work teams of surplus laborers under government aegis or with government support. This approach works best when there is a large project, such as the building of a dam or the construction of an airfield, in an area not too distant from the manpower-surplus villages. Under these conditions, when men can look forward to a job that may last for many months or even years, an organized effort at recruitment, mobility assistance, and even preemployment training may prove successful. But the juxtaposition of surplus laborers and unmet labor requirements is the exception, not the rule. The more typical situation is a seasonal requirement for additional farm workers. However, at harvesting time, villages characterized by surplus manpower usually have work at home for all who have spare time. When it comes to matching manpower in distant communities with different seasonal requirements, the resolution is more complicated because of the distances involved, the costs of transportation, and the necessity to live away from home, often among strangers.

To this intractable problem of surplus manpower located in rural areas must be added the additional manpower imbalances growing out of the mismatch between the educational and economic systems, the personnel policies of large organizations, and the dysfunctional results of faulty economic policies that artificially reduce the cost of capital.

Aside from the strong assumption that in most developing countries the whole of the higher education system is overexpanded, there is a poor fit between the training of the graduates and the demands of the labor market. High school, college, and university graduates with backgrounds in the arts and humanities are usually in oversupply, while employers in the modern sector, both government and private, are looking for graduates with technical competence. The sources of this misfit are the greater ease with which the educational establishment can cope with large numbers of arts students, the disinclination of many students to undergo the rigors of technical education with its heightened danger of failure, the higher status and greater opportunities that in earlier years went to the most successful of the arts graduates, and the slow adjustments in salary structures that often discourage a shift to technical fields.

These difficulties are more severe at the secondary schools, since technicians and craftsmen must be trained wholly or in part on the job and these training opportunities are often lacking or are of poor quality. Moreover, the existing wage structure slows the increase in the numbers of skilled personnel. Young people with the capabilities of becoming technicians shy away from entering these occupations and attempt to enter the university because skilled jobs usually carry low status and often relatively low wages.

We called attention earlier to the tendency of developing countries to encourage employers to hire more workers than they need and to be circumspect about discharging surplus workers when they realize that their work force is swollen beyond their needs. Since jobs are hard to find, those on the payroll are determined to remain. And employers are loath to engage in the conflicts that would result from an effort to cut back staff. They look to expansion and attrition to solve their problems. The tendency toward overstaffing is pervasive throughout the modern sector in LDCs, and it is chronic in public enterprises because politicians are afraid of public reaction to cutbacks. As a consequence of swollen staffs, it is difficult for a bank, a factory, or a government office to improve its productivity, since management is precluded from introducing organizational changes that will result in reduced staffs.

An additional manpower imbalance in many developing countries is the result of faulty economic policies which keep the interest rate artificially low, which provide incentives to enterprises to import capital equipment, and which give priority to capital-intensive undertakings in the development plan, which in turn distorts the relative prices of capital and labor and slows the growth of employment opportunities. This does not mean, of course, that a developing country should avoid investing in capital-intensive undertakings, such as improving the transportation system or expanding the production of basic minerals, often a key foreign exchange earner. Without large capital investments, development might be even slower.

A further source of imbalance is the persistent and often worsening salary differentials between persons employed in the modern sector and those employed in the traditional sector, differentials that speak more to the dead hand of the past and the exercise of political power than to considerations of relative productivity. Senior bureaucrats are determined to protect and, if possible, improve the salary scale and perquisites of the civil service. Over an extended period, the market forces operating in the private sector, a shift in the distribution of political power, or erosion resulting from inflation may moderate this imbalance. But in the interim, the favored few earn more and live better, while many others, who could make a greater contribution or would at least do as well and would gladly work for lower salaries, cannot find jobs.

These imbalances, which result from the salary distortions between the modern and traditional sectors, are reinforced by the pattern of governmental expenditures. Most governmental services are concentrated in urban areas, with the result that more and more rural folk are attracted to the cities. The large inflow of migrants to the cities leads to environmental deterioration, such as the hazards that overcrowding precipitates. If the flow becomes a cascade, there is a clear danger that the city will be inundated, and the countryside will continue to lag to a point where commerce between the two will be hobbled, and this will lead to a corresponding brake on development.

We have now identified a series of manpower difficulties that developing economies face beyond the generic shortage of jobs and income-earning opportunities, and some of the impediments to a successful resolution of these difficulties have been pointed out. The solutions are difficult to find because any quickening of the urban economy will attract large numbers from the stagnant hinterland. An increased inflow of rural migrants to the city will force the society to use part of its modest surplus to contain the resulting urban ills.

These and similar manpower imbalances are not limited to the developing world. They are present in developed economies as well. In point of fact, developed nations confront a great number of manpower imbalances despite the considerable success that most of them have achieved in keeping their economies operating at a high level of employment.

The conventional measure for assessing the success of a modern society in providing employment is its unemployment rate. For a long time, an unemployment rate of 3 percent was considered a target, at least in the United States. Experts have held that when allowance is made for the fact that some people are entering the labor force while others are leaving, that some workers voluntarily change jobs, and that personal and social mishaps cause others to become temporarily unemployed, a 3 percent unemployment rate, at least in the United States and Canada, can be accepted as prima facie evidence of balance in the labor market. For the better part of the quarter century after World War II, the leaders of the developed nations of Western Europe, at least the more affluent nations, were able to improve on the 3 percent target. By the mid-1970s, a revisionist view made substantial headway in the United States, and to a lesser extent also in Europe. Under the leadership of certain academics, the new doctrine holds that the natural rate of unemployment in the United States has moved up to 5 percent or even higher. An attempt to depress it below that rate would generate inflationary pressures.

Putting the target question to one side, a critical issue is, how do we measure the numbers interested in working who are not currently employed? For instance, the many who are not actively seeking work are not counted among the unemployed. This group includes many young people who are not looking for jobs because they believe that employers do not need additional workers and that, even if they did, they would not hire adolescents. Similarly, many married women would like to work if the opportunity were available, but they do not look for jobs because they know no suitable jobs are available. The same attitudes and behavior characterize many persons with one or another handicap who, after a long and fruitless search, decide that nobody will hire them. Another large element among the uncounted is composed of older persons in good health who have had to retire but who would prefer to continue working. Realizing that employers will not hire retirees except in emergencies, they reconcile themselves to not working. These are among the groups who are not counted in the labor force because they are not actively looking for jobs.

Another group of potential job seekers consists of the many enrolled in special training programs. Some are in training because they want to acquire a special skill in order to enter a particular field. Many others, particularly in the United States, however, are in training because they are unable to find employment and believe that they are better off keeping busy (and receiving training stipends) than doing nothing.

The developed nations have done well in meeting the overt demands for employment of regular members of the work force, particularly married men who are heads of households, and also of increasing numbers of women and young people, many of whom want to work only part time. But it would be an exaggeration to say that these nations have created job opportunities for all who desire and are able to work.

A related aspect of the imbalance between jobs and workers in advanced economies is whether these economies provide full-time employment throughout the year for all who desire it. While many people prefer part-time jobs, this is not true of the many who remain in such jobs only because they cannot find full-time employment. A few are able to find two part-time jobs or move from one seasonal job to another, thereby reducing, though seldom eliminating, spells of unemployment.

The extent of this particular shortfall should not be exaggerated. The data suggest that at any one time only about 3 percent of the American labor force works part time out of necessity, not choice. But once again the reporting system may be deceptive. We know that when the economy strengthens and the number of full-time jobs increases, a considerable number of persons who previously worked part time, presumably out of preference, shift into full-time employment.

Many seasonal workers would prefer year-round work. In construction, the prototype of an industry characterized by seasonal employment, many workers are unable to work for weeks because of inclement weather. This means that in a temperate climate they may work for only nine or ten months in the year. However, seasonality is only partly explained by the weather. It is also a result of the ways in which contracts are let and work is scheduled. We know that some workers have been steadily employed in commercial construction in a number of large American cities for the last quarter century. They have not suffered any involuntary layoffs. And some countries, such as Canada, have designed special incentives to reduce seasonality, with at least partial success.

Another source of imbalance grows out of the lack of effective articulation among important manpower institutions; many countries encounter difficulties in educating and training the numbers and types of people the market seeks to employ. Many European universities have produced an oversupply of arts graduates despite the unmet needs of the economy for scientifically and technologically trained personnel. Although the employment market and, occasionally, even the educational system send out signals that point to the need for a shift in focus with regard to training, the students ignore them.

The student riots in France in 1968 and the increasing difficulties that Sweden faced at the same time in absorbing the vastly expanded number of its arts graduates attest to a serious imbalance. The difficulties are a result of the societies' inability to meet the expectations of university graduates for status and income and for assignments where the skills they have acquired can be used productively. Frustrated graduates, if their numbers grow, can become a major force leading to social instability.

Other imbalances between the educational system and the labor market often follow upon a significant shift in public and private expenditures. This occurred in the United States in the 1950s and 1960s when vastly increased federal expenditures for research and development greatly stimulated the demand for scientists. The universities responded to this demand, only to find that their increased number of graduates reached the market when the spending patterns had leveled off or declined, turning the long-term scientific manpower shortage into a new and disturbing surplus. Imbalances among groups of specialists resulting from sudden shifts in demand and delayed responses in the supply of trained manpower are inevitable in a society dedicated to the freedom of occupational choice, although improved educational and manpower planning should be able to reduce them.

A related imbalance which no developed society has succeeded in avoiding stems from the mismatching that occurs between available manpower and the manner in which the society utilizes that manpower. Employers in the private sector learned long ago that one way to increase their profitability is to reduce their labor costs through increased investments in technology, through improved organization and management, and through improved manpower utilization. But they have been slow to devote adequate attention and resources to improving utilization, and employers in the not-for-profit sector have generally been even slower. Experimentation with different mixes of manpower from the most specialized to the unskilled has not attracted the attention of management that it deserves. Employers understand the opportunities of substituting capital for labor, but they have been slow to explore the potentialities of substituting less trained and less expensive personnel for high-priced specialists. In the preceding chapter we noted the extent to which employers give free rein to their preconceptions and prejudices in screening out applicants of the "wrong" sex, with the "wrong" credentials, the "wrong" social background. The unwillingness of most employers to assess an employee in terms of his skills and potential rather than in terms of his social and academic characteristics is an important contributor to manpower waste.

Another source of waste results from managers' practice of assigning people to work which does not make an adequate demand on their training and skills. In all industrial countries large numbers of professionals—physicians, engineers, managers, government officials—spend a considerable part of each day engaged in work that can be carried out just as well, if not better, by people with less training. Part of the explanation for this anomaly lies in the restrictive practices followed by the professionals themselves, who want to keep others from infringing on their preserves in order to protect their work and income. But this is not the whole of the story. Employers have been slow to recognize the critical importance of trained manpower and accordingly have been slow to explore ways to utilize it more effectively.

When the jobs that people have do not yield them an income sufficient to support themselves and their dependents, that too can be defined as a manpower imbalance, since adequate employment opportunities imply adequate incomes. A significant minority of workers in both rural and urban settings are unable to earn enough from their work to escape from physical and social deprivation. The low-income earners include farmers who have been left behind on worked-out land. No matter how hard they work, they cannot earn enough from their exhausted land. The most deprived own neither land nor a house, and their only work experience has been in agriculture. They often piece together a bare living by hiring out as day laborers during certain months of the year, and at other times they join the groups of migrants who follow the crops.

Likewise, many non-farm laborers and service workers cannot earn enough to support themselves and their families. Without skill, and frequently because of additional handicaps, these marginal workers cannot find regular jobs. The jobs they do find often do not pay enough to enable them to raise their family above the poverty level. If they experience, as many do, one or more spells of unemployment during the course of the year, their predicament is even worse.

The situation is more difficult for a female head of household with young children to support. Many women, lacking skills, can qualify only for unskilled jobs that carry low wages, often grossly insufficient to cover the family's minimum needs, which include child care when the mother goes to work. As long as unskilled work pays as poorly as it does, there will be a relatively large number of workers, many regularly employed, who remain trapped in poverty.

This discussion of the problems facing the unskilled worker provides a backdrop for another imbalance characteristic of industrialized economies. Full employment and increasing labor productivity can be in conflict, especially in the short run. We know that when the labor market is tight, employers are loath to let skilled workers go even if they temporarily have inadequate work for them, since those discharged or furloughed will probably find other jobs and consequently will not be available when their former employers need them in the future. There is considerable evidence that European employers kept a great many excess workers on their payrolls during the booming 1950s and 1960s. The counterpart American experience was the hoarding of specialists and technicians by employers in the aerospace industry where companies realized that their ability to secure large government contracts would be enhanced if they could demonstrate that they had the requisite personnel on their payrolls. The fact that they were able to include in their reimbursable costs the salaries of redundant personnel encouraged this practice.

In several Western European countries, as well as in Japan, law and tradition have made it difficult for large employers to discharge workers, especially those with records of long employment. The high cost of severance tends to keep employment above required levels.

The principal arena where additional employment wins out over increased productivity is in the not-for-profit sector. While economic and financial considerations are not disregarded in the management of the post office or the operation of a hospital, managers in the nonprofit and governmental sectors are under substantial political and community pressures to maintain or expand their work force.

It is not implied that advanced economies are constantly accumulating more and more redundant workers because of the risks and difficulties of discharging them. But powerful pressures are pushing them in that direction, while countervailing forces are operating on the productivity side of the equation. All employers must pay close attention to their labor costs. Moreover, when their operations expand, especially after a recession, most employers will try to keep tight controls over new hirings, since expansion presents them with an opportunity to improve productivity. Difficulties arise, however, when a company or an industry enters a period of a stable or declining demand for its products. If precipitous personnel reductions are to be avoided and reliance placed on attrition, it may take a decade or even longer to bring about the desired shrinkage in payroll costs.

The interface between overfull employment and increasing productivity indicates that, in an advanced economy, there are often institutional factors that use part of the growing national surplus to protect the interests of long-term employees over the cost cutting objectives of employers.

Another rubric for analyzing manpower imbalances involves changes resulting from shifts in demand. The first aspect relates to spatial imbalances. Workers must find employment within commuting distance of their homes unless they relocate to an area where job openings are more readily available. In any case, the closing down of plants in locations which have lost their competitive advantage will leave some workers stranded, such as older workers who are unable or unwilling to relocate.

Even in countries such as France, Switzerland, the Netherlands, Sweden, and the United Kingdom, which have recruited large numbers of foreign workers to help meet their urgent manpower requirements, significant numbers of native workers remain rooted in areas where the economic base is eroding. While some eventually move, usually in response to repeated promptings of family members and friends who have relocated earlier and made a satisfactory adjustment to their new locations, and further impelled by offers of governmental assistance, a significant minority, especially among middle-aged and older workers, will stay put. In many instances they own their homes, and this helps to anchor them. If their skills are not readily transferable or convertible, as with miners, or if they are too old to contemplate retraining, they will remain where they are and manage as well as they can. Their children are likely to leave when they reach working age. And when young people leave, the prospects for the area to attract new companies worsen.

Areas that are undergoing rapid expansion are usually able to attract the workers they need to fill the jobs that are opening up. Governments have responded to the challenge of regional imbalances by designing programs aimed at encouraging industry to locate in declining areas and to speed the relocation of surplus workers. The first approach involves the use of subsidies, tax rebates, free or low rent, and other inducements to encourage enterprises to locate in a distressed area in the hope that the declining employment cycle can be reversed. The United Kingdom has made extensive use of relocational policy, and most West European countries have also resorted to subsidizing plants in depressed areas.

The counterpart approach has been for governments to design special forms of mobility assistance for persons who, in the face of the decline of the local economy, are willing to relocate. In Sweden, the government, in addition to providing a wide range of assistance from job training to covering moving expenses, has been willing to purchase the homes that the migrants leave behind.

Despite considerable governmental experimentation, aided and abetted on occasion by corporate initiatives, to help workers relocate, the process of reaching a balance between men and jobs is relatively slow, especially in areas that are suffering an erosion of their economic base. Governments have found it difficult to put together effective packages of incentives and inducements to counterbalance the decline in private-sector enterprise. Once an area starts going downhill and young people begin to leave, new enterprises are not easily persuaded to locate there.

Recent events in the developed economies have brought another spatial dimension of the manpower problem to the fore. There has been a steady relocation of jobs in manufacturing and consumer services from the city center to the periphery of large urban concentrations or to new towns nearby. To date, burgeoning suburban enterprises have been able to attract the labor supply they require by drawing on the expanding suburban population and the residents of outlying communities, many of whom are willing to travel considerable distances to work. But the people in the low-income neighborhoods in the inner city remain cut off from these new jobs because of inadequate public transportation, their lack of private cars, and the absence of low-income housing in the suburban ring. While the juxtaposition of a trapped urban population and an expanding suburban job market may be a peculiarly American problem because of the added racial component, achieving and maintaining an optimal employment level is always difficult in a dynamic economy because of the uneven expansion among jobs, housing, and transportation. For example, if the real standard of living, personal savings, and various types of governmental benefits are high in one area, workers are less willing to accept jobs in other areas where they cannot obtain minimally acceptable housing or have access to other basic amenities.

The substantial success that advanced nations have achieved in eliminating periodic shortfalls in the general level of output and employment has not, however, eliminated specific imbalances resulting from radical shifts in demand affecting particular industrial and occupational subsectors. Economists have assumed for many decades that a new equilibrium would be established through the flow of capital and labor out of the declining sectors into the expanding sectors. The conventional model postulated a basic homogeneity in the manpower resource so that balance was conceived primarily in quantitative terms. However, advanced economies are increas-

ingly characterized by manpower that is differentiated in terms of specialized skills. Consequently the equilibrating process is more complex. When
the demand for one or another type of trained manpower expands rapidly,
one or another of the following adjustment devices is likely to operate.

When the economy is on the upswing, interoccupational and inter-
industry mobility, new patterns of utilization for the trained manpower in
short supply, and a speedup of the educational-training cycle are likely to
follow. These devices can help moderate the imbalances but are seldom able to
prevent them. A striking case in point was the substantial increase in federal
funding in the United States in the mid-1960s for the medical care of older
persons and low-income families. This expanded substantially the effective
demand for medical services, markedly in excess of the system's capacity to
respond, at least in the short run. The initial result was vastly increased revenues for the providers of service, physicians and hospitals alike, accompanied
by only modest increases in the total services provided the public.

Although manpower adjustments to sudden and large-scale increases
in demand are often difficult to achieve, they present less of a problem than
adjustments to large-scale reductions. A sudden falloff in the demand for
engineers and scientists occurred in the United States in the late 1960s and
early 1970s as the level of governmental expenditures for defense and defense-related activities declined substantially. Many scientists, engineers,
and technicians who had become highly specialized suddenly found themselves without jobs, living in regions where the aerospace industry was concentrated, at a time when the civilian economy went slack.

While some of the newly unemployed had recently been hired and had
graduated only a few years earlier, many others had ten to twenty years of
experience in the defense sector and had come to look upon their jobs in
this sector as their careers. The sudden and dramatic cutback in governmental expenditures removed the ground from under them. Having been
encouraged in their early years to consider themselves as patriots working
to strengthen the security of their country, many felt that they had been
misled and let down by an insensitive government. In light of their defense-
specific skills, home ownership, relatively high salaries, preference for the
region of the country where they were located, the sluggishness of the private economy, and employer prejudice against hiring technologists in their
forties and fifties, it is not surprising that many who lost their jobs found it
difficult to make a satisfactory readjustment.

Another imbalance can be the result of changes in the composition of
imports, especially those that impinge on companies and industries which
are losing their competitive position. Sweden, observing a free-trade policy,

has permitted its least-competitive textile, shoe, and other consumer goods companies to close, on the assumption that domestic producers could no longer compete in the small home market with products imported from countries characterized by lower wages. But even in Sweden, with its taut labor markets, the closures of long-established plants confronted older workers with the need to find new jobs in new industries, often in new communities. Many workers who failed to find new jobs were forced into subsidized public employment.

At the beginning of the 1970s, American trade unions retreated from their support of free trade in favor of protectionism. The unions believe that if American employers are freely permitted to move their plants abroad or import parts manufactured in low-wage countries, the result will be an accelerated loss of jobs for many workers in such diverse industries as textiles, clothing, footwear, electronics, and automobiles. No labor leader can be indifferent to the erosion of his member's jobs in the short run on the assumption that the nation's total employment will be greater in the long run.

The growth of multinational corporations with their worldwide production and marketing strategy, the speed of industrialization of many hitherto nonindustrialized countries, the cooperation between national governments and their exporters in penetrating new markets, the rapid transfer of technology, and the increasingly rapid shifts in consumer tastes can undermine established companies and industries in an advanced economy so that they may have to discharge a large part of their work force. This is one more source of manpower imbalance.

An additional source of manpower imbalance is found in the conflicts that arise among different groups in the labor market and in the population as a whole as they seek to alter their relative positions in response to changes in goals and power. For example, the latent and overt conflicts between employers and workers or among competing groups of workers over jurisdictional issues create critical tensions that often result in manpower imbalances. It was the proud boast of the Swedes up to the early 1970s, when unexpected labor conflicts erupted, that they had found an answer to serious labor conflict through their bipartite collective bargaining between the Employers Association and the Labor Organization. In contrast, the United Kingdom has been plagued during most of the post-World War II period by wildcat stoppages; many last for only a few hours or days, while others last considerably longer. British workers have also periodically resorted to working to rule and other forms of slowdown and shutdown which have reduced the effective use of the nation's human resources, with resulting losses in output and earnings.

A major concomitant and consequence of the successful organization in the United States in the 1960s of many civil service and professional workers has been their leverage to rewrite existing work rules relating to work schedules, work loads, work standards, and other conditions that were formerly under the control of management. The short- and long-run consequences for manpower utilization of this substantial thrust to unionize civil service workers are increasingly obvious. If public managers fail to protect their managerial rights or bargain them away, workers will make significant gains, at least in the short run, at the expense of taxpayers. But over the long pull, unionization need not result in lowered productivity.

Confrontations between labor and management make up only one area of conflict. Another, the cause of growing difficulties in many advanced economies, relates to changes in the relative positions of different groups of workers—blue-collar and white-collar; skilled workers and operatives; professional workers and nonprofessionals; and, in the United States in periods of recession, workers with seniority and newly hired employees from minority groups. Management is increasingly caught in a dilemma: if it responds affirmatively to the demands of one group, it sets the stage for new demands by another group which resents the loss in its relative position. This situation is worse in countries where the trade union leadership, confronted with factionalism, is driven into extreme positions in order to safeguard its power.

One more consideration about labor-management strife and manpower imbalances. Since industrialized countries are increasingly forced to use governmental powers to restrain inflationary pressures, and since governmental intervention frequently results in the perpetuation or worsening of existing wage inequities, the arena for conflict is often widened. Since no nation, to date, has succeeded in fashioning an effective incomes policy, we must anticipate that until substantial progress is made in developing new institutions capable of helping to adjudicate conflicting claims, conflicts will continue and will be accompanied by manpower wastes.

There is widespread concern in the United States, and to a lesser degree in other technologically advanced societies, that the elaboration of a broad system of social security and related welfare benefits is reducing the pressure on people to seek and remain at work. In times past, a man had to work in order to eat. He had no alternative. But today he may be able, without working, to obtain from government the minimum amount of money he needs to feed and shelter himself and his family.

The concern in the United States with the erosion of the work ethic is centered on the large number of female heads of households who remain on public assistance for many years and who raise their families on the tax-payers' money. But a closer look discloses that many others rely on public funds, particularly workers who voluntarily reduce the months they work because they then become eligible for unemployment compensation. A third group consists of early retirees from the public or private sector, some of whom have sufficient income from their pensions to spend their mature years outside the labor force. Then there are men, mostly from disadvantaged groups, who drop out of the labor force in their forties and fifties and who manage to exist by working irregularly or through the assistance of relatives.

The sources of manpower imbalance delineated in this chapter are the result of the shortfalls in employment opportunities and the consequences of job segmentation. Although modern economies operate most of the time at a relatively high level of employment, they have not succeeded in avoiding significant sources of manpower waste.

Sudden changes in the national or international economy as a result of the outbreak of war or the imposition of an embargo can result in significant imbalances which will be reflected in manpower surpluses or shortages. An equally important source of imbalance is the lack of articulation between a dynamic economy and the other societal systems. A change in values, in the pattern of governmental spending, or in the output of the educational-training system is often out of phase with changes occurring in the labor market.

The analysis has pointed out that job segmentation contributes to manpower imbalances by creating or maintaining unfavorable conditions for many workers. Because of adverse conditions, workers suffer periodic spells of unemployment, are unable to find jobs that pay a living wage, or are employed in jobs where their skills cannot be effectively utilized.

While none of these sources of imbalance alone may account for more than a modest shortfall in the effective use of the manpower of a developed nation, together they create a sizable gap. A more important finding is that in a dynamic society the forces which determine the utilization of manpower do not tend to move toward equilibrium. The improved articulation between a changing economy and the other principal societal systems remains a continuing challenge.

PART IV

« « « · » » »

THE ORGANIZATION'S MANPOWER STRATEGY

Is this improvement in the circumstances of the lower ranks of the people to be regarded as an advantage or as an inconveniency to the society? The answer seems at first sight abundantly plain. Servants, labourers and workmen of different kinds, make up the far greater part of every great political society. But what improves the circumstances of the greater part can never be regarded as an inconveniency to the whole. No society can surely be flourishing and happy, of which the far greater part of the members are poor and miserable. It is but equity, besides, that they who feed, cloath and lodge the whole body of the people, should have such a share of the produce of their own labour as to be themselves tolerably well fed, cloathed and lodged.

—ADAM SMITH, *The Wealth of Nations*

· II ·

The Employing Organization

IN THE PRECEDING PART, our focus was on the macrodeterminants of employment, that is, on the forces which determine the level of job opportunities a society is able to generate. In this part we will shift our concern to the manpower strategies pursued by the prototypic institutions in developed societies—the large organization and its counterpart, the trade union. We will address three critical issues: how large organizations procure the trained manpower they need to realize their goals, the objectives of middle management and workers who seek a career with a large organization, and the conflicts that arise between the organization's goals and the employees' goals and how these are compromised.

No organization, no matter how large, how profitable, or how powerful, can move solely on the basis of its own momentum without considering the forces in the macroenvironment that impinge upon it and to which it must remain alert and responsive. For the purpose of the present analysis, however, the interactions between the large organization and the economy and society within which it operates will be treated only in passing; primary attention will be directed to the internal forces that shape the organization's manpower strategy.

This approach has been adopted for several reasons. First, the discipline of economics has only recently recognized the large corporation as the principal unit which organizes activity in developed societies, and it is finding it difficult to modify its tools and theories to encompass the dynamics of these large aggregations of resources and power. Consequently, the gap between theory and reality remains wide. Secondly, the extant theories do not address the congruence and conflict among the different sectors of the work force of a large organization and the consequences thereof for efficiency, profitability, and work satisfaction. And finally, even the best managed organizations have only recently realized the importance of developing a manpower strategy and adapting it to changing opportunities and threats.

The concern here with the manpower strategy of large organizations is a direct outgrowth of the basic theme of this work, namely, the preeminent importance of the manpower factor, which can be understood only within an institutional context. This chapter will outline the opportunities and constraints that large organizations confront in assuring that they have the manpower resources they require now and in the future—at every level, from janitors to the chief executive officer—to discharge their several functions effectively. We start with the extant large organization which, on the basis of experience, has subdivided its functions into a number of job assignments which call for workers with specific characteristics and skills. The nub of the organization's manpower strategy is to fill these positions with suitable applicants and assure that the organization contains in its work force individuals with the requisite skills and experience to fill openings in the higher ranks in the future.

While there are clear differences among large organizations such as General Electric, the U.S. Navy, and Massachusetts General Hospital, there are also important structural and operational parallels, especially relating to manpower, which permit us to treat all large organizations under the same rubric. Some of the important parallels follow.

Every large organization has both a decision-making center and a number of operating units which, in turn, have varying degrees of freedom to determine their own goals and particularly how best to accomplish them. There never has been and there never can be a large organization in which all decisions, small as well as large, are made at the center. These two loci of decision making—top central and lower divisional—are integral to the structure of every large organization and, more importantly, they establish the basic tension in all large organizations which surrounds the allocation of scarce resources, particularly manpower resources: the center seeks to restrict allocations, while the operating divisions press for more.

A second aspect of large organizations is their reliance on career personnel, especially for middle and top management. Each large organization has a distinctive history, preferred ways of operating, and an admixture of formal and informal policies which determine the manner in which its people act and react. The effectiveness of every large organization depends on whether the middle and top management share a common understanding about how work is to be carried out and decisions reached. This implies mutual understanding and trust, which can be achieved only among people who have been exposed to the same environment over a long period of time.

In a dynamic economy in which there are expanding opportunities, especially for persons with energy and talent, a large organization can attract and retain able persons only by offering them a combination of inducements in the form of attractive work, adequate compensation, promotional opportunities, security, and deferred benefits—a total compensation package which on balance is equal or superior to what persons with similar skills could command elsewhere. Since the working life of an executive may encompass thirty-five to forty years, the fortunes of the organization and the economy are likely to undergo several major shifts during a man's working life. Consequently, every large organization must balance its commitments to its career managers with the need for continuing flexibility to respond to new conditions.

The allocation of resources, the critical importance of career personnel, and the conflicts between commitments to them and changes in the internal and external environment establish the parameters which determine how the manpower strategy of all large organizations must be designed and implemented.

Before addressing the components out of which a corporate manpower structure is built, we will review briefly certain structural and functional characteristics of large organizations to which a manpower strategy must be responsive. The strength of a large organization rests in the first instance on the fact that its existence is not constrained by the span of one person's life. The Catholic church can point to an unbroken history of almost two millennia. Many industrial and commercial corporations in Western Europe boast, in their advertising, that they were established in the eighteenth century or earlier.

Although survival is the leitmotiv of large organizations, growth via specialization and diversification is not far behind. In fact, survival and growth are ineluctably linked. In a world in which organizations, like nations, must struggle to survive, an organization can assure its future only by adding to its strength. To do so, it must diversify and expand.

Organizational survival and growth are linked to the quality of leadership, including its provision for succession. The principal advantage that a large organization has over a family enterprise is its freedom to go farther afield in seeking talent. In selecting its potential leadership, it is not constrained by ties of blood or marriage.

The critical importance of a talented leadership derives from the vulnerabilities of every large organization to inertia, factionalism, and incompetence. The strength of a large organization derives from its proven capacity to survive and function, but it cannot rest on its record. To find the proper balance between policies which should be continued and strengthened and innovations which must be introduced is a critical challenge to every leadership.

The leadership must also ensure that its activities continue to provide useful goods or services, the test of which is the willingness of government to allocate funds to support its activities or the willingness of consumers to buy its output at a price that provides a profit. In addition, the leadership must create and maintain an effective manpower system. Thus, another continuing challenge to the organization's leadership is to find the balance between responsiveness to its clientele and providing conditions for its work force which elicit acceptable performance.

These, then, are the five principal elements generic to all large organizations: the need to survive, the need to grow, the need for talent, the need to balance continuity and innovation, and the need to be responsive to both their clientele and their work force.

The social sciences have not yet developed a useful model for the study of large organizations; they are even farther away from a model for the systematic analysis of their manpower resources. Conventional economic theory, which considers the corporation as an income-maximizing entrepreneurial unit, provides little guidance for ordering the realities of corporate life, which involve conflicts over goals, resources allocations, and investment decisions—the issues which continually engage competing groups. Therefore, this chapter and the two that follow should be read as an effort to identify and structure the key elements in an early theory of manpower strategy in large organizations.

A first step in understanding the shaping of an organization's manpower policy is to consider the implications that flow from the goals that have just been identified. Since survival is the first objective of every large organization, and since large organizations depend on the willingness of thousands of people to work cooperatively in pursuit of their disparate goals, senior executives must avoid actions that could weaken or undermine the basis of cooperation. However, the leadership cannot pursue policies of placating the work force if the consequences of doing so are likely to jeopardize the organization's economic survival. Many profitable small companies which were absorbed by conglomerates were liquidated shortly thereafter because of the dismissal of their people at the top and the ensuing confusion and discontent among those who remained. The post-World War II experience of Great Britain points to the opposite danger. Both private and public management were so concerned about maintaining industrial peace that, in attempting to placate their work force, they incurred such high labor costs that they eroded their financial base.

Every large organization is composed of large or small units which see the organization's future from their own vantage. A critical task of top management is to prevent one of the parties from shoving the organization too far in one or another direction. For example, prior to World War II, the U.S. War Department was niggardly in making resources available to the Air Corps. During the war, however, when the importance of air power was belatedly recognized, the General Staff sought to meet almost every request of the Air Corps. Again, in science-based companies it is never easy, especially in years of poor profits, for top management to allocate sufficient funds to the research department in the face of arguments presented by other departments that with increased resources they can provide a quicker payoff. The "old school tie" on which Great Britain relied to such a marked degree for its leadership cadre in the heyday of the empire was a source of pronounced strength. A high proportion of those in leadership positions was related to or was a school chum of everyone else, which greatly facilitated the decision-making process. This inbreeding, however, even though it was diluted by a few talented outsiders, simply did not provide Great Britain with a sufficient pool to meet its total leadership requirements.

The leadership of every large organization must constantly assess new external challenges and opportunities. The more an organization is rooted in tradition, as is the Catholic church, the more caution its leaders exercise in responding to changes, but an excessively conservative policy carries its own costs—witness the problems which faced Pope John XXIII when he sought to close the gap that had developed between the leadership of the church and the laity. The corporate world provides a contrasting illustration of companies which are so committed to growth for its own sake that they pay little heed to maintaining continuity of structure, policies, and managerial personnel. A large organization that seeks to change more quickly than do the people who work for it may run into trouble, because most people can absorb only a limited amount of change within a limited time period.

We see then that top management must shape its manpower strategy in such a manner that it facilitates the organization's drawing strength from continuity while retaining flexibility to respond to the new. A management that is insensitive to the legitimate claims and expectations of its personnel is as likely to undermine the organization as one which, in an effort to avoid the costs of conflict, is so supine that it jeopardizes its economic future.

These brief considerations have sought to highlight the interface in every large organization between its basic goals and its manpower policy options. While top management always has some, and often a considerable, degree of freedom in shaping its manpower policies, it operates within two fundamental constraints: those introduced by external factors over which it has little or no direct control, and those embedded in the enterprise's past— its collective experience which is both a source of strength and an important constraint on its rapid transformation.

A better understanding of the elements that constitute an organization's manpower strategy will be derived from a brief consideration of the differences between a true strategy and the conventional view that employers obtain the skills they need in the labor market. First, we must note that the large employer goes to the market to recruit workers for entering jobs. But, with few exceptions, that is the beginning and end of his direct recourse to the market.

A second difference is embedded in the mere acceptance of a job offer by the applicant and his interest in making a long-term organization affiliation. To the extent that the latter is his concern (and it usually is), he will place less importance on the initial salary offer and more on the developmental opportunities that may be open to him and the prospects of his profiting from them. Recruiters of college graduates in the United States have repeatedly noted that these young people, at the beginning of their work life, raise questions about the company's pension system, the benefits of which often become available only after thirty years of employment.

The employer on the other hand realizes that the contribution of the employee after his initial assignments will depend in no small measure on the opportunities available to him to broaden his knowledge, skills, and competences. These opportunities, in turn, depend in large measure on the assignments, on-the-job training, and formal instruction that the organization provides.

The newly hired employee who seeks a long-term affiliation early understands that his progress up the job ladder will be a result not only of the assessments of his performance made by his supervisors but also of the judgments of his peers and subordinates. He will consequently pay attention to such matters as organizational style and behavior, since his successful accommodation to these will have as great an influence on his future as his technical proficiency.

Basic to the market theory of employment is the belief that people are recompensed at a rate that reflects their productivity. However, the manpower systems of large organizations are predicated on a hierarchical structure of positions which conventionally carry specified salaries. While trends in the market exercise some influence on an organization's manpower strategy, market trends do not determine the specifics of a large employer's manpower policy.

The schema which we will use to analyze an organization's manpower strategy focuses on three major dimensions: assignment, including the antecedent steps in the process—hiring, orientation, and indoctrination; evaluation and promotion, including rewards and benefits; and educational and training experiences which are linked to assignments and promotions to the higher ranks. Since considerable variability exists among large organizations within the same sector and even more among those in different sectors, a quasi-schematic approach will have to be followed in describing the dominant practices and procedures characteristic of large organizations in an advanced economy such as the United States.

Except in periods of severe financial stringency, every large organization annually adds young trainees to assure itself future, middle, and top management. Its requirements may vary substantially over time, depending on the rate of its losses through resignations, retirements and deaths, and, further, on its present and prospective rate of expansion. At times, some large organizations may be unable to increase their trainee pools because of limitations in the existing educational-training structures which provide the new supply. But in general this is not likely to be a major problem, since they can usually tap alternative sources. For instance, although the Armed Forces may prefer to have more graduates of the service academies in a period of rapid buildup, they can increase the flow of officer personnel by drawing on the reserves or expanding officer candidate schools, and by direct commissioning.

There is considerable variability in the amount of effort large organizations devote to actively recruiting executive personnel, both at the entrance level and for higher positions. To take the last point first. As we have noted, most managerial positions routinely are filled by insiders. However, from time to time an organization may decide to fill certain key positions from the outside. For example, the top positions in the federal government turn over almost completely with each change of administration. In addition, many corporate and nonprofit organizations frequently look beyond their own staffs to find a chief executive, a senior operating official, or a key staff specialist. On rare occasions a large enterprise may bring in a new senior team, as happened in the immediate post-World War II period, when the Ford Motor Company reorganized and established a management consisting primarily of key executives who had previously worked for General Motors.

The dominant pattern of obtaining trainees in the United States, surely among large corporations and increasingly among large governmental agencies and nonprofit organizations, is to send representatives to college campuses to recruit young people as executive trainees or junior specialists. After making a first selection, the recruiting organizations invite the more interested and attractive candidates to visit their headquarters or a branch for further screening in the form of interviews, testing, or other exercises and exposures. Thereafter, offers of employment are made to the most promising candidates.

In hiring specialists, that is, young men and women who have been trained in accounting, chemistry, information systems, economics, marketing, or other fields of specialization, recruiters place considerable weight on the student's academic record, his work history and extracurricular activities, and the recommendations of his teachers. Although considerable information about the applicants is collected and sifted and additional efforts are devoted to intensive individual interviews, the inherent limitations of even the most thorough screening efforts must be pointed out. There is no firm basis for judging how a young person who has not held a regular job will react to a specific company and particularly to a specific unit within that company. The high turnover rate of newly hired college graduates—between 30 and 50 percent leave during the first three to five years of their employment—speaks to the limitations of the selection procedure. Observation of the process of college recruitment suggests that large organizations might do almost as well and possibly better if they were to ask the registrars of the institutions where they recruit to list the graduates by their general and specific grade averages and then, after eliminating the lowest fifth or sixth on grounds of possible intellectual or emotional limitations, make offers to the rest on a first-come basis. In light of the considerable sums spent every year on college recruiting, large organizations with high recruiting costs might well consider a controlled experiment.

Although it is difficult to generalize about the recruitment-selection process, a few tentative conclusions can be advanced. Every person with the authority to hire tends to consider himself an expert, surely about his own needs and, if he serves in a staff role, about the needs of those for whom he recruits. The usual pattern is that young men and, recently, young women who appear to fit the organizational prototype tend to be selected. The attempted matching of newcomers to insiders implies that a preference is given to individuals who will "fit in." In the seminary, all novitiates are kept under close supervision, and those whose faith begins to weaken are separated before they are ordained. In the service academies, the cadets ostracize the deviant in the hope that he will resign. The search for congeniality is universal, and since organizational performance and personal satisfaction depend on easy and relaxed relations among the members, this emphasis is understandable. But no matter how much effort is made to find young people who will "fit in," the success rate is not likely to be high because both the choosers and the chosen are making decisions largely in the dark.

The manpower policies of most large organizations are predicated on the assumption that productivity, morale, and loyalty will be enhanced if the organization has the opportunity to indoctrinate its new members. The church and the military long ago established a tight control over the indoctrinational systems through which all newcomers must pass. Medicine, the most closely knit of the professions, has fashioned an extended educational-training process, a principal aim of which is to shape the young physician in the image of the established professional.

Many large corporations spend considerable time, effort, and other resources in orienting and indoctrinating their newly hired executive trainees in their philosophy and policies. An occasional company may rotate a new employee through various assignments, including a spell of formal education and training, for a period of up to two or three years. But this extended orientation has a disadvantage because most recent graduates have been passive for many years, listening to lectures, conducting experiments under direction, or writing assigned themes, and they look forward to putting their knowledge and skills to work. Consequently, they are unhappy if they are sent from one division to another for three to six months at a time; the arrangement has more in common with their experiences in college or graduate school than with their idea of a real job where they have an assignment which they must complete within a stipulated period of time. The high rate of early resignations among trainees confirms the shortcomings of this approach. The units which are obliged to make room for trainees question the effectiveness of an orientation process that requires them to find assignments for the trainees, even if they are "make-work" from which they receive little useful output. Finally, top management has increasingly realized that morale building is a long-term process which cannot be condensed into special efforts concentrated during the initial period of an employee's career.

Many corporations now believe that a more constructive approach would be to establish and keep open lines of communication with all key groups, including young executives. They believe that if they clearly state their aims, the plans and programs that are being readied for implementation and the likely changes that will follow from these new initiatives, the young executives are likely to support and identify with their corporation's goals. However, although little corporate identification is likely to occur without effective communications, communications must not be confused with successful indoctrination and persuasion. New members of an organization, especially those whose education has stressed a skeptical approach, will pay more attention to actions than to words. No matter how clearly top management communicates the criteria upon which it evaluates performance for the purposes of promotion, the young executives will wait to see whether the actions and results conform to the promises. Only if they do will top management have made its point. If a gap develops between what is communicated and what actually occurs, morale is weakened. Lyndon Johnson's loss of credibility with the American people as a result of his repeated optimistic assessments of the course of the war in Vietnam is only an extreme case of attempted morale building which backfired because there was no basis in fact.

A man's initial assignment is crucial, since it determines the first work he does and his pay and perquisites and also foreshadows the probable next stage in his career. As we have seen, large organizations are subdivided into operating units which have varying degrees of autonomy, including control over their manpower resources. While top management can assign and reassign individuals among its divisions, it seldom does this without consultation and negotiation with the divisions involved. Top management cannot hold a divisional manager responsible for meeting his production quota or his profit goal if it can unilaterally remove key persons from his control and press him to accept a replacement who is unacceptable to him. Even during a war, the Chief of Staff may find it difficult to obtain the release of a key officer from a theater commander.

The underlying sources of tension in the arena of assignment can be readily identified. The individual with the potential for advancement can add to his skills and experience only if he is reassigned after he has extracted what he can from his current assignment. However, if he performs capably, his superior will not be inclined to release him. The third party of interest is the personnel staff which has responsibility for assuring that the organization will have an adequate pool of qualified persons ready to assume senior positions when they become vacant. The development of such a pool requires broadening the experience of individuals with potential, which in turn requires their periodic reassignment.

The larger and more complex the organization, the more difficult is the assignment process. No one at higher headquarters can know personally more than a small proportion of the total managerial and technical group. Moreover, the assessment of an individual's competences and skills which is stored in a computer is frequently misleading. Some social scientists believe that the computerization of the personnel function can improve the use of human resources, but even when many details are logged into a computer, obstacles remain. Hard decisions are required about what factors should be entered and at what frequency, how the stored information is to be tapped, and what additional inputs beyond the computerized record are needed for selecting individuals for new and important assignments. Without a strong centralized personnel system, most individuals remain the hostage of the division to which they are assigned, at least until they themselves take the initiative to relocate, until their supervisors relocate them, or until the central staff decides to act.

Such a restricted personnel attachment process lies at the heart of every large organization. People identify with the division, sometimes with a small unit within the division, where their work is centered, their friends and associates are located, and their career prospects lie. This can be demonstrated by reference to such diverse organizations as the Catholic church, where members relate first and foremost to their order or diocese; the military, where a man is first a "submariner" and only thereafter a member of the U.S. Navy; the university, where a professor considers himself a historian and a member of the history department rather than an employee of Harvard or Stanford; the government, where federal civil servants see themselves as employees of the Social Security Administration or the National Institutes of Health rather than as employees of the Department of Health, Education and Welfare; and industry, where the executive introduces himself as working for Cadillac or Chevrolet, not for General Motors.

Assignment is one of three legs of the personnel stool. The second is evaluation and promotion; the third, education and training. In every large organization, there are many people in the lower ranks and successively fewer toward the top. Thus, the process of promotion is crucial to both the individual and the organization. In many large organizations, promotion up the first two or even three rungs of the ladder may be quasi-automatic: in the military, initial promotions depend on time spent in grade; at many universities, the earning of a doctorate leads automatically to promotion to the rank of assistant professor.

But when automatic criteria can no longer be used and several individuals are left behind for every one who is advanced, the organization must resort to some form of acceptable evaluation system to support its decisions. The conventional approach is that a man's superior grades him on various aspects of his performance, and the next higher supervisor reviews these evaluations and confirms or modifies them.

However, the personnel literature is replete with evidence that no matter what type of evaluation system is used, there is a strong tendency for supervisors to make favorable evaluations. Many more people are rated as excellent or very good than as fair or unsatisfactory. This "halo effect" reflects the difficulty of maintaining confidentiality in a large organization where many people have access to the records. Supervisors anticipate that their ratings will soon become known to those whom they have evaluated, and in many organizations provision is made for formal feedback. While the supervisor may have ample evidence to back up a poor rating, he is reluctant to enter it upon a man's record because of the tensions it will create, unless he plans to reassign or discharge him. Large organizations make their peace with employees with borderline competence. Consequently, as long as the superior does not feel that his own position will be endangered by a poorly performing employee, he is likely to avoid taking action which could lead to the discharge of the worker.

Relatively few persons in the managerial ranks are discharged for inefficiency. Even if some who leave "voluntarily" are eased on their way by friendly advice that they had better look elsewhere, the total number of managers who are eased out is small.

Evaluation procedures are almost as limited in selecting people for promotion as they are for identifying those who should be discharged. The "halo effect" singles out as suitable for promotion a number usually in excess of the opportunities available. Moreover, most openings are in units of the organization which have specialized requirements. While top management may favor or even encourage lateral movements among production, marketing, and various staff assignments, the supervisor responsible for filling a specific opening may be less inclined to gamble; he wants the new man to carry his new responsibilities as quickly as possible. This helps to explain the adage that the successful applicant is often the man in the right place at the right time. Most openings are filled by persons in a lower echelon of the same division. As men move toward the top, they are likely to become linked with others higher up who then consider them their protégés. These alliances work both ways. As the sponsors move higher, they help to pull their followers along. On occasion, however, when two senior groups become locked in conflict, the key members of the losing team may have to leave.

The foregoing emphasis on allegiances, alliances, and conflicts helps to illuminate the extent to which the critical promotional process is governed less by objective evaluations of competence and potential and more by the coincidences of experience, exposure, and political considerations. Both the men who lead large organizations and the scholars who study them tend to downplay or ignore this reality, possibly because to acknowledge it would undermine the belief in fair and open competition in which the best man wins.

The third strand of the personnel process, education and training, is linked to both assignment and promotion. Executives, like other workers, learn by doing; they need to have different assignments to broaden their understanding of the complexities of the organization and to increase their skills in coping with them. A middle manager is more likely to be appointed to a senior position if he has had an opportunity to acquire broad experience. In the Armed Forces, the career development system aims at the early identification of officers with the potential to move toward the top, followed by the provision of successive assignments that will broaden and deepen their exposures and experiences. Only in this way will they be prepared for a top position. Every large organization must develop a group of experienced personnel from which to select its top management. But for various reasons, including rapid growth, unexpected losses of key personnel, and belated evidence that some of the aspirants will not be able to perform successfully in top positions, senior management may suddenly find that it has no eligible candidates within its own ranks, and it must look outside to fill key assignments. Some companies, of which General Motors is the prototype, believe in multibackup for each executive in the upper ranks. But this approach has limitations because it is difficult to keep able men in a holding pattern for long. Even if they can be bribed by high salaries and other perquisites to stay with the organization, their abilities and skills will obsolesce if they do not have sufficiently challenging assignments.

Although learning is built into the assignment process, most large organizations, especially since the end of World War II, have resorted increasingly to various types of continuing education and training of a more formal nature, an approach that has long been followed by the church, the military, universities, and the professions. Despite the considerable resources that corporations invest in executive management training programs, little is known about their effectiveness. Most companies, however, continue to underwrite these programs, even in years of poor profits. If those who attend these formal courses are promoted soon thereafter, a favorable ambiance is created about these educational efforts. But when men who have been introduced to new ways of thinking and analyzing their problems are returned to their former assignments with little or no opportunity to put their new knowledge to use, they are likely to become frustrated.

Many large organizations believe that they will achieve enhanced productivity and morale by making more educational and training opportunities available to their managerial staffs, who, in turn, soon consider these opportunities a fringe benefit. The organizations may be right in this judgment, but it would require more feedback and analysis to be certain that the outcome is positive. To encourage managers to attend courses and seminars or otherwise participate in learning situations may be counterproductive if the goals are not clearly delineated and the rewards are problematic.

To attract and retain competent management, a large organization must provide competitive opportunities and rewards. There tends to be a rough comparability in the hiring salaries for the same types of position among large organizations in different sectors of the economy, that is, business, government, and the universities. But the reward systems among different organizations become increasingly differentiated at the middle and higher levels of management. The rate of advancement, salary levels, working conditions, and fringe benefits differ substantially among organizations and sectors, and consequently only rough comparisons can be made. If a man has many options by virtue of his native ability, education, and experience, he can afford to respond to different inducements, depending on his values and goals. Those who desire status and money are likely to shift jobs and careers for relatively small income differentials within the same company, between companies, and even among sectors of the economy. Others, more committed to a particular pattern of work or perhaps more concerned about long-term security, will forgo an opportunity to increase their immediate earnings, even by a substantial amount, if it requires that they change the nature of their work or accept the risk of lessened job security.

Different organizations seek to design reward and benefit packages which are responsive to their special needs. For many decades, the federal government paid relatively low salaries but sought to make long-term service attractive through reasonable assurance against job loss, liberal fringe benefits, and good retirement income. On the other hand, certain large department stores offer the opposite: little job security but quick promotions and high salaries for the successful merchandiser. In fact, success in retailing involves a commitment on the part of the young, and even older, executives to work long hours, including nights and Saturdays.

In prestigious universities, the principal attraction has always been the relative freedom of the faculty member to be master of his own time. His formal teaching responsibilities may require less than 100 hours a year, and his responsibilities to his university, including committee work and consulting with students, may be discharged within a total of 300 hours. But the very individuals who devote so few hours to their formal duties are likely to be constantly engaged in reading, lecturing, experimenting, and writing, which makes them among the hardest working members of society. But they work for themselves, for scholarship, and for science, not for their dean or president. And that makes a difference.

In a pecuniary economy, large business organizations rely primarily on monetary incentives to attract and hold competent people. The federal government and nonprofit institutions now realize that the salaries they offer must be competitive with those offered by industry if they are to find, attract, and retain competent people. Since the mid-1960s, the pay scale of the U.S. Civil Service has been adjusted annually so that it remains abreast of changes in the private sector. Moreover, it is no longer exceptional for the head of a large hospital, museum, or foundation to earn between $75,000 and $100,000, which is additional evidence of the importance attached to high salaries in attracting capable managers. Marked variability continues, however, in the earnings of the chief executives of major American corporations. The model range in the mid-1970s is about $250,000 to $300,000, but many receive only half that amount, while a few earn three times the average. There is no simple explanation for this wide disparity, but company and industry traditions hold part of the answer.

Because of the much larger numbers of middle managers, even highly profitable companies keep a close eye on competitive salaries. They are less concerned about the generous salaries earned by the relatively few at the top than about the distortion of the entire salary scale that results from the fact that high salaries for the senior group will exercise an upward pull on the scale for middle management.

Increasingly, the salaries executives receive are related to the positions they hold rather than to the specific contributions they make. While executives in sales may be rewarded in direct relation to their performance, this is not, nor can it be, the general pattern, because so much of the work in a complex organization reflects the joint efforts of a group. In such an environment it is difficult to identify the high producer.

Another trend in organizational compensation is to provide perquisites in addition to salaries for executives. They include liberal expense accounts, company limousines, and travel at company expense to attend meetings in exotic places (to which wives are also invited). Since most of these benefits are tax-free, large companies have increasingly resorted to these fringes; they are highly valued by the recipients, and their cost to the organization is relatively small. As with many aspects of personnel policy in large organizations, relatively little is known about the extent to which liberal salaries and benefits contribute to important goals, because these goals are often not specified with sufficient clarity to make a meaningful analysis possible. A safe assumption is that the prevailing patterns are determined largely by an admixture of company tradition and market trends.

To assure a steady supply of managerial personnel who can be advanced to higher levels of responsibility, most large organizations have relied increasingly on compensation systems which tie important benefits to long service. The objective has been to make it costly, in the form of lost benefits, for a manager to leave once he has spent a decade with a company. Many company retirement and pension plans require relatively long service—from fifteen to twenty-five years—before the individual becomes eligible for benefits. The outstanding exception has been the Teachers Insurance and Annuity Association which, through the assistance of the Carnegie Corporation, has made all professorial retirement benefits portable.

In recent years, the logic of tying benefits to long years of service has come under increasing criticism; moreover, considerations of equity have also come to the fore. To take the last first. A plethora of evidence has been presented to various congressional committees concerned with pension reform that many long-term workers have been "cheated" of their retirement benefits because, through no fault of their own (business recesssion, company bankruptcy, illness, plant closure, fraudulent action by the employer), they have not worked the specified number of years. For this reason, new legislation has been passed which establishes tighter public control over pension systems and which provides for earlier vesting.

But the issues go deeper. The logic of deferred benefits aimed at locking executives into a company has been challenged by both experience and theory. Many large organizations have discovered that some of their older managers find it increasingly difficult to meet their responsibilities effectively and, worse, they stand in the way of younger people who are ready and waiting to be promoted. As a consequence, many large organizations are moving to adjust their personnel policies to facilitate the early retirement of managers whose energies have waned. This process has been accelerated by the realization that it is deadening to an organization to have high-salaried executives merely waiting until they reach the age of retirement.

The broad outlines of the manpower strategies pursued by large organizations in the United States, especially the corporation can now be set forth. A barrier now separates the mass of blue-collar employees from those with managerial responsibility. Manufacturing foremen still are drawn from the rank and file, as is an occasional plant superintendent. But for the most part, the future executive comes from a different pool and is treated differently. In order to find new employees, most large employers tap into the pool of recent college and university graduates. Although company recruiters seek to identify young men and women with the qualifications and potentials for becoming effective managers, the high rate of early turnover of junior executives underscores the tenuous assumptions and fragile procedures that characterize the selection process.

We have found that the critical assignment function is hobbled by the difficulty that most large organizations have in assembling and keeping up to date relevant information about their managerial personnel and, equally important, by the tensions between divisional units with direct control over some personnel and the central staff's concern with long-range career development.

Shortfalls also exist in current approaches to evaluation techniques and promotional procedures, educational efforts, and compensation. In each case, the large organization seldom knows enough about the complex elements involved in the process. It does not have adequate instruments to differentiate reliably among those in competition for promotion. There are no reliable follow-up studies of managers who have participated in executive development programs which would enable the corporation to reach sound conclusions about the costs and benefits of these efforts. A review of established policies and practices with respect to salaries, fringe benefits, and pensions also indicates that current approaches are vulnerable on both conceptual and procedural grounds.

The weaknesses in the manpower strategies of large organizations which have been identified suggest alternative explanations. The least radical holds that these weaknesses reflect first the relatively recent date at which top management began to appreciate the importance of developing a manpower strategy, and it suggests that these weaknesses will be addressed if not remedied in the years ahead. A second interpretation focuses on the obfuscations which result from the presumably scientific nature of the theories and techniques employed in the personnel arena and which help to insulate established practices from criticism by outsiders. A third interpretation predicates that since all large organizations are by nature complex political organisms, their manpower strategies cannot be put on a scientific basis. This interpretation implies that critical personnel decisions, however they are rationalized, inevitably follow the ebb and flow of power among competing organizational cliques.

Belated recognition of the critical importance of the manpower factor, poor conceptualization, questionable personnel practices, and the neglect of the political element in large organizations are not mutually exclusive explanations. The present state of the manpower strategy of large organizations probably reflects them all. The more important question is, what will happen in the future?

Ad hoc approaches to manpower are likely to be subjected increasingly to critical scrutiny, since top management now recognizes the complex arrangements required to assure an effective corps of able and competent managers. Recognition of the importance of manpower resources and the complexity of managing them presages the investment of additional time, effort, and leadership to improve an organization's manpower strategy.

Recognition of the need for a manpower strategy is an essential first step. The second step is more difficult: it is the challenge to top management to fashion a strategy and assure that it is sensitive to the changing environment within which the organization operates. Each organization must develop its own strategy, which must include a responsiveness to its idiosyncratic experiences. A generalized manpower strategy for all large organizations, even those operating in the same sector of the economy, is no more possible than is a common strategy of financial or facility planning for all profit-seeking enterprises. If large organizations share broad experiences and are exposed to similar environmental stimuli, their manpower strategies will include common elements. Nevertheless, each strategy will also be characterized by elements which are unique to each organization's experiences and circumstances.

Although attention from top management and improved staff efforts can go part of the way to strengthening the manpower systems of large organizations, a final challenge remains. The goals of the leadership of an organization are not necessarily congruent with the aspirations of those lower in the hierarchy. Many in the ranks of middle management eventually realize that they will never reach the top, and their subsequent goals and actions reflect this. As will be made clear in the next chapter, no manpower strategy can avoid the necessity of reconciling the goals of the organization with those of the managers and workers who are affiliated with it.

· 12 ·

What Employees Want

THIS CHAPTER WILL CONCENTRATE on middle management and the rank and file. It will be less concerned with the work they perform and more with the goals they seek to realize through their work. To incorporate this shift, our framework will be enlarged to include the trade union, which now plays a critical role in helping the rank and file achieve its objectives in the workplace.

What do employees want? They want to earn enough from their work to meet the needs of their families and to enjoy a rising standard of living. Secondly, they want reasonable assurance that if their performance is satisfactory, they can look forward to holding their jobs and to the special benefits which will accrue to them by virtue of their long-term affiliation with the organization. Thirdly, in light of the long hours they spend at work, they want their jobs to provide the satisfactions that come from meaningful activity. Finally, workers expect that those who supervise and direct them will not infringe on their rights as human beings and as citizens.

Reworded, workers want more money, more job security, more benefits, more satisfactions from the work itself, and more freedom in the work setting. This catena comes very close to Samuel Gompers' formulation that workers strive constantly for "more."

The traditional approach of economics to workers' goals is to consider the issue almost exclusively in terms of current earnings. This approach does allow for some extra compensation when a job has particular drawbacks, such as instability, danger, and irregular hours, but it largely ignores the importance that workers attach to such long-term aspects as job security and deferred benefits, to direct satisfactions which can be derived from working, and to their desire to enlarge their scope for determining the conditions under which they work.

When the traditional approach takes account of the importance that workers attach to their job-related goals, it looks to the structure of wages to reflect these considerations. For workers with comparable competence and productivity, the theory sees a trade-off between the current wage and other benefits; the fewer the benefits, the higher the current wage, and vice versa.

One reason for differentiating middle management and the rank and file from top management is to point up that only the latter have good prospects of getting most of what they want—good pay, good benefits, interesting work, and freedom. The situation is less favorable for middle management and much less favorable for the rank and file. As we shall soon see, what workers want is in considerable measure determined by their estimate of what they can hope to achieve.

We will explore sequentially the goals of middle management, those of the rank and file, and the modifications in the objectives of the rank and file which arise as a result of the actions of trade unions, which have a dynamic of their own.

A first step in the consideration of the goals of middle management is to review the sequencing of the employment process, from initial hiring to retirement. After an employment offer has been made and accepted, the new employee needs orientation and support, especially during his first weeks and months on the job. Going to work for a large organization for the first time can be traumatic. The newcomer has difficulty in mastering the special language, symbols, and behavior patterns that characterize the organization he has joined. If he must rely on himself, he is almost certain to make errors along the way.

He needs, expects, and looks for guidance from his superiors and peers. If guidance is forthcoming, the acculturation process can proceed without difficulty, but if it is not available, the newcomer is likely to flounder and become increasingly anxious and confused. Managements differ in their approaches to the novice. The Armed Forces, for instance, believe in a "cold shower" approach. The prospective officer-candidate is under pressure to perform from the moment he enters the academy or the officers training school, since the tradition holds that his capacity to absorb and adjust to pressure is an important diagnostic clue to his potential capability to perform effectively under stress. At the opposite extreme, a few managements, recognizing the newcomer's need for special support during his early weeks of employment, have identified a group of sensitive supervisors to whom newcomers are assigned.

Since the orientation a man receives is linked to the nature of his assignment, the initial matching of men and jobs often has a determining importance for long-run adjustment. Even if a new employee has no pronounced preference among several types of work, he may still want to be asked. More importantly, most new employees look forward to receiving an assignment which will enable them to demonstrate their capability, one that will enable them to use for the first time the knowledge and skill they have accumulated during their years of preparation. Many new employees become disheartened when they are given routine work which offers them no challenge. The opposite danger, when a new employee is given work far beyond his capacities, also occurs, but infrequently.

Even if new employees make their peace with an initial routine assignment which fails to challenge them, they remain concerned about the future. Most trainees early realize that their best chance to advance up the leadership ladder is to broaden and deepen their knowledge and experience, and to do so they need challenging assignments.

Large organizations with national or international operations often find it necessary to move a junior manager from one location to another when they change his assignment. This is true of many corporations, the Armed Forces, and the diplomatic service. Although some individuals look forward or become reconciled to a gypsy existence, others find the necessity to make repeated moves too disruptive and are willing to sacrifice a promising career for greater stability.

Every large organization has some mechanism for evaluating its managerial and technical personnel. Whatever system it uses must be acceptable to those who are evaluated, or it will lose its legitimacy. Many employees do in fact question whether they are being fairly judged, just as many supervisors who make the ratings have qualms about their own objectivity. If one were to speculate about why flawed appraisal systems do not cause more organizational dissonance, the answer is probably to be found in the cautionary manner in which the results are used for critical decisions, that is salary determinations and promotions. Top management uses formal rating systems in reaching important personnel decisions, but it also uses other inputs. If employees conclude that the persons selected for promotion represent reasonable, if not necessarily the best, choices, the integrity of the formal system is not jeopardized.

One reason young people join a large organization is that they place value on the educational and training opportunities provided by their prospective employer. They understand that these opportunities are linked not only to initial managerial assignments but also to the promise of later advancement. The less specialized their prior education, the more they rely on in-house educational training opportunities for career advancement.

The technically trained college or university graduate also sees the continuing educational and training opportunities offered by prospective employers as critical factors in his employment decision. It is difficult for such a person to stay abreast of developments in his field of specialization unless he has continuing opportunities to learn about new ideas and methods.

Most young managers expect that the time and other costs involved in their continuing education will be carried by their employer. They expect, at a minimum, that if they attend classes at a university, their employer will rebate their tuition payments upon proof that they have satisfactorily completed the course. They also expect their employer to give them time off from work to pursue course instruction that is job-specific.

When managers make a mid-career change, as do military officers who are not moving to the top, or when a radical shift in governmental financing reduces or closes out a major procurement program, access to "retraining" can be important. While few large organizations have yet accepted "conversion training" as a contingent liability in long-term employment contracts, there are signs that various professional, managerial, and technical societies are beginning to seek this benefit for their members.

When young people enter managerial careers, many consider only tangentially the range and quality of the organization's personnel policies and practices, from work assignments to pensions since they are convinced that their future will be based on their own performance. But after five to ten years with a large organization, many reassess their potential for further career advancement and, at that point, compensation levels, fringe benefits, job security, and related matters become increasingly important.

During their initial years of employment junior executives frequently receive a raise in salary every year or two as their title is changed and their responsibilities are enlarged. Later, when changes in titles and assignments are less frequent, those in the middle of the managerial hierarchy still look forward to receiving at least an annual upward adjustment in their salary. If the company which employs them is expanding rapidly, and there are corresponding increases in its profitability, these expectations are even stronger, since the managerial group feels that it is largely responsible for the organization's successful performance.

If not-for-profit enterprises are to attract capable executives, they must at least approximate the conditions prevailing in the market. This does not imply that their salary levels must be as high as those in the profit sector; however, offers of professional and managerial positions, including the nature of the work, status, and total compensation, must be competitive with opportunities in other sectors of the society. Although the profit-making sector usually takes the lead in improving the level of compensation, the pattern is not rigid. In the 1960s, the rapid expansion in the demand for higher education and health services led to differentially more rapid increases for academic staff and medical specialists in the not-for-profit arena.

The high personal income tax rates have led many managerial personnel to become almost as interested in fringe benefits as in their salaries. For example, it is expensive for a family to buy on the open market comprehensive health insurance that now often includes outpatient psychiatric care and dental services, but certain large organizations provide superior coverage at little or no cost to the employee. Large private universities usually waive tuition for the wives and children of regular members of their faculty, and many, in addition, pay half the tuition of children of faculty members who elect to attend other institutions. The federal government has been extremely liberal in its provisions of time off for illness, which, together with earned vacations, approximate one-sixth of the work year. Many large companies, recognizing the disruption they cause by their frequent shifting of executives from one part of the country to another, have sought to reduce the opposition and resentment caused by relocation with a panoply of financial supports and assistance. These include liberal travel and interim living expenses, coverage of the full costs of moving household effects, and, most important, assurance that the employees will suffer no financial loss from the sale of their houses.

Valuable saving plans, including the purchase of the company's stock below market price, are additional benefits to which many below top management have access. Once a family knows that it is well protected on such important fronts as health care, higher education for the children, housing, and savings for the future—the most important of the fringe benefits—an executive's preoccupation with the annual adjustment in his salary is somewhat reduced.

Steadily increasing salaries and valuable fringe benefits are critical objectives for those who seek careers with a large organization, but equally important are their concerns about job security and assurance against arbitrary and capricious actions. Most executive personnel do not have the protection of a formal employment contract. On the other hand, a powerful attraction of a large organization is the likelihood that a manager will have a long career with the organization if he performs satisfactorily. Even without a formal contract, he knows that in the normal course of events he can look forward to lifetime employment.

This implied promise is relative, not absolute. If, instead of growing and becoming more profitable, the corporation runs into prolonged difficulties, it may be forced to cut its managerial staff. A second threat to executives is the upheaval following a merger, which often leads to a thinning of the managerial staff. Executives in the company that was absorbed are often declared redundant. Men with good records of performance are discharged through no fault of their own, often, solely because the takeover organization wants to place its own personnel in control.

A third problem, increasingly recognized by some top managements, is how, with a large number of able young people in a holding pattern, to unblock the promotion process. This can usually be accomplished by accelerating the early retirement of senior personnel. Executives at age forty who formerly could look forward to another quarter century of employment now must recognize that they may be separated within a decade or less.

While the expectation of many middle managers of continuing their organizational affiliation until the conventional age of retirement can be threatened by adverse economic trends, mergers, or new personnel policies, the anticipation of long-term career stability has not yet been broadly undermined. If it were, one would have to anticipate the growth of new arrangements, such as early vesting of pensions, special separation allowances, and subsidized conversion training and education to facilitate the occupational readjustment of people in middle and senior management who are let go in their mature years. This conclusion grows out of the assumption that all personnel, except the few who earn very large incomes, are always concerned, first and foremost, with job security. Since top managements will continue to compete to attract young talent and to hold on to large numbers of managers for several decades, the probability is strong that they will be pushed to alter their present benefit systems.

There are growing indications that managerial and technical personnel concerned about job security are joining one or another type of professional organization to enhance their bargaining positions. Although the American Association of University Professors has always given precedence to protecting the tenure system, in recent years a small but growing number of faculty members, particularly at public institutions, have seen advantages to joining trade unions to improve their negotiating positions.

There is also evidence of greater militancy among scientists, engineers, lawyers, nurses, and teachers who work for large corporations, nonprofit organizations, or government. While the proportion who are union members remains relatively small, many professional organizations have become increasingly active in bargaining arrangements involving salary levels, job security, working conditions, fringe benefits, and retirement plans.

The most striking development has been the organization of physicians and dentists into trade unions for the explicit purpose of containing the threat they see in the increasing role of government in determining fees, working conditions, and other aspects of medical and dental practice. With national health insurance on the horizon, these professionals see an ever more interfering governmental bureaucracy as the principal danger to the continued well-being of their profession and their personal careers.

From the viewpoint of the professional or managerial employee, then, there is a tripod of career objectives—compensation; fringe benefits, including retirement plans; and working conditions. The more time and effort a man devotes to preparing for work, the more his career objectives are likely to be central to his life style.

Except for those who have highly technical assignments, that is, in law, accounting, or research, most managerial personnel perform supervisory functions. Despite the strenuous efforts of many top managements to push decision-making responsibility onto lower echelons, there are powerful forces operating in the opposite direction which tend to draw the critical decision-making process back toward the top. The principal reason for the relatively limited success of recent attempts to enlarge the powers of divisional leaders is the need to keep the multiple activities of the organization in alignment, and this can be done only at the top. Accordingly, there comes a time in a middle manager's career, usually by his tenth or fifteenth year of service, when he realizes that he is unlikely to move much closer to the top. With this growing realization, a man who had formerly invested a great deal of his energies and interest in his work and in the pursuit of his career goals is likely to start a search for a more satisfying balance among his job, his family, and his other interests.

The fact that large organizations are hierarchically structured implies that the few successful managers soon become increasingly differentiated from the larger numbers whose progress is considerably slower. It is difficult for a middle manager to remain interested in his work in the absence of challenging assignments. But challenges are available primarily to the small numbers who are on the fast track. One issue neglected by organizational analysts is the large organization's inability to keep more than a minority of their managerial cadre deeply involved in their work. The restricted opportunities available to the majority helps to explain why they attach so much importance to matters of compensation, fringe benefits, and job security. Any other response on their part would be unrealistic. A man whose organizational role, assignment, and prospects constrain him from investing his full energies, skills, and interests in his work will seek other compensations and rewards. And that is what most managers do, once they realistically reassess their prospects in light of organizational realities.

This extended consideration of the aims and objectives of the managerial cadre is justified not in terms of the numbers of managers, since, even broadly defined, they account for only a small percentage of the total work force in most large organizations, but because of their influence in shaping the dominant environment in which work is carried out in advanced economies. Although only those at the top hold critical decision-making positions, they understand that their middle and lower managers must be provided with sufficient satisfactions and rewards so that they will identify with the organization and carry out their duties satisfactorily. No large organization can function effectively unless middle managers are reasonably satisfied with the conditions of their work and their rewards. Occasionally, those at the top become isolated from their supporting staffs and no longer understand what is happening to the organization. Only after an organization is thrown off balance (witness the Catholic church after the reforms of Pope John XXIII, the universities after the student riots of the 1960s, and the U.S. Armed Forces during the unpopular war in Vietnam) will top management recognize and respond to the smoldering discontents, often expressed in overt attacks on the organization's value system or personnel system, or even on the competence of top management itself.

The foregoing recital of many points of dissonance between the expectations of young people entering the lower ranks of management and the realities that confront them during successive stages of their career helps to illuminate the emergence of a new kind of discontent, the discontent of middle management.

Let us turn to a consideration of the worker with modest education and little skill. His first goal is to be hired by a large organization where, in the normal course of events, he can look forward to a progression up the job ladder which will result in his eventually receiving a wage at least twice what he earned on his first job. In the event that the economy turns down and some part of the work force is furloughed or discharged, the order of those laid off, as well as the order of those called back when business improves, is governed by the length of service of each person within the unit. Consequently, the second major advantage which accrues to the worker with seniority, particularly in large organizations which experience only modest declines in employment during recessions, is the likelihood of continuous work experience or, at worst, only short periods of layoff. A third advantage enjoyed by the worker with long service is his right to bid for the more pleasant and less strenuous work assignments. The seniority system contributes directly to assuring that older workers who experience declining health and stamina will be given preference for work assignments where they can more readily meet the norms. Finally, the long-term worker accumulates additional fringe benefits, such as longer vacations; he builds up his equity in the company's savings plan and, most important, by the time he is ready to retire he is eligible for a pension which may equal half or up to three-quarters of his maximum earnings.

Although young people just beginning to work may not be aware of all the advantages of employment in a large organization, it is not long before most of them learn enough about the labor market to recognize these advantages, particularly after they marry and start a family. Large organizations provide a range of opportunities to enable recently hired workers to advance into better jobs. In a steel mill or utility plant, the blue-collar worker sees a path to successively higher job levels. Such an opportunity is more limited in an automotive assembly plant, where only a minority of the workers can look forward to getting off the line and into skilled jobs, but most workers can, in time, move to less demanding positions. In such a setting, where seniority is less likely to lead to a better paying job with better working conditions, the principal attraction is the considerably higher initial wage. For many years, Detroit has been able to attract large numbers of new workers to meet its expanding labor requirements and to compensate for its heavy turnover by being a pacesetter in the area of wages for the newly hired, most of whom can qualify for work on the assembly line within a few hours of being hired. From Henry Ford's $5 daily wage in the early 1920s to the $5 an hour offered in the mid-1970s, the large automotive companies have been out in front. In addition, the strong trade union in the industry, the United Automobile Workers, has played a major role, particularly since World War II, in obtaining for its members not only higher wages but also improvements on other fronts, including better working conditions, grievance procedures, fringe benefits, and pensions.

There are several reasons, of course, that workers are always concerned about their pay. First of all, the amount of money they earn is a major factor in determining the kind of life they can provide for their families. And in a society in which an ever higher level of personal consumption is the principal goal, workers are determined not to be left behind.

Other forces help to keep the working man's focus on his wages. One measure of his progress is the rate of increase in his real wages. The worker who earns the same today as he did a year ago, allowing for inflation, recognizes that he is not bettering his condition, and this realization will undermine his self-confidence. If his failure to progress is paralleled by larger profits for stockholders and higher salaries for managers, insult is added to injury, since the worker will conclude that others are making gains at his expense.

When the cost of living rises rapidly, as during most of the post-World War II period, workers press for substantial increases in their money wages. Unless they receive more money, their standard of living will erode. And even continuing large increases in money wages is no guarantee that they will be better off, because the price level may advance more rapidly. Since government is unable to control inflationary pressures, workers have few alternatives to demanding higher money wages, although this itself intensifies the inflationary pressures.

An additional reason that workers seek to increase their wages even after they have achieved a comfortable standard of living is their desire for a share of whatever additional profits result from the increased productivity to which they have contributed. Bargaining over wages has been institutionalized, and all parties—management, workers, government, and the public—now tacitly endorse the recurrent efforts of the laboring man to improve his take-home pay.

Since fringe benefits account for between 25 to 30 percent of the total wage packet of most workers in large American organizations, this is a second arena in which workers seek to improve their position. The fact that Social Security is not a pension but merely aims to fill the income gap of workers who leave the labor force at the age of sixty-two or sixty-five helps to explain why the American working man, especially if he belongs to a strong union and is employed by a profitable company, is concerned about his pension rights. He is likely to receive as much from his employer as from government, or even more.

There is literally no limit to the range of fringe benefits now available to the rank and file. Some workers receive one or two meals a day which are heavily subsidized by their employers. Others can buy company merchandise at substantial discounts. Still others can obtain company stock below the market price. Some employers match a part of the savings that employees put into the company's savings plan. Some companies provide college scholarships for the children of their employees. Others will match the gifts their employees make to eleemosynary or educational institutions. And some companies grant vacations of up to three months to employees with fifteen years or more of service.

Although the conflict over wages remains central to the employment relation, it is by no means the only factor about which the parties are periodically locked in combat. The issue of "working conditions," a euphemism for a range of concerns including safety, the speed of machines, and social amenities such as eating and recreational facilities, continues to play a leading role in the work life of most employees. After all, most men and more and more women spend the largest part of each day, five days a week, at their jobs. It is not surprising therefore that conditions at work, especially conditions that threaten their safety, comfort, or self-respect, command their attention.

Every worker aims to control the pace of his own work. He will try to thwart every attempt by management to increase his output, since he sees such efforts as a "speedup" whereby the employer wants him to produce more for the same pay. The conflicts with respect to pace are in part physiological, in part psychological. In assembly-line operations, production engineers are constantly recalculating the time required for each operation in an effort to reduce labor costs. In more conventional work settings, work norms are determined less by objective measurement and more by tradition. The concept of a fair day's work for a fair day's pay is anchored in a norm informed by experience. The adage implies that the worker who receives the going rate of pay will work at what has come to be the accepted pace. But arguments and conflicts arise because of changes in technology, labor market conditions, and collective bargaining agreements. Yesterday's norms do not provide adequate guidance for tomorrow. Consequently, management and the union must periodically renegotiate the number of units of work the employee is required to produce. Management argues that every improvement in technology makes the worker's task easier and that this should be reflected in higher output on his part. The worker, on the other hand, knows that a new machine often requires that he add to his skills and increase his concentration and speed. Since a man's wage is supposed to reflect the total demands made on him, workers insist on wage adjustments as new or improved technology is introduced.

Conflicts over work norms are even more acute when the basis of wage payments shifts from piece work to hourly or day work. When wage payments are geared to the clock, management must be concerned about the number and quality of the units the work force produces. But, as we have seen, workers will seek to protect themselves from having to produce more for the same wage. This concern goes beyond considerations of equity which lead them to demand a fair return for their labor. It also speaks to the critical matter of job security. If workers do not thwart management's efforts to increase their output, they may become party to their own unemployment at some time in the future. Small wonder then that conflicts over work norms continue, since they are directly related to the worker's desire for higher earnings, his determination to have a share of the increased output from any process in which he cooperates, and his fear of contributing to his future disemployment.

Workers are particularly sensitive to all approaches that bear directly or indirectly on their job security. We earlier called attention to the rules governing force reductions and pointed to those which are mandated in most collective bargaining agreements and which are also often followed in the absence of a formal labor agreement. We have just noted the extent to which the conflicts over output norms are influenced by fear of unemployment.

There are additional dimensions to job security. A critical objective of all worker protests is to reduce the scope for arbitrary employer actions, especially when it comes to matters of discharge. Workers are determined not to be at the mercy of the employer's whim, whereby they might be cheated of their rights to their jobs and to their deferred benefits. The best way of protecting themselves is to insist that the employer recognize the "rule of law" in the workplace with explicit penalties for improper behavior and a system of due process for workers charged with breaches of discipline. Until workers succeeded in enlarging their control over the workplace, they were subject to arbitary dismissals, limited only by the pressures of the market which placed some constraint on the employer's actions.

While the establishment of a formal system of grievance procedures is linked to job security, its reach goes beyond. Throughout all the hours a worker is in his place of employment, he is subject to the directions of his supervisor. This setting invites harassment, pressure, denigration, and indignities imposed by supervisors who, often under pressure from their own superiors, take advantage of the men under their control. Since any physical attack by a worker on his foreman is cause for immediate discharge, and since even verbal attacks carry penalties, the scope for foremen to abuse their powers is considerable. There are ample opportunities for a sadistic or insensitive foreman to abuse workers whose jobs depend on his goodwill. Since many workers have built up valuable rights and benefits which they are loath to jeopardize, they continually strive to restrict the foremen's power and to insist on additional safeguards against arbitrary actions on the part of management. Unless workers succeed in these efforts to restrict the power of supervision, all their gains with respect to job security and deferred benefits are at risk, because they would then hold their jobs by sufferance, not by right.

Since the employment situation implies a conflictual relationship between workers'and management, pressure remains high in several areas. In addition to seeking periodic increases in pay, enhanced job security, and greater control over working conditions, workers also keep pushing for such gains as additional holidays with pay, pay for setting up machines in the morning and cleaning up at night, and pay when machines are down.

We have seen that there is little basis for contending, as some scholars have, that once workers achieve a living wage their concern shifts from monetary considerations, and they become more interested in improving their working conditions. We know instead that all workers want more wages, more time off with pay, more retirement benefits, more amenities, and more control over their work.

Some employers, realizing that their employees will attempt to improve their working conditions and rewards, have sought to meet this challenge head on by trying to engage them in a cooperative effort to increase work satisfaction. The principal thrusts of this type of effort have been to enlarge the tasks that workers perform and to delegate more decision-making responsibility to them. These employers assume that worker dissatisfaction is the result of the routinized nature of the workers' tasks and of the fact that workers have little role in determining the pattern of their work. Consequently, reforms have been directed at job rotation, job enrichment, job enlargement, team assignments, increased consultation between work teams and supervisors, and the delegation of responsibility for a range of specific decisions to the workers themselves.

These efforts have been more aggressively pursued in Scandinavia and Western Europe than in the United States, although experiments in work restructuring have been undertaken in most industrial nations. A major site for experimentation has been the assembly line, where the burden of routine is reinforced by the brief work cycle, which is sometimes as short as ninety seconds. The reports of the experiments suggest that most workers who shift to new patterns of working find them preferable to more tightly structured processes, but this favorable reading must be interpreted cautiously, since the experiments usually rely on volunteers, and only a few have been under way for a sufficient time to cancel out the favorable response to the experimental situation itself.

Workers have always been interested in the conditions under which they work, and, as we have seen, they have applied major pressure on management to improve health and safety conditions, to restrict the pace of their work, and to improve the amenities in the plant. The new focus on increased job satisfaction is only the most recent manifestation of one of the oldest objectives of workers, which is to achieve improvements in their work environment. Whether job satisfaction becomes a key area for future negotiations depends on the assessment that workers make about the gains that can be accomplished. Although many workers find their jobs uninteresting, even boring, the open question is whether even cooperative employers can introduce sufficient changes in the production cycle to alter significantly the quality of the work environment. Certainly, constructive changes can be introduced, but it is uncertain whether the changes that are feasible in terms of costs and returns can make a real difference from the viewpoint of the worker.

The continued importance that workers ascribe to improving their earnings, current and deferred, reflects both the high value they attach to improving their standard of living and their recognition that they are better positioned to do so than to assure their job security, increase their work satisfaction, or keep management from solely determining the work environment.

So far only passing reference has been made to the fact that, in most industrial countries, the trade union is the principal instrumentality through which the needs and desires of workers become known and subject to negotiation with the employer. The fact that in some countries only a minority of the entire work force belongs to trade unions does not downgrade their importance. They play a separate and significant role in advancing the interests of workers while simultaneously responding to the dynamics of their own institutional structures.

The union leadership must be constantly alert to retaining the support of the majority of its members; if it loses that support, it will be forced out. To maintain the majority's support, the leadership must obtain higher wages and improved or new benefits for the rank and file. As in all political settings, the leadership must seek to balance different interests and groups. In modern industrial unions, there is a continuing tension between the minority of skilled workers and the semiskilled work force. While the leadership must be responsive to the wishes of the majority, it cannot afford to ignore the demands of the skilled groups, for if they secede, they will deprive the union of one of its major sources of strength in future negotiations with employers.

If the workers become disgruntled because they believe that their wages and benefits are not increasing at a sufficiently rapid rate, the odds are strong that the incumbent leaders will be forced out by a group of challengers who promise to do better. Despite the belief that trade union leaders can manipulate the rank and file and maintain themselves in office, this is not the case in unions where the leadership does not resort to criminal tactics to secure and maintain itself in power.

A second source of internal tension to which the leadership must respond is the differences in the goals of older and younger workers. The former are likely to press for improved retirement and pension arrangements. The younger workers are more interested in the size of their weekly wage packet, since they need all the income they can get to meet the needs of their growing families.

During a period when public opinion and governmental efforts are reinforcing each other to remove various forms of discrimination in the society, including discrimination in the workplace, trade union leaders must respond to these pressures without coming into conflict with the strongly held views of the members, many of whom resent losing any of their prerogatives or privileges in favor of blacks or women. Unless the law of the land forces the issue, the leadership is potentially vulnerable to rank and file reprisals if it pushes reforms too fast. On the other hand, a leadership that acquiesces to existing discrimination runs the risk of losing prestige in the community and may even face court action.

In large unions, the leadership is continually reconciling anew the goals of discrete interest groups. To negotiate effectively with management, the central leadership must have broad scope for decision making. However, many points of friction which concern the rank and file stem from unsatisfactory local conditions. No top leadership, especially of a large union, can hope to settle in its major contract the myriad sources of worker discontent, which more often than not reflect specific local conditions. But unless provision is made in the master contract for the review and resolution of local issues, no contract terms, no matter how favorable, will satisfy the rank and file.

In this analysis of what the worker wants from the organization to which he is attached, an effort was made to enlarge the conventional framework. First, attention was directed to the special interests and concerns of middle and lower managers, who represent a group apart from the top leadership of large organizations. Secondly, in reviewing the goals of the members of the rank and file it was found that their continuing emphasis on wages and fringe benefits reflects in large measure their inability to bargain as effectively for job security, work satisfaction, and freedom in the work setting. Finally it was noted that the continuing confrontation between employees and employers must make room for the trade union, whose activities introduce a new dimension. The chapter that follows focuses on the congruence and conflict between the organization's manpower strategy and the interests of its work force and the manner in which the issues that cannot be resolved are compromised.

· I3 ·

Conflict and Compromise

WE HAVE CONSIDERED top management's concern for the organization's survival and growth and the equal desire of the work force for job security, good wages, and attractive benefits. This chapter will explore how the conflicts inherent in these objectives are compromised so that each party can look forward to sufficient benefits to justify its continuing cooperation.

Evidence of the overlapping interests of management and workers is the continuing vitality of large organizations in an advanced economy along with strongly organized trade union. Nassau Senior, the first professor of political economy at the University of Oxford (early in the nineteenth century), prophesied that capitalists would soon be bankrupt if the workday were reduced from twelve to eleven hours; he believed the employer made his profits in the last hour of work. But in the century and a half since Senior made this forecast, workers have worked much less and have earned much more, and competent employers have had no difficulty in surviving, making profits, and expanding. Nassau Senior and his fellow economists looked upon the employer-employee relationship as a conflict in which the gains made by one party had to be paid for by the other. If workers succeeded in achieving an increase in wages, the profits earned by employers would inevitably be reduced, they believed. But the classical economists and, later, Karl Marx and his followers, left out of their forecasts the inevitable, if unforeseeable, changes in the employment relationship which are inherent in the dynamism of modern societies.

A review of six arenas will help to clarify the conflicts between management and workers in a modern economy in both profit and nonprofit organizations and will delineate the ameliorative influences capable of narrowing the differences between them. The six points at issue involve work norms, discipline, hiring and promotions, technological innovations, wage determinations, and strikes.

There has always been conflict in and around the issue of work norms, since every employer understands that if his employees do not produce sufficient output, his costs may become uncompetitive, or his profits will erode. At the same time, his employees are reluctant to either work at a pace which they feel is too strenuous or increase their pace without increased compensation.

The issue has become newly important in advanced societies because so many workers are engaged in producing services, and in the service arena it is difficult for an employer to establish output norms and police them. Nevertheless, the following reality should be noted: in a great many service areas, employers are able to use norms based on output—the number of telephone calls completed, automobiles repaired, hotel rooms readied, or meals served—and their own experience or that of competitors. And most workers recognize the right of the employer to use such output norms for personnel control purposes.

It remains a management prerogative to determine the preferred combination of employees—highly skilled, semiskilled, and unskilled. Particularly in periods of expansion, a competent management has an opportunity, through altering its staffing pattern, to control its wage costs. For the most part it will not be challenged by the workers if it thins its supervisory ranks. Finally, workers understand that management must be able to cover its costs with revenues, however they are obtained—from sales in the competitive market or through governmental appropriations. This understanding operates to moderate the demands that workers advance.

The second arena of confrontation between management and the rank and file relates to matters of discipline. Every large organization must have a set of rules which the members must follow or be penalized. Not many decades ago, managers were able to use physical force to keep their employees in line. They were able to extort money and demand personal favors. A primary objective of trade union organization was to reduce the almost unlimited power that management wielded. Unions sought to bring the rule of law into the workplace.

Despite the considerable success that unions have achieved in reducing arbitrariness, management still has the right to discipline workers who violate established rules and regulations, although physical abuse and summary dismissal have been outlawed. Workers and their trade union leaders recognize the necessity for discipline; they know that hundreds or thousands of employees cannot work together in a single establishment unless each person understands and meets his obligations. Men cannot come to work late without being penalized. Altercations between one worker and another or between a worker and his foreman must be proscribed if naked strength is not to become the rule of the workplace. Safety regulations must be followed if fellow workers are to be protected from unnecessary risk.

Management believes that it should continue to exercise wide discretion over the rules that are established and over their enforcement. But workers insist that they be party to both rule setting and rule enforcement, since they stand to lose the most from faulty actions. This results in their continuing pressure to expand the rule of law in the workplace to ensure that management cannot establish or maintain capricious rules and regulations which can intimidate or punish members of the work force. The primary concern of employees is to be consulted before rules are enacted and to have a role in their enforcement.

The third arena relates to the freedom that management seeks to retain with respect to hiring, assignment, training, and promotion. Management ascribes great importance to retaining discretion in carrying out these personnel functions. But workers have learned from experience that a management that is unconstrained can use its power to their disadvantage. Accordingly, in the construction and maritime industries, unions insist that all hiring be funneled through them. The employer must accept any worker whom the union refers in the absence of clear-cut evidence that he is incapable of doing the job. In most sectors, however, employers retain the right to hire, even when there are strong unions present.

Unions have concentrated their efforts on restricting the employer's freedom after the worker is on the payroll. Their primary aim is to establish an orderly procedure for promotions, in the belief that if the employer is free to pick and choose whom to advance, workers will compete rather than cooperate with one another, thereby weakening their bargaining position vis-à-vis the employer. Collective bargaining agreements customarily provide that the man within the unit with the highest seniority has the first right to bid for an opening, and if, he is adjudged qualified, he will move up and have a reasonable period in which to master his new assignment. According to many contracts, the employer must provide training opportunities on the basis of seniority so that senior workers will be qualified for promotion. Most managements resent this restriction on their right to select the best qualified person for promotion, but the unions fought hard to substitute the objective criterion of length of service. Nevertheless, in fighting and winning on this issue the unions understand that the person advanced must be qualified to do the work—if not immediately, then after a trial period. If he fails, management is free to return him to his former position and promote the next senior person.

The same general pattern prevails in the case of layoffs. Here, reverse seniority governs, and, under many contracts, workers have "bumping rights" that go beyond their immediate unit. But even under conditions of extended intraplant mobility, which provides additional protection to workers with the longest service, the employer's interest is not overlooked. Workers with greater seniority who bump others must be able to perform at their new assignments, or they cannot claim the new jobs.

In attempting to improve its competitive position and its profitability, management repeatedly seeks to introduce labor-saving devices. When a firm is growing rapidly and workers feel secure about their jobs, it may be relatively easy for management to reach agreement with the union about introducing new machinery or making other changes. As long as workers see no threat to their jobs or wages, they are likely to acquiesce to such changes. They may disagree about the speed at which the new machines should be run or the new wage rate that should be established, but such issues are usually settled amicably.

Workers will fight to prevent the introduction of new technology if they believe that their jobs are at stake, as happened in the United States in coal mining, railroading, newspaper composition, stevedoring, and meatpacking when these industries with declining employment sought to modernize their operations. A man with ten, fifteen, or twenty years of experience with the same company is likely to be relatively high on the skill and wage ladder and to have acquired considerable deferred benefits. If he concludes that all this is in jeopardy, he will certainly urge his union to adopt an uncompromising position against the proposed change. The claim of the employer that unless he is permitted to modernize he will be unable to compete effectively does not carry conviction. No single change, no matter how radical, can by itself assure the company's survival any more than a delay in introducing the change will necessarily assure its demise. The worker who may be displaced by a machine within one year cannot be sympathetic to the plight of an employer who, denied the right to innovate, may be forced out of business five years or a decade later.

Although these conflicts can reach fever pitch because each of the parties sees its survival at risk, accommodation is usually achieved. Even radical technological changes seldom threaten the jobs of more than a minority of the work force, perhaps as high as 25 percent, but seldom more. In the course of a year, workers die, retire, or leave. Consequently, strict control over new hiring can ease the adjustment process. And if management underwrites early retirement and provides separation allowances, workers in the higher age groups can be encouraged to leave voluntarily.

Since the major technological improvements are often introduced when a company is expanding its sales, this implies that even substantial labor-saving machinery will not lead to a loss of jobs. At worst it may result in the necessity to retrain part of the work force.

The most common and persistent area of conflict between management and the work force relates to wages, including the many types of fringe benefits that have come to be part of the total compensation packet. Workers and their leaders start from the premise that unless they press continuously for higher pay, more and more of the gains from increasing productivity will be preempted by the owners and management. The working man and his leaders have never accepted the model of the equilibrating labor market in which competition assures that the real earnings of labor will increase in response to advances in productivity because employers will be able to retain their workers only if they meet a steadily rising market price for labor. Although competition for labor will increase the level of real earnings in a country undergoing economic growth, the relationship between macroeconomic trends and the position of any specific group of workers is too tenuous to encourage workers to look to broad economic trends for their continuing progress and well-being. Accordingly, most workers seek to exert as much leverage as they can on their employers to obtain improvements in their wages and benefits.

Although workers can resort to the threat or reality of a strike to back up their demands, employers are not without countervailing power. They are often able to shift production to a different location, close down their plants for a time and meet their customers' needs from inventory, or resort to a range of other measures to avoid capitulating to wage demands that they find intolerable. Since workers and their union leaders know that the employer has these possible defenses against unacceptable demands, they take this into account when they put forward their claims. Only a few employers are forced into bankruptcy because of the exorbitant and inflexible wage demands of their workers.

An important moderating influence is the prevailing wage rate for comparable work in the same locale. The demands that workers make are anchored in the broader reality. Moreover, the fact that many collective bargaining agreements run for two or three years implies that the upward pressure on wages is periodic.

Workers and their leaders also become knowledgeable about the economic circumstances of their employers; they know whether the firm is operating close to the margin or whether it is highly profitable. Workers, profiting from the experience of other workers, seek to avoid wage demands that may force their employer to shut down or relocate. Important as higher wages are in the goals that workers pursue, even more important is their concern with safeguarding their jobs. Accordingly, many workers and unions have learned that they must accept relatively low wages because of the particular circumstances of their employers or the industry to which they are attached.

The ultimate pressure that workers can exert on management is to strike. But the costs of striking are high to the worker as well as to the employer. When workers go out on strike, they do not know how long the strike will last or whether they will win all or most of their demands. Thus, the decision to strike carries potentially high costs to workers, even for those who belong to unions capable of paying strike benefits.

The employer runs risks if he accedes to what he considers excessive demands of his workers, and he runs risks if he decides to fight. In the first instance, his increased wage bill may reduce his competitiveness, and the company may be severely weakened. Alternatively, if he decides to fight he must be prepared for the multiple losses that can result from a strike, especially a prolonged one, including the loss of customers, the erosion of working capital, the possibility of violence, and the loss of the community's goodwill, and, most critical, the hostility of his work force that may adversely affect its productivity long after the strike has been settled and the workers have returned to work.

The potential losses from a strike to both workers and management speak to the caution with which both parties are likely to enter wage negotiations and the pressures on them to reach a compromise rather than fight it out. On occasion the union leadership may conclude that management's last offer is the best it can extract, but, knowing the mood of the rank and file, it may also conclude that the workers will not accept the proffered terms until they have gone out on strike and found out for themselves that management is intransigent, at which point they may be ready to ratify the contract if a face-saving formula can be found. This gambit carries a risk for the union leadership, since a strike offers ambitious men, standing in the wings, an opportunity to challenge the incumbent leadership. Once again, the decision to strike or not presents a hard choice for the union leadership.

The broad arena of labor-management relations, with its formal agreements and informal arrangements, provides ample opportunities for misunderstandings. Unless these are cleared up expeditiously or at least started on the road to adjudication, they can bring the work process to a halt. In the United States, an elaborate structure for the expeditious handling of grievances has been put into place to assure that work continues even while conflicts involving interpretations of the contract, actions proscribed by the rules or traditions of the plant, or possible violations of rights guaranteed by law are reviewed jointly by representatives of management and labor; in the event that they are unable to agree, the matter goes to an arbitrator whose decision is binding.

This elaborate structure and process do not guarantee the peaceful and equitable solution of the myriad grievances that arise in the work situation, in which each of the parties seeks to protect and advance its rights at the same time that it tries to fend off any extension of the rights of its opponent. Over time, workers learn which issues their shop stewards are willing to push and which they will let slide, knowing that they cannot win them. In turn, foremen and other supervisory personnel modify their behavior as they realize that their top management is unwilling to back them up beyond a certain point. In general, both parties usually see an advantage to reaching a settlement without going to arbitration, which is often a drawn-out and costly process. Moreover, once the parties go to arbitration, they run a risk that the decision of the arbitrator may lay down new principles which go beyond the needs or desires of one or both of the contestants. Since this possibility is always present, it represents an additional restraining influence. The elaborate structure of grievance procedures and arbitration cannot obviate conflicts, but it goes a considerable distance to containing conflicts when they arise.

In each of the six arenas where disagreements between management and workers can arise, the emergent conflicts are likely to be contained because the principals understand that they have more to gain from compromise than from carrying the struggle to a point of no return.

The framework within which these conflicts arise and tend to be compromised is not fixed but is subject to change, which introduces another important dimension into the relationships between management and workers. Management's willingness to accept a strike, for instance, may hinge on its inventory, the state of the market, the position of competitors, and the attitude of government. In turn, workers and their union must weigh whether they have the financial resources to pay strike benefits, whether strikers will be able to find temporary jobs, the attitudes of the dominant labor organization, and the mood of the community. With so many important parameters in flux, neither management nor the workers are likely to be in the same position in any two successive periods. This introduces a potent dynamic into the conflict-resolution process.

The role of the trade union as a distinct element in the relationship between workers and management must be taken into account, although the union depends on the worker for its rationale, existence, and survival. Many conflicts do not stem from differences between workers and their employers but instead reflect interunion and intraunion dynamics. Some of the most bitter fights in the labor arena grow out of struggles between competing unions to control a particular group of workers or a particular type of activity. Although the national union leadership endeavors to keep jurisdictional conflicts and interunion raiding to a minimum, the existing mechanisms occasionally break down and internecine struggles intensify. Management is often an innocent bystander, unable to intervene, yet victimized by the disruptions that occur.

The repeated failure of top union management to be responsive to the complaints of the members of a specific local can lead to disruptions in the workplace, particularly if the aggrieved workers decide to engage in a slowdown, a wildcat strike, or other disruptive tactics.

Although many top labor leaders remain in office for long periods of time, others, especially those lower in the hierarchy, must maintain a guarded watch against challengers who are waiting for an opportunity to unseat them. Most union leaders are under constant pressure to demonstrate that they are delivering for the union members as much as or more than other leaders. This competition among labor leaders helps to explain why gains achieved in one settlement become guidelines for the next.

Attention has been called to two sets of forces which operate in favor of compromise in conflicts between management and workers. The first is the instability in the power relations between the principals which suggests to both parties that the lessons of experience cannot be uncritically projected. Despite their confidence about the probable outcome on the basis of earlier trials of strength, if the conflict is permitted to escalate, they cannot be sure that their calculations will be correct in the new situation. Secondly, the existence of a union, especially a mature one, is a strong force for the reduction of major conflict. The leadership of every bureaucratic organization knows that additional risks attach to all strikes, since their outcome can never be foretold. Consequently the leaders usually opt for compromise.

However, we must note that additional potent elements operate in favor of accommodation. These elements involve the opportunities for accommodation in such diverse matters as hiring policies, retirements, the specifics of the compensation packet, and the conditions governing overtime.

Although management is careful to retain wide discretion over its right to hire new employees, it will generally follow the preferences and prejudices of the dominant group among its work force unless it forsees special disadvantages. Few employers will lean against their dominant work group and insist that, for reasons of efficiency or equity, opportunities be broadened for employees from minority groups who have been discriminated against in hiring, assignments, or promotions. This means that the dominant group of workers has considerable scope in determining both who will be hired and how they will be treated once they are on the job. As long as the employer can recruit qualified applicants and can keep his labor costs competitive, he is likely to follow the conventions that command support from his work force.

Management also tends to accept workers' preferences about the retirement age of blue-collar employees. Although some managements stipulate the age at which all workers must retire, this is the exception, not the rule. Many union members, through their bargaining agreements, have succeeded in retaining the option of when to retire, subject only to an understanding that a worker who elects not to retire must be capable of meeting the requirements of his job. Nevertheless, many managements are willing to go a fair distance to find jobs within their organization for their older workers.

A third area of accommodation is the willingness of management to follow the union's lead in distributing pay increases. Management's primary concern is with the total dollar costs, including fringe benefits, arising out of a wage settlement. Union leaders have additional concerns. They must be alert to the relative position and the relative power of the groups which comprise their several constituencies. Labor leaders know that they must avoid upsetting the relative wage scales that are in place. Most experienced managements are aware of the difficulty that union leaders face in this regard and are willing to follow their leads with respect to how the increases should be divided.

Much the same accommodating posture obtains with respect to the division between wages and fringe benefits and among different types of fringe benefits. Here again, management's primary concern is with the total dollar costs of a settlement, currently and in the future. But union negotiators must be sensitive to the competing demands of different groups of workers; as noted earlier, younger workers are more likely to be concerned with the amount of their take-home pay, while those in the upper age brackets prefer to see the retirement package sweetened. Once again, management is inclined to follow the leads of the union in dividing the negotiated increases.

The same pattern of accommodation prevails in such matters as overtime or assignments to second or third shifts. The primary concern of management is to have an adequate and balanced work force to meet its requirements. Over the years, most managements have recognized the necessity for incentive pay to assure the availability of labor at other than regular hours of work. But once the size of the wage differentials has been agreed upon, management often leaves it to the workers to decide how to distribute the extra work and cover the less attractive shifts. They determine how overtime is shared and whether shift work is to be permanent, semipermanent, or rotating.

The analysis up to the present has focused on conflicts between management and the rank and file, both blue-collar and white-collar workers. But a new and pressing arena of conflict and compromise in advanced economies centers around the growing differences between the interests and goals of middle and top management. Although top management in both corporate and not-for-profit organizations is usually drawn from persons who begin at the lowest level of the managerial hierarchy (for example, the Chief of Staff of the Army who began his service as a second lieutenant, or the university president whose first academic post was as an instructor), there is a wide gap between the responsibilities and rewards that attach to the top group of decision makers and those of the much larger numbers who become permanently locked into subsidiary positions. In John Gardner's trenchant formulation, middle management is like the Van Allen belt; nothing gets through in either direction. Because of this significant gap in power between top and middle management, it is essential that the conflict-resolution mechanisms are understood. There are trade-offs between those at the top and those in middle management whose continued participation is required if the organization is to thrive.

The first trade-off involves the cost to the individual of entering the competition for a top position, which requires that he devote all his energies to his job and career over a long stretch of years and be willing to accept frequent changes of assignment that require family relocation. Such a commitment requires the aspiring manager to commit his body and mind—and to some extent those of his wife and children—to the corporation. Since the numbers who compete are many and the top positions few, large corporations have encountered relatively little difficulty in developing a large pool of candidates who can be kept under continuing surveillance; from this pool, management can pick the few who show the greatest promise of eventually moving all the way to the top.

In every large organization, middle managers tend to accumulate. This accumulation reflects, first, the determination of responsible officials to build up their staffs to ensure that they can meet critical organizational objectives on time. Secondly, the power and prestige of a top manager usually depends on the numbers over whom he exercises direct authority. Thirdly, although the total dollar costs of overstaffing are high, they are often sufficiently small in the context of the total budget to escape tight control. Both the lack of authority which most personnel divisions have to monitor the accumulation of managerial manpower and the primitive stage of the monitoring techniques reinforce the tendency toward overstaffing.

The presence of surplus personnel has several consequences, the most important of which is the shortage of meaningful work to engage the potentials and talents of the staff. For every manager who brings a briefcase home, ten others easily make their commuter trains at 5:15 P.M. An organizational environment in which there is little pressure is likely to give rise to the make-work syndrome in which people pretend they are busy or engage in work which has no useful output. Even more destructive is the fact that managers with time on their hands tend to invest it in offensive and defensive actions to protect and expand their respective domains.

We have seen that the manpower surpluses characteristic of most large organizations derive in considerable measure from the tendency of supervisors to stockpile people and the absence of control mechanisms to keep manpower resources in balance with requirements. Behind this lies a trade-off. In the absence of an organizational crisis, middle managers can be reasonably certain that as long as they do their work competently and avoid conflicts with their superiors, their jobs are secure. They may have little prospect of advancing further, but they can be reasonably certain that they will not be cashiered. Since most middle managers have family responsibilities, they value their job security. Men are willing to put up with many unsatisfactory elements in their work, if they realize that on the critical issue of job security they have little to fear.

Another trade-off relates to the reward system. Top management pays itself five to ten times more than what those in the middle ranks receive, a sufficiently large spread to precipitate periodic tension and ill will. But top management has sought to contain the discontent by providing a limited number of positions in the upper reaches of middle management at salaries two to three times higher than the average for the group. Moreover, top management has provided a wide range of benefits and appurtenances for those who receive only modest salaries, including nicely furnished private offices, secretaries, and the use of the executive dining room; these benefits are in addition to the other usual fringe benefits, such as long vacations, good health insurance plans, retirement benefits, company contributions to savings plans, and bonuses. These multiple benefits do not change the underlying reality that the few at the top often make inordinately large salaries, but they help to moderate the potential restiveness and discontent of many in the middle ranks who value their "extras."

A related phenomenon is the matter of forced separation or early retirement. In periods of declining profits, top management may find that it can no longer ignore the slack in managerial staff at various levels of the hierarchy. At such times, it may feel compelled to tighten the supervisory structure, both for reasons of cost control and to improve future performance. Many companies allocate substantial amounts to help ease out their least effective managers or those with the longest service. Those who had looked forward to working until the conventional age of retirement are seldom assuaged by the liberal settlement which they receive, but their departure is surely less painful because of it.

Brief reference was made earlier to managerial issues that are linked to the process of decentralized decision making. A company with a hundred thousand or more employees in a hundred different locations cannot have all its operational decisions made by a small headquarters group. Considerable scope for decision making must be passed down the line, but the top group retains the essential decision-making power which will shape the future of the company. The decisions of the top group involve control over investment policy, relationships with government and organized labor, research and development, acquisitions, and new-product development and above all the appointment of key personnel.

Power remains concentrated at the top, first, because those who have succeeded in reaching the top want to hold on to their position and, secondly, because only those at the top have the breadth of perspective to balance the multiple opportunities and risks that face the organization, today and tomorrow.

Accordingly, there is an inevitable chasm between the work performed by top management and the work done by those lower in the hierarchy. A relatively few people, perhaps a hundred in a large organization, actively participate in making the key decisions. Many down the line understand this fact and are able to make their peace with it. However, those at the top realize that they must continue to engage the interest and commitment of their middle managers, since the organization's successful functioning depends on their effectively performing a great number of routine operations.

This helps to explain why top management continues to explore an array of approaches aimed at improved communications between itself and the middle managers; it understands that the commitment and morale of its middle managers are essential for the continued success of the organization.

Top management is slowly becoming aware that while money, status symbols, fringe benefits, and participatory devices are important in helping to retain the loyalty of large numbers of middle managers, this panoply of attractions may not suffice to compensate for the lack of excitement and power which characterizes the work of those trapped in the middle of the managerial hierarchy. In an attempt to ease potential discontent, some corporate leaders have started new experiments; they make blocks of time available to underutilized groups of managers in the expectation that they may find compensatory satisfactions away from their jobs. The new departures involve regular time off for participation in public service activities, such as serving on the board of an important community organization; a leave of absence for a one- or two-year stint with government; and a paid leave to take advanced work at a university. So far, only a small number of organizations have acted to broaden the opportunities for middle managers, but if discontent and disenchantment with managerial work should intensify, as appears likely, top management will have no option but to institutionalize new programs.

We have identified a number of tension points between top and middle management including the organization's need to attract trainees who will tolerate a substantial number of relocations within a relatively short time span, who will accept the fact that they are busy for only part of each day, who appreciate that luck will largely determine whether or not they move toward the top, who will not feel exploited because of the gap between their earnings and those of top management, and who are increasingly willing to seek their major satisfactions in areas outside their regular place of employment. These stresses and strains are real and are likely to worsen. Top management may soon discover that its manpower difficulties are no longer restricted to the rank and file but permeate the core from which their successors are drawn.

The thrust of the foregoing analysis can be recapitulated. Each of the three major groups involved in the operation of a modern organization—the rank and file, middle management, and top management—is concerned with achieving similar objectives and goals: security, equity, and freedom (self-determination). But each is in a different position to accomplish its goals, and each pursues a different approach.

The rank-and-file worker is first, and mostly concerned about his job security, not only because he knows that it may be difficult to locate another job if he loses the one he has, particularly in a period of slack business, but also because of the many valuable benefits that he has accumulated. A loss of employment usually carries with it the loss of these benefits. Consequently, American trade unionists have put job security at the top of their bargaining objectives.

Workers constantly seek to acquire a larger share of the additional revenues which they have helped to create. Without denying that the owners and managers of capital are entitled to a return for their contributions, the rank and file sees its own efforts as crucial. A concern with equity also helps to explain why workers are particularly sensitive to sudden shifts in their relative earnings. The workers who are more skilled expect significantly higher wages to compensate them for their longer period of training and their greater contribution to the output. Skilled workers understand that those in the poorest paying jobs need higher wages if they are to have an acceptable standard of living. But they feel that an increase in the wages of the lowest earners should not erode the legitimate differentials to which they are entitled.

Every man seeks to exercise as much control as possible over his life. To expand his freedom, he must restrict the authority that others can exercise over him. Workers everywhere, and particularly in democratic societies, attempt to restrict the powers of management. While workers and their union leaders acknowledge that management has the primary responsibility for organizing the way in which work is carried out, they insist on their right to participate in all decisions that directly affect them.

Middle management has a different stance with respect to its goals of job security, equity, and freedom. Since many young people seek careers in large organizations, with the aim of competing for top positions, their initial concern is less with job security, and more with opportunity for advancement. But once they realize that they are out of the race for the top jobs, they attach heightened value to continuity of employment and look upon the promise of job security and attractive salaries and benefits as compensation for not making it to the top.

Because of their initial interest in competing for one of the top positions, young executives are seldom bothered by the wide gap between the pay of top managers and that of middle managers. Their concern with equity is more likely to center on evaluation and promotion procedures. Young managers want to be sure their superiors are not favoring others on purely personal or political grounds.

With respect to freedom, most middle managers are likely to become accustomed to the ways of a large organization and to accept as reasonable the demands that are made on them. The relatively small numbers who balk at the restrictions placed on their freedom are likely to leave early in their careers.

Middle managers, by virtue of their higher salaries, greater privileges, considerable status, and job security, are less likely than the rank and file to be antagonistic toward the top leadership and the demands it makes on them. But if a time comes when the organization is no longer able to provide the career security which middle managers take for granted, or if other rewards to which they have become accustomed are reduced, tensions and antagonisms will intensify and dissonance will increase.

Senior executives, who have high salaries and many other perquisites, including the satisfaction of having been successful in the competitive race, and who exercise broad decision-making powers, are likely to manifest the least dissatisfaction. Many among them have regrets because they realize that they will never become the chief executive officer, because they do not have the time and energy to enjoy fully their considerable income, or because they are uncertain about whether, if they had pursued a different career, they might have had greater satisfactions. But these doubts and regrets are seldom pervasive. We know that few men who come close to the top, or who reach the top, voluntarily leave the arena for other fields.

We find, then, that large organizations have developed the capacity for meeting some of the primary goals of the three goups which compose their work force. They have been able to do this despite deep-seated and continuing conflicts. However, developed societies have established procedures which help to constrain the conflicts and push the contestants toward compromising their differences. Among the important constraining influences is the recognition by both management and workers that they can realize their individual goals best if they can develop accommodations when they come into direct conflict with each other. Next, workers know that if they go on strike, management has certain defensive options, from shifting production schedules to relocating; these options act as a restraining influence.

Most importantly, a modern society such as the United States, knowing that conflicts are inherent in the work situation because of differences in interests among the principal parties, has developed a system of conflict resolution that has become institutionalized. The system facilitates a redefinition of rights and responsibilities among the parties, which permits an accommodation to changing realities and power constellations while assuring that the organization can continue to meet its performance objectives.

Finally, top management, recognizing the potential restiveness of middle management, whose continuing support it needs, is constantly experimenting with new ways of organizing work and with new systems of compensation to assure organizational effectiveness. There is no guarantee that reality constraints, the development of the common law of the workplace, or operating initiatives will be able to contain indefinitely the conflicts that arise between management and the workers and between top and middle management. But the record to date supports a cautious optimism at least for the near term.

PART V

«« « · » »»

POLICY

Though the state was to derive no advantage from the in-
struction of the inferior ranks of people, it would still deserve
its attention that they should not be altogether uninstructed.
The state, however, derives no inconsiderable advantage
from their instruction. The more they are instructed, the less
liable they are to the delusions of enthusiasm and super-
stition, which, among ignorant nations, frequently occasion
the most dreadful disorders.... They are more disposed to
examine, and more capable of seeing through, the interested
complaints of faction and sedition, and they are, upon that
account, less apt to be misled into any wanton or unneces-
sary opposition to the measures of government. In free
countries, where the safety of government depends very much
upon the favourable judgment which the people may form of
its conduct, it must surely be of the highest importance that
they would not be disposed to judge rashly or capriciously
concerning it.

—ADAM SMITH, *The Wealth of Nations*

· 14 ·

Conceptual Foundations for Manpower Policy

IN THE NATURAL SCIENCES, the development and strengthening of theory is the principal approach to deepening knowledge and improving the prediction of outcomes. Improved theory often leads to improved applications. There is no analogous method for studying social behavior. Although theory remains the critical instrument for increasing knowledge, no social theory to date has been strong enough to guide changes in social behavior. The internal and external forces which operate on societies, particularly dynamic societies, constantly introduce new elements which the existing theory has not encapsulated. And since men have different goals and methods for pursuing them, there is seldom agreement among them about which lessons should be extracted from the theory as a guide for practice.

There is another, perhaps a more useful, distinction to be made among the varieties of social theories. Some are structured to speak directly to policy issues; others are concerned with methodological improvements. A critical distinction among competing social theories is the extent to which they are sensitive and responsive to the institutional and other changes that are constantly transforming societies and to the new opportunities and difficulties that these changes bring in their wake.

Up to this point, this book has presented a step-by-step elaboration of the critical processes involved in skill acquisition and utilization. The approach is predicated on the fact that the extant theories have not adequately accounted for the critical importance of these processes for individual fulfillment, the efficiency of the economy, and the well-being of society.

There are two barriers to developing an effective relationship between theory and policy in the social realm. One is that theory is insensitive to policy considerations and that therefore theory is unlikely to illuminate practical alternatives. The other is that theory seeks to speak to policy, but since it has not incorporated the relevant elements or their interactions, it carries the inevitable consequence that its prescriptions are faulty.

This chapter has a single objective: to recapitulate the principal mechanisms that underlie the basic processes of skill development and utilization. This will strengthen the foundations for policy formulation in the following two chapters.

Conventional economic theory has applied a market model to the study of manpower resources, in terms of both their development and their utilization, but it generally ignores other influences that affect men in their search for work and income. It looks upon the employment relation as an isolated transaction similar to the purchase and sale of any other commodity, thereby minimizing the role of such potent forces as social class, discrimination, and the power of large organizations in the allocation of jobs and the distribution of rewards. Further, it assumes that macroeconomic policy in advanced societies is capable of providing the required level of employment opportunities. Finally, it tends to ignore, to consider irrelevant, the extent to which the changing values and expectations of people alter the place of work in their personal goals and the goals of their society.

The conventional theory is comfortable with its formal demonstrations that the market rewards more liberally those who contribute more; that the market compensates individuals for the expenses they incurred in preparing for work; and that discrimination is largely an illusion, since the employers' interests assure that they will place profits ahead of prejudice.

But the theory runs directly counter to everyday experience, which provides indisputable evidence of a market which endorses large differentials in earnings based on power, not productivity; which makes a mockery of the efforts of many young people to improve their circumstances through education and training; and which reeks with discrimination.

When the application of market theory to manpower is analyzed, several loopholes are found; theory ignores the multiplicity of goals that men seek to achieve in addition to their primary aim of improving their material circumstances; it is insensitive to the shaping influence of the principal institutions within which men live and work to accomplish their several goals; it tends to consider the employment relationship as a market transaction without antecedent or consequence rather than as a process. Moreover, conventional theory ignores the fact that individuals, families, employers and even societies live in three dimensions; their behavior in the present is linked to their experiences in the past and to their aspirations for the future.

The first specification of the manpower development process is the sequencing of the acquisition of skill, partly because of the developmental needs and potentialities of individuals and partly because of the existing social structure and institutions. The physical, emotional, and mental aspects of the development of human beings are geared to nature's time clock. Although some individuals are precocious and others are retarded in one or more of their basic functions, the surprising fact is that there is substantial regularity in the developmental cycle.

Implicit in this sequencing is the fact that those individuals who do not acquire during the appropriate stage the prerequisites that will enable them to cope with the demands and opportunities of the next stage become handicapped. It is one of the belated and sad insights acquired from modern investigations of nutrition among low-income peoples that children who experience malnutrition in the first two years of life are likely to suffer irreversible retardation in their physical and mental development; the more severely deprived are unlikely to be able to profit from attending school, if and when they have the opportunity. At best, they will be unable to learn at the same pace as the average child who did not experience nutritional deficiency.

Related to but distinct from the sequencing aspect is the cumulative nature of the skill development process. The more elongated the process, the more likely it is that the achievements and failures that mark the individual's development will become irreversible. After a young man or woman who graduated from college magna cum laude has been accepted by a leading law school, served as a member of the school's Law Review, and been chosen to clerk for a justice of the Supreme Court, his or her cumulative record practically assures a satisfactory career.

Compare the successful law student with a youngster who dropped out of high school, barely able to read at the sixth-grade level; who was sent to reform school for two years as the result of his conviction for robbery; who, not finding a job upon his release, joined a gang engaged in transporting stolen goods and then was sentenced to jail for three to five years. He also has a cumulative record. The earlier stages of his developmental process did not predetermine his later behavior and outcomes, but they surely were powerful forces leading in that direction.

It must be added that these two facets of the process—sequencing and cumulation—transcend the developmental cycle and continue into the working years. Two accounts help make the point. One concerns a young man who, finishing his apprenticeship, becomes a high wage earner for a period of years. He then goes into business as a contractor and, with the support of his local bank, branches out into diversified ventures which, because of his growing capital, experience, and circumstances, become highly successful. The second case concerns a young man who starts a small enterprise with his family's savings, goes into debt to his suppliers and his bank, and, failing to meet his payments, is forced into bankruptcy. He repeats this cycle a few years later. By the time of his second bankruptcy, his future prospects are indeed dimmed.

Another dimension of the manpower development process is that its several stages are age-relevant. Within every society there is an appropriate time for a person to attend school, to work, to marry, and to retire. While these patterns change in response to shifts in the underlying reality and the value system, the process is indeed time-related.

A few illustrations will help to illuminate this dimension of the process. In most advanced societies the admission of students to professional training, especially to medical schools, has been limited to those between their eighteenth and twenty-eighth years. This restriction was predicated on the assumptions that, first, older persons would not have a sufficiently long working life to justify the substantial social costs of their preparation and, further, that individuals who decide only in their mature years to enter the study of medicine are likely to be poor risks, since they must compete with the much larger numbers who early know that they want to go that route.

We have seen that there are strong reasons for an organization to establish a compulsory retirement age; in addition, however, this arrangement is reinforced by the common assumption that older persons are incapable of performing as effectively as younger ones, notwithstanding the scattered evidence of outstanding accomplishment of older persons in politics, the arts, and business.

There is an additional piece of evidence of the time relatedness of the developmental process. For many generations it was assumed, especially in developed societies, that as women enter the menopause, they suffer periods of illness and ineffectiveness and that this argues against their being regularly employed. The fact that much of their instability might be directly related to their lack of useful function, once their children are grown, was not understood until the demand for their labor power opened new opportunities for them, and at that point the folklore that surrounded the middle-aged woman lost its credibility.

An associated dimension of the process is its spatial attributes. The opportunities available to people to develop their skills and to make effective use of them depend in no small measure on where the people live.

Although in most countries adults are free to relocate, the costs involved are never small, and they increase according to the number of the adults' dependents. Reference has been made to the handicaps under which most rural people live because of their limited access to developmental opportunities and because of the limited demand for workers in rural areas. However, the importance of the spatial factor derives from more than such gross differentials as those between urban and rural locations. The spatial factor often operates within a narrow geographic area and leads to differentials in the developmental opportunities available to the children of families in low-income neighborhoods and to children in high-income neighborhoods within the same metropolitan area.

The critical elements underpinning the spatial factor are these: the differential ability and willingness of governmental units to provide developmental opportunities for their citizens and the location of certain groups in the expanding sectors of the economy where new jobs are opening up.

The appropriateness of considering manpower development in terms of a process analysis has been demonstrated. The underlying dynamic of human resources development and utilization has been explicated by calling attention to such critical components as sequencing, cumulation, time relatedness, and spatial characteristics, which together constitute the process.

The second building block consists of the major institutions, specifically the family, the school, and the employing organization, and related structures such as youth organizations, the military, the church, trade unions, and professional associations.

Although no society, regardless of how primitive its economy, organizes all its activities around a single institution, the principal concomitant and consequence of development is the establishment and growth of specialized institutions which take over an increasing number of functions earlier performed by the family.

In addition to recognizing that manpower development and utilization occur within an institutional framework and that multiple institutions are involved in the process, we must note the critical dimensions of the institutional structuring, which include access to the several institutions, the consequences that flow from their multiple functions, the diverse interest groups which direct them, and the quality of their performance.

With respect to access, we note first that every newborn child immediately becomes a member of an institution, the family, and that during his critical early years he is completely dependent on his family, obviously for sustenance and survival. Membership in a family does not require any action on the part of the newborn, and the care he receives during the many years of his dependency is not subject to negotiation or exchange, beyond the pressures on the child to conform to the standards of the family.

Although access into a family is automatic, that is not true of any other type of institutional affiliation. Even in highly developed societies, not all persons have equal access to public education, the Armed Forces, or employment affiliations. The reasons for limitations on access are, first, the limitations in the resources that a society is able and willing to devote to the support of a particular institution. For example, it may simply not be able to make places available in school for all who seek to enroll. This holds for primary schools in many developing nations and for colleges and universities in developed countries. The same principle governs access into the military. Despite the desire of most nations to build up their armed forces, budgetary constraints often limit the numbers who can be accepted. The most pervasive limitation on access results from the discrepancy between the numbers seeking jobs with large employing organizations and the number of openings available.

We note, then, that most institutions provide restricted access usually because of limitations of resources but also because of their belief that unrestricted access would jeopardize their ability to function effectively. When governments create an educational system, they look to the schools to teach young people basic knowledge and competences, and they also expect the schools to play a leading role in the indoctrination of civic values and in the socializing process. Consequently, if a child cannot adapt to the school environment and engages in disruptive behavior, the educational authorities endeavor to remove him, whether or not there exists a more suitable institution to which he can be assigned.

Since institutions have multiple goals, including a primary concern with survival, each continuously assesses whether providing access for certain persons or groups or holding on to them after they have been admitted is desirable. Decisions governing the acceptance and retention of people in an organization depend on a multitude of factors in both the larger environment and the specific microconstellations. The sudden opening and closing of the sluices into the U.S. Army in World War II reflected the changing estimates of the military leadership of its manpower requirements, which were affected by the public's and the Congress' views on who should serve in time of war.

The leaders of all major institutions must assure their organization's effective performance and future well-being. Therefore they attempt to create conditions that are attractive to their career staff in an environment that is constantly changing in terms of competing values and alternative uses for resources. Consequently, the decisions they reach seldom represent the optimal contribution of their organization to either skill development or its utilization.

A third element in an institutional analysis of the manpower development process is the fact that every organization is a composite of diverse groups whose interests are both congruent and conflicting. To illustrate: the organization of a medical center may be satisfactory from the vantage of the chiefs of service and the supporting medical staff, reasonably good from the viewpoint of the nurses, and quite unsatisfactory as far as most of the paramedics are concerned. Similarly, the discontent of workers on an automobile assembly line may not be paralleled by those at the top or even by those in the middle-management of the company.

There is a further aspect embedded in the structure and functioning of major institutions which should be at least briefly noted because of their impact on manpower development and utilization. This aspect relates to the general environment within which the organization operates, that is, whether it faces an expanding or declining demand for its output. There is a presumption that organizations that expect a strong and growing demand for their output will attempt to improve their personnel policies and procedures to make more effective use of the people on their payroll. They understand that if they resort to recruiting, it will be a considerable time before the new employees are able to assume important responsibilities. Certainly, a decline in the operations of an organization usually results in redundant personnel, anxiety about job security, and lowered morale, all of which are antithetic to effective manpower development and utilization.

The fact that the manpower arena is characterized by a developmental process and institutional structures provides the backdrop for another characteristic—the role of affiliation. We have noted that, for a variety of reasons, including the limitation of resources, the specialized functions performed by different institutions, and the idiosyncratic behavior of individuals, the affiliation process is not automatic.

We have seen that every institution, the family alone excepted, is able to determine within limits whom it will accept and whom it will reject. Every important institution, then, performs a screening function. While political, economic, and social factors may restrict the freedom of an organization to select its members, that freedom is nowhere so restricted that a reasonably managed organization is unable to obtain the people it needs to perform its functions.

We have seen that the principal institutions are able to exercise varying orders of discretion in selecting from among the people who seek to affiliate with them. In addition, they set the terms under which affiliation is permitted to continue by specifying the standards of acceptable behavior and performance. Moreover, all organizations must over time remain in budgetary balance; that is, their expenditures cannot be in excess of their revenues for long. This means that at times part of their work force may be let go, temporarily or permanently, simply on grounds of financial necessity.

In general, affiliation with institutions for the purpose of manpower development is usually for a limited number of years. In developed countries, the educational system is usually divided into a series of discrete units, and separate affiliation is required for each division. Each segment may involve a period of from three to five years. Relatively short periods of affiliation are also characteristic of military service, formal occupational training, and preventive and rehabilitative arrangements made by the courts or the medical authorities.

The time period is more extended in the employment relationship, where the preferred affiliation is not short-lived but quasi-permanent; that is, a job with career prospects may extend over a person's working life or at a minimum over a period of twenty years or so, long enough for the worker to acquire rights to a pension.

The desire for a quasi-permanent employment affiliation, as pointed out earlier, stems from the concern of most workers with promotional opportunities, job security, and deferred types of compensation that often accrue to those who accumulate many years of service with one organization.

In a world characterized by uncertainty and instability, in which most persons are unable to assure by their own actions the well-being of their dependents and themselves, it is scarcely surprising that they seek an employment affiliation which holds promise of reducing the risks attached to participating in an economy in a continuing state of flux.

A satisfactory employment affiliation, however, is more than a simple risk-reducing relationship. The career employee of a large corporation, a university, a governmental agency, or a large nonprofit hospital finds that his role as a worker affects other important aspects of his life, including where he lives, with whom he associates, and how he spends his leisure time.

Important as affiliations are for manpower development and utilization, substantial variability in outcomes derives from the considerable degree of freedom of the individual to select among alternative goals and to devote more or less time and effort to realizing them. Important as are the societal and institutional forces in opening opportunities for individuals and in establishing standards of performance, we must take into account the options that most people in modern democratic societies have to structure their work and lives. People have different energies and drives, and, equally important, they have different values and goals. All these factors influence their actions with respect to both developing and utilizing their skills.

A few move toward a clearly delineated goal as if driven by the furies. Their every move is directed toward the furtherance of their primary objective. In contrast are the considerably larger numbers who do not choose to make special efforts to acquire specialized skills or seek out opportunities where they can most effectively utilize their competences. Experience has assured them that they will be able to earn their livelihood. Many among them seek their principal satisfactions in intrafamilial pursuits; athletics; hobbies, from chess playing to yachting; or involvement in religion, politics, or eleemosynary activities. People can do many different things with that part of their time which they do not spend at work earning an income. It is clear that only a minority spend most of their energies in self-development and fulfillment in the arena of work.

It should be added that the choices that people make differ not only according to their energy, values, and goals but also according to the stage in their life cycle. Just as the external reality is continually changing, so are the perceptions that people have of themselves and their future, perceptions that have an important role in directing their actions.

Since most adults live as members of a connubial family, disruption or dissolution of a marital relationship frequently leads to important changes in how they approach their work and careers. Moreover, as more and more married women in developed countries prepare for and pursue active careers, important and far-reaching changes will occur in the decision making of the conventional family, which until recently stressed the overriding importance of facilitating the husband's employment prospects. In the future, it is inevitable that wives with strong career orientations will insist upon a family strategy with respect to both development and work that takes their needs and desires into account.

One further observation relates to the choice of options. The goals of an individual or a family are determined not only by the advantages people see in pursuing particular lines of activity but also by the estimate they make of the risks entailed. Consequently, the manner in which the economy performs and the system of transfer payments that is in place can alter the risks attendant upon alternative work and career decisions. For instance, many individuals would be more ready to leave secure jobs which fail to use their skills or stimulate them if the track record of the economy suggests that the employment level would remain stable. Their willingness to take a chance on relocating would be greater if the society were to make pensions transferable (as in Sweden) and if it provided a series of labor market supports, from liberal unemployment insurance to mobility allowances, which would contain the risks facing a person who decided voluntarily to seek a new job or make a career change.

The conceptual foundations for manpower policy, we have found, rest upon four basic elements: the existence of a developmental process, the critical role of certain institutions, the importance of affiliation, and the existence of options. Embedded in this analysis are the building blocks of a theory of manpower development and utilization.

The development of skills and competence is a process involving a long period of preparation which, for those whose skills are highly specialized, is practically coexistent with their effective working lives.

The process involves a series of sequential steps or stages.

Developments in the early stages of the process have a cumulative effect upon later outcomes.

The several stages of the process are age-related in that every society expects its members to undertake and complete particular tasks within a certain time frame.

Spatial considerations play an important role in the opportunities that people encounter with respect to both the acquisition and the utilization of skills and competences.

The process of skill acquisiton and utilization is dependent on a group of interdependent institutions which, in advanced societies, includes at a minimum the family, the school, and employing organizations. Also included in varying degrees are such institutions as the church, the military, youth groups, and various professional and employee organizations.

Since most organizations attempt to adjust their goals and operations to meet the constantly changing internal and external realities, the decisions they make frequently detract from their manpower development goals.

With the exception of the family, access to these institutions is not automatic. The extent to which a person's skills are developed and utilized depends in no small measure on his success in obtaining access to these institutions.

With the exception of being born into a family, affiliation with an institution depends on whether the individual is able to pass its screening criteria and meet its performance standards.

While affiliation with developmental institutions for the purpose of skill acquisition is usually for a limited number of years, affiliation with respect to employment is frequently for a person's entire working life.

Such a long-term affiliation is sought by many to enhance their prospects of job and career security and to obtain valuable deferred benefits. A long-term arrangement is also favored by many employing organizations because it facilitates the building up of a career work force.

Many persons whose skills are undcrutilized and who see few prospects of further development in their current employment setting hesitate to look for new jobs because of the risks of leaving, including the potential loss of valuable benefits. Societies differ in the efforts they make to reduce these risks by providing supports for those who seek new employment opportunities.

In every society, different people attach different degrees of importance to pursuing work and career goals. The amount of energy they are able and willing to invest in their work largely determines their success in developing their potential.

Most persons seek to reach a balance among the several goals they pursue. If they can improve their prospects in the work arena, they know that additional earnings and job security will contribute to the realization of their other goals. Others, who realize that they can do little to improve their position in the labor market, seek their satisfactions elsewhere.

Since more married women are pursuing careers, the selection of options will be increasingly aimed at setting a balance between the needs of both spouses rather than only at advancing the career of the husband.

If the risks that attach to a worker's leaving his job are reduced, the worker will be more willing to explore new approaches aimed at acquiring new skills and to seek out opportunities that will make greater use of his potentials.

To complete the foregoing schema of the critical elements in manpower development and utilization, reference must be made to the level of employment opportunities that a society is able to provide relative to the number of active and potential job seekers. The implicit assumption underlying the manpower schema that has just been developed is that advanced societies recognize the importance of a continuing high level of employment opportunities. The further assumption has been made that although no advanced society has yet met this challenge completely, most advanced societies have passed the important milestone of successfully avoiding large-scale and persistent shortfalls in employment opportunities.

These are the principal building blocks of a theory of manpower development and utilization in an advanced society. The conceptual approach that has just been delineated stresses process rather than transaction, institutions rather than the market, affiliation rather than current wages, and options rather than an income-maximizing strategy. It challenges the conventional theory on every critical point. As we will see in the following chapters, the differences between this approach and conventional theory are important for both manpower policy and the well-being of the citizenry and the society.

· 15 ·

The Broadening of Options

THE ANALYSIS HAS SOUGHT to specify and clarify one predicate—that the progress of men and nations depends in the first instance on the development and utilization of their potential and skill. As they succeed in this undertaking, they will be more likely to accomplish the goals they have set.

Several subsidiary themes have emerged which should be briefly recapitulated so that the thrust of this chapter, the broadening of options, is placed in context. The first of these themes is that men are largely the creatures of the institutions they have built and through which they accomplish their ends.

A second theme is that in an environment in which change is pervasive, such as the Western world during the past half millennium, it is inevitable that the articulation among the principal societal systems will become so distorted that disequilibrium rather than equilibrium will dominate the scene. Under these circumstances, men can accomplish their near and long-range objectives only by modifying their institutions or putting new ones in place.

Another proposition is that the goals a society pursues at any point in its development will inevitably be modified and altered as a result of the society's experiences in pursuing them. This implies that all dynamic societies, by virtue of their internal dynamics and external settings, are open societies in that their values and goals as well as their institutions are constantly being transformed.

An additional theme is that every individual, as well as every society, constantly faces situations which demand that choices be made. Since the values of men and institutions are not always congruent and are sometimes in contradiction, and since there are disagreements about goals and how best to accomplish them, consensus about options is hard to achieve.

When a diversity of values, goals, methods, and options abounds, the question arises whether there are better ways for a society to enhance the well-being of its members. This chapter propounds an affirmative answer. Moreover, it stipulates that the basic guideline should be the broadening of options. With this as the criterion of societal development, an attempt will be made to adumbrate and explicate it and then establish its relevance for policy guidance.

We will first review how the human resources system and the other societal systems delineated earlier can be informed by this criterion. We will then review the criterion of the broadening of options in relation to the three principal types of societies that have earlier engaged our attention: traditional, transitional, and developed. In the concluding section we will consider the uncertainties that attach to any normative principle of societal development, including that articulated here, the broadening of options.

One reason for selecting the broadening of options as the basic criterion of societal development is that since individuals and societies have competing values and competing goals, they need an ordering principle which will enable them to distinguish the more important opportunities and challenges from those which are less important in order to guide their behavior.

The last two centuries provide a second perspective. The Western world has developed competing principles. Where individual well-being has been the center of concern, the seers and statesmen have emphasized the importance of personal freedom, the pursuit of material gain, and the optimization of pleasure. The goals for the collectivity which were formulated were the aggrandizement of the power of the national state, accelerated economic growth, security for all citizens, and the building of a new society based on equality.

But neither of the foregoing principles has been able to command more than limited allegiance. The passage of time has indicated the inevitable changes in the undeviating pursuit of these goals; experience has also revealed the hidden costs that became manifest only as each goal was actively pursued. Moreover, when leaders saw the goal of society as the greater fulfillment of the individual in terms of freedom, wealth, or pleasure, their attention was deflected from the effectiveness with which societal systems and institutions were performing their critical functions. When the thrust of development was directed toward the realization of communal objectives under the momentum of nationalism, imperialism, and communism, the needs and desires of the individual were submerged. The millions who were injured or killed in wars and revolutions undertaken in the name of achieving important collective goals gave telling evidence of the dangers of leaving the individual out of any system of social accounting.

Finally, our criterion of the broadening of options is based on the dynamics in the lives of both individuals and societies. The values that guide their actions and point to the goals they pursue are modified and transformed by the experiences they undergo and the lessons they are able to extract from these experiences. No criterion of societal development which ignores the principle of continuing transformation and change can be effective.

There are, then, four potent factors that support, at least initially, our choice of the criterion of the broadening of options: the need for a principle which can help to order conflicting and competing values and goals, the limitations that have become manifest in the criteria that have guided the Western world during the past two centuries, the need for a criterion that is responsive to the nature of both man and society and that is not exclusively preoccupied with the one or the other, and the importance of selecting a criterion that can take account of the transformational dynamics that characterize the life of both the individual and society.

The broadening of options is presented as the guiding principle of human resources development by pointing to its supports: it can moderate competing values and goals; it is free of the demonstrable weaknesses of the principles that have misled its adherents in the past; it is responsive to both the individual and society; it can encapsulate change.

The concept of broadened options implies that both individuals and societies are in a better position when the range of their goals is extended beyond those previously available to them and, further, that enlarged horizons will enable both to make greater use of their potential. The broadening of options does not imply that people or nations will necessarily utilize their enlarged range of opportunities to achieve more satisfactory existences. It merely postulates that an enlargement in the range of their choices could lead to desirable outcomes.

Now the relevance of this criterion for policy will be established. A first step is to note that the human resources system, similar to the other societal systems, has a basically instrumental quality. The several institutions, from the family to the employing organization, can help the individual to develop his potential, skills, and competences. But the human resources system is neutral about the uses to which the individual's skills will be directed.

The same distinctions can be made about the other societal systems, particularly government and the economy. Each was treated instrumentally. We noted that a well-functioning political apparatus, with an accepted process for the selection and succession of leaders, an effective bureaucracy, and the ability to command adequate resources, can serve effectively as a consensus-forming organ which is able to facilitate the citizenry's deciding upon common objectives and the preferred methods of pursuing them. But this consensus-forming apparatus is silent with respect to the substantive goals that a people seek to accomplish.

Similarly, our analysis of the economy noted the importance of various institutional arrangements that can facilitate increases in output, employment, and surplus, but it remained silent on the ends to which increased surpluses are deployed. The manufacture of armaments, the proliferation of recreational activities, and simple transfers of income are all potential claimants for the surplus.

The principal societal systems, consisting of government, the economy, and the manpower development institutions, are mechanisms that men have created for the purpose of serving their individual and collective needs and desires. But a mechanism implies that it is an instrument to be used in helping to accomplish common objectives and goals. As instruments that command the time and talent of men, the principal societal systems often exercise an influence far beyond their initial purpose. Unless those who fashioned and use them assume responsibility for directing their own lives and that of their societies, these systems can never surmount their instrumental role.

Policy implies selection among competing goals, and it also implies the modification of existing institutions and the establishment of new ones so that the selected goals can be realized.

We will now review the relation between the instrumental nature of the principal societal systems and the policy uses to which they can be directed within the framework of a broadening of options. In this connection, we will enlarge our framework to include the value structure in addition to the other societal systems, since the stress on free inquiry that characterizes Western societies plays an instrumental role in these cultures.

In the absence of free inquiry, the choices available to the individual and the society are circumscribed. We can assume that most societies where free inquiry is precluded continue to pursue goals which were determined at some time in the past, sometimes far in the past, without allowance for the changes that have occurred in their own development or in the external environment. Secondly, those who control the levers of power, including the communications media, are able to inflict their preferences on the body politic, since competing points of view are proscribed or cannot be broadly disseminated. Since the application of critical thought and free inquiry themselves are potent tools in the broadening of men's minds and spirits, limitations on their use stunt men by constricting their choices.

We find then that the value structure, particularly free inquiry, has an important instrumental role to play in societal development. How important is suggested by the narrowing of options that results from its absence. Additional insight into the intersection of the principal societal systems and the broadening of options can be obtained from a summary consideration of the inevitable narrowing of options that occurs as a consequence of the faulty performance of the other principal societal systems.

The central function of government, we contended earlier, is to provide a medium through which the citizens of a country, or of a political subdivision, can decide upon common goals, choose among alternative ways of achieving them, and determine how the costs of the undertaking are to be borne.

What are the consequences, direct and indirect, when people sharing a common territory have not been able to put into place an effective organ of government? What are the consequences of this deficiency for options that are likely to be available to them? The answers are obvious. They will not be able to engage in many communal undertakings. They will not be able to make plans or introduce changes. A weak government may be insurance against foolish and costly social experimentation, but a weak government is also a major barrier in the way of people's modifying their existing institutions and building new ones so that they can better meet the challenges that time has brought. People without an effective government are constrained. Many options are cut off from them.

The level of development of the economy is the third basic instrumentality that can constrict the options available to people. If individuals must devote most of their efforts and energies to raising food and obtaining the other essentials they need for subsistence, they will not be able to engage in other endeavors. Moreover, if the economy yields little surplus, it will be difficult for the people to make collective investments in infrastructure to facilitate a higher order of specialization, which is the only effective basis for raising the productivity of the economy and increasing its surplus.

People who must work ceaselessly to keep hunger at arm's length cannot enjoy broadened options; options follow only after a surplus has been achieved. Men trapped in poverty have little opportunity to explore other dimensions of existence. Unless and until they are collectively able to strengthen their economy so that it yields at least a modest surplus, they are enslaved. All that goes under the name of civilization rests on the existence of an economic surplus.

This brings us to the fourth and last of the basic societal systems that plays a critical role in the broadening of options—the manpower development system. Knowledge and, equally important, the pursuit of knowledge require learning. Each child must be instructed. Moreover, the skills and techniques required for physical and social survival and well-being must be learned. The ease or difficulty of transmitting a tradition depends on its history and creativity. The greater its accomplishments, the more difficult but also the more rewarding is the task.

Of all the societal systems, the institutions involved in developing the potential of each new generation are the greatest contributors to the broadening of options. The educated man who has learned about the successes and failures of earlier generations can better appreciate the range of his options; the theory and techniques that were at the heart of his own education provide him with the tools he needs to appraise critically the attractiveness of alternative options open to him and to the society to which he belongs. Trained intelligence is the vaulting pole which enables men to extend the height of their leap.

When a society can enable all its members to develop their potentialities to the full, its members will recognize the range of their options and, equally important, will be better able to explore and pursue them. Illiteracy, like the poverty with which it is so closely linked, prevents men from developing their principal resource, their intelligence, which alone can free them from bondage and broaden their options.

With these general considerations of the intersection of the major societal systems and the broadening of options before us, we can now review briefly the extent to which societies at different stages of development encounter broadened options and the manner in which they respond to them. Specifically, we will consider the three types of societies which have had our attention earlier—the traditional agricultural society, the traditional society in the process of transition, and the advanced technological society which is either centrally controlled or market-oriented.

The outstanding characteristic of traditional societies is the almost complete absence of options, reflecting the almost complete absence of any margins that allow for departures from the established ways of doing things. The values that are in place leave little room for individual discretion; communities are also tradition-bound because of their fear that any deviation might result in costs that they would simply be unable to bear. The great strength of tradition is that it encapsulates for the society the ways to adjust to nature and to man that have been tried and tested. Although adherence to tradition may carry many hidden costs, people trust their tradition not to place them at mortal risk.

A second reason for the absence of options in traditional societies is the limited strength of the governmental structure, particularly in large countries with diverse ethnic groups. A weak central government and independent satraps in the several regions preclude the reaching of a consensus about most matters; in large underdeveloped countries it is next to impossible to achieve agreement about important next steps.

The low productivity of these economies results in an annual surplus of such modest proportions that with the exception of a few rich families, no individual or organization, not even government itself, has sufficient uncommitted resources to support a major new departure.

The small annual surplus, reinforced by the weakness of government and the strength of the value system that is in place, determines the low level of skills and competences characteristic of the population and the lack of leverage to increase them. A significant attempt to raise the skill level would involve, first, large-scale investments in the establishment and expansion and improvement of the educational systems, but even under the best of circumstances these efforts would not be reflected in significant gains in the economic and social performance of the population for decades. Even then, the gains might be modest, unless other favorable developments also occurred, such as a quickening of the economy and a strengthening of government.

These few illustrations reinforce our earlier analysis which indicated that each of the principal societal systems in a traditional society is unable to respond to new ideas or new realities. The difficulties that traditional societies face in broadening options can be read in their experiences in seeking to reduce their rate of population growth. The underdeveloped state of intermediaries in the health arena, in community relations, in the manufacture and distribution of contraceptives, in communications, and in research means that almost the whole burden of effecting change is placed on the government bureaucracy, which is poorly structured to carry out such a complex task. In countries which were willing and able to add a large number of family-planning staffs to their payrolls, it soon became clear that numbers alone were not the answer. The meager training of these public health workers, their unwillingness to carry the message into the hinterland, their limited skill at persuading local leaders, and their inadequate resources critically limited their effectiveness. The inability of traditional societies to respond effectively to an option that they recognize, such as family planning, underscores the constraints that bound their existence.

Occasionally, these constraints are loosened by a concatenation of circumstances, usually favored by the emergence of an economic surplus which provides the leverage for change. When more and more people are able to change their residence and their work and increase their earnings and their standard of living, they confront options which were previously not within their purview. To the extent that they, and especially their children, have access to more and better schooling, still further options develop. Much that a traditional society takes for granted and considers fixed and immovable becomes the object of critical reappraisal.

Accelerated development is usually accompanied by changes in power relationships at every level of the society—within the family, between husband and wife and parents and children; between landowners and tenants and employers and workers; between government and the citizenry. Here, too, assumptions about power, authority, legitimacy, and participation are likely to be reassessed, and as a consequence, new and broadened options are recognized and pursued. As we noted earlier, in a transitional society, the new bourgeoisie is likely to press for a role in the political decision-making process.

A transitional society is characterized by a substantial broadening of options, particularly for those members of the society who are exposed to the forces of modernization and who are able to accumulate some wealth and benefit from more extended education. The society in turn is able to establish programs previously beyond its capabilities, including those aimed at altering the basic value system, strengthening the government so that it can extend its effective sovereignty over dissident groups, accelerating investments in the economic infrastructure with consequences for linking more closely the rural and urban areas, and establishing various developmental institutions that can add to the health, education, and training of the population.

A society in transition must attempt to keep its critical systems in tolerable balance. As long as it succeeds in this, the process of development is likely to continue and carry with it a further broadening of options.

What can we say about the broadening of options in a developed society, centrally controlled or market-oriented? The central management of an industrialized society, as exemplified by the U.S.S.R. and its neighbors, points up the relative ease with which it is able to generate a considerable surplus. This surplus allows the ruling group discretion to pursue priority goals, including speeding the process of economic growth, expanding the developmental institutions, achieving changes in the value structure, and strengthening the governmental system.

These pervasive changes in the principal societal systems are also reflected in a broadening of options for many individual citizens, especially those who have benefited from the society's enlarged investments in human resources development, such as campaigns to eradicate illiteracy and the expansion of institutions of higher education. By virtue of more education, better training, higher earnings, and other advantages, many citizens in these state-controlled economies are able to benefit from broader options.

However, the leadership of a controlled society must maintain strict control over the flow of ideas and over the levers of political power. In addition, it must keep close control over the allocation of resources and the output of the economic system. Because of the leadership's concern with exercising continuing close control and supervision over these many sectors of activity, the freedom available to the individual is constricted. There are a great many decisions which are not his to make, including decisions about what he can discuss, write, and read; the career he prepares for; and where he is permitted to live. These decisions are made by the authorities.

In democratic, market-controlled societies the individual has a much wider area for self-determination. As long as he does not violate the law he is more or less free to follow his own wishes and pursue the options which the society has made available.

However, here, too, there is another side. Many options are open only to those who command considerable financial resources. Most members of the population have only a modest amount of savings, which means that they are bound to their jobs and to the pattern of life that their earnings permit them to sustain. Bounded by their work and income, they have considerable freedom about which options to pursue, but the income constraint is a major deterrent to a true broadening of their options.

Furthermore, in the market-oriented societies, with so much property and power in the hands of intermediaries, particularly the large corporations and trade unions, government can command only a limited amount of the surplus, and it can pursue only limited options. A democratic society usually needs many years of discussion and political maneuvering before it can pursue new goals.

But the continuing creation of additional surplus which is characteristic of advanced societies, the importance that both market and state-controlled societies attach to encouraging larger numbers to pursue higher education, and the stimulation that comes from improved communications with the outside world provide added momentum for the continual broadening of options in developed societies. Unless a developed nation runs into a major disequilibrium among its basic systems, the odds are favorable for a broadening of options for both the individual citizen and the larger society.

We now face the last and most important aspect of the analysis. The criterion of. the broadening of options has been defined; its relevance for policy has been explored; it has been used to assess the direction of change in different societies. What can be ventured about its strength as a normative principle?

One proposition must be recapitulated here. Since all societal systems are inherently, if not exclusively, instrumental, individuals and communities must find some principle that will enable them to choose among their options now and in the future. Since experience has demonstrated that the principles that men and societies have used for guidelines in the past are ineffective—from the search for national power to the individual accumulation of wealth—there is a strong presumption in favor of a new guideline—the broadening of options—particularly one which enlarges the criterion from a specific goal to a process through which multiple goals can be realized.

Since our inquiry has stressed the mutual interaction among four basic societal systems, each with its own dynamics and goals, the presumption in favor of a normative principle which is sensitive and responsive to this diversity in individual and societal behavior is reinforced. A man wants not a single option but several—personal freedom, the opportunity to participate in a government to which he pays allegiance, the ability to earn a reasonable income, and an opportunity to develop fully his potential and skills. Since men differ in their capacities and performances, the greater their degree of freedom to determine the mix of options they can pursue, the greater is the likelihood that they will be content with the outcomes. Herein lies one of the greatest advantages to the criterion of broadening of options.

But the process of widening the range of choices for the individual carries costs. Since individuals cannot operate in an industrialized society primarily on their own, they seek many of their goals through cooperative action. They must decide which constrictions they are willing to endure by forgoing certain options in order to gain the advantages of joint action which hold promise of broadening other options.

Since there can be no a priori determination of the respective agendas of individual and public action, adherence to the principle of broadening options, which includes an abiding respect for free inquiry and participation by all citizens in the political process, establishes the preconditions for people to learn, on the basis of continuing experimentation, where to set the dividing line between social intervention and the arena for individual decision making. The line may be shifted, first in one direction and then in another, but the adjustments should be considered a source of strength, not weakness, since they can contribute to the broadening of options.

The principle of broadening options rests unequivocally on the assumption that it is preferable for the individual to take as much responsibility as possible for his own life and welfare and play an active part in shaping the future of his society. We need not exaggerate the extent to which men have relied on reason, tolerance, and sympathy in shaping their lives and that of their societies. But most men only recently emerged from the shadows of poverty and ignorance. It is a reasonable presumption that their broadened options will further enhance their freedom and well-being.

· 16 ·

Directions for Manpower Policy

THE CONCEPTUAL SCHEMA on which the present work rests points to the need for a social policy which includes a manpower policy. All societies, particularly developed societies, must constantly adapt their institutions to the forces of change which impact upon them from within and without. Although every institution strives for stability, major tensions arise when new forces weaken and undermine the existing societal systems. Unless we become fatalistic and assume that despite collective action men are unable to influence, contain, and redirect the forces impinging on them, an active policy in the arena of manpower, as in other social arenas, is mandated.

Even when a society recognizes that forces are unsettling its basic institutions, it has no firm basis on which to fashion policies and programs aimed at solving the problems that change brings in its wake. However, since societies, like individuals, always confront a present and a future different from the past, the fact that policies are elusive does not permit them the luxury of not attempting to formulate them. Failure to develop a policy is itself a policy that gives free scope to the forces of change to work their will. As long as men are concerned with shaping their own lives and the life of their community, they must engage in the never ending task of goal selection, refinement, and redirection and the concomitant task of choosing among the alternative mechanisms which are most likely to help them to accomplish their high-priority purposes.

The underlying assumption that informs this concluding chapter is that men who want to be masters of their fate, who want to control their future as much as possible, must shape and reshape manpower policy. This mandate derives from the fact that the institutions which determine the skills that people acquire and the institutions which govern the use of these skills will inevitably lose their alignment because of the forces unleashed by change.

Manpower policy is here defined as the actions that a society can take to increase the opportunities available to its members to develop and utilize their skills. The elements of manpower policy can be distinguished as, first, the actions directed to providing developmental experiences, including skill training, for the members of each new generation. The second element of manpower policy involves the opportunities available to all members of a society to obtain productive employment, which is a precondition for their utilizing their skills and competences. The third dimension of manpower policy relates to the opportunities available to people after they start to work to further develop their competences. Such opportunities usually involve both additional training and education and, most important, a succession of job assignments, each of which challenges the individual.

In addition to the preparatory period, work, and the continued growth of adult competence, manpower policy must be sensitive to the critical dimension of equity. As the earlier discussion of social class (Chapter 6) and the parallel discussion of job structures (Chapter 9) sought to make clear, the opportunities that societies, capitalist and communist alike, make available to different groups for both the development and utilization of their skills and competences are conspicuously unequal. Some young people and adults are in better positions than others to obtain access to institutions which can facilitate their development. Because of these gross inequities, a manpower policy which is committed to the optimal development of a nation's human resources must aim to remove the barriers that block young people from developing their skills and that prevent adults from obtaining the type of employment in which they can effectively use their talents and skills. An effective manpower policy must be sensitive to the pervasiveness of unequal opportunity which characterizes the society and attempt to eliminate discriminatory practices.

Since men and women are unable to live fulfilling lives without the opportunity to work, a critical responsibility for societies which produce sizable surpluses every year is to assure that all members of each new generation are afforded the opportunity to acquire the skills and competences they will need to engage in productive work when they reach adulthood. While this principle appears to have been accepted and implemented by developed, and an increasing number of developing, societies, all of which have committed sizable resources to financing a system of public education, a closer look reveals that mere acceptance does not mean implementation.

We note, first, that if the family is unable to carry out its nurturing responsibilities satisfactorily before the school takes over, the child may be unable to take advantage of the formal educational system. Consequently, the implementation of the principle of providing every child with effective preparation for adulthood requires that provision be made for assisting families which are unable to meet their child-rearing responsibilities; this help may involve a wide range of supports, from income supplements to assured access to health services. In the event that, even with such supports, families are still unable to cope, the community must be ready to remove children from their dysfunctional parental environment, but it should do this only if the substitute homes are clearly superior. To permit children to remain with incompetent or cruel parents or to fail to develop suitable alternatives for poor homes spells trouble for the child and the society alike. In addition to having a distorted personality, the almost certain consequence of sustained neglect in childhood, the damaged child is likely to grow into an incompetent adult unable to support himself through work. Accordingly, when the parental family fails, a society which aims to have a self-sufficient and productive citizenry has the responsibility of assuring all children a childhood which is as close to normal as possible.

In addition to the moral imperative that every child should be protected from neglect and abuse, the criterion of efficiency reinforces the necessity that the society adopt a policy of constructive intervention. The sizable investment that an advanced society makes in the education of all its children is likely to be wasted unless young people live in a supportive environment during their formative years. Moreover, the disturbingly large number of neglected youths who later run into trouble with the law enforcement authorities or who break down and require prolonged institutionalization in a mental health facility is further reason for a society to prevent this kind of pathology from arising in the first place.

Another dimension of the application of the principle of effective preparation for adult work is the malfunctioning of the educational-training process for a substantial minority of young people who, despite good home environments, they still fail to acquire satisfactory orders of competence. The malfunctioning is manifest in the numbers of young people who, after many years of school, have not mastered the basic skills required for adulthood and who, instead of being helped to learn to control their emotions and live in a society that demands conformity, harbor resentment and hostility against a system with which they are unable to cope. No school system has mastered the task of assuring that all young children capable of learning to read, write, and count can do so. There is no simple explanation for this failure, but the following factors should be noted: the educational establishment has not directed adequate efforts to designing appropriate curricula; the assignment and teaching of young children follow inflexible rules; the educational authorities do not insist that principals and teachers perform effectively.

There is little point in moving children through the system if their failure to master the essentials, especially reading, in the early grades prevents their later progress. If children pass through grades without having learned to read, the school system should at least avoid compounding the consequence of this failure and provide these youngsters with meaningful alternatives for skill acquisition. Learning from books may well be the preferred way for people to increase their skills, but it is clearly not the only way.

The major drawback, especially in the United States, of the elongated compulsory educational cycle is that meaningful alternatives for the nonbookish young person have not been provided. The classroom is such an oppressive environment for many fourteen- to seventeen-year-olds that the truancy rates reaches 50 percent and higher during these ages. These young people need a bridge to the world of work. They need to have real jobs where they can interact with adults. Such a program need not sever all relationships to the school; it might provide a combination of training and work with continuing didactic instruction to which the youngsters would respond more positively when they recognize how learning in the classroom is related to the workplace.

To substantially increase work-study programs for adolescents would be difficult, especially in an advanced technological society in which employers are not pressed for additional labor and are wary about assigning immature young people to work on expensive machinery. But a society that continues to ignore the inadequacy of its existing institutional structures for facilitating the transition of young people into adulthood pays a high price. The unproductive investments in secondary education are the smaller part of the loss. The more significant costs reflect the stunting of the development of large numbers of young people, many of whom in protest or desperation may enter a life of vandalism, alienation, and crime that carries substantial individual and social costs. The greatest social cost would result if, even after a period of floundering, they fail to make a satisfactory transition into the world of work, with lifelong inadequacy and dependency as the likely consequences.

A third aspect of adequate preparation for adult work is the need of every advanced society to improve the articulation between the later stages of the educational-training system and the changing career, job, and occupational structures. Since the preparatory institutions are characterized by inflexibility, they are increasingly out of contact with the changing contours of the economy, unless they exercise constant and close surveillance. It is not simple to ensure that the development and employing systems are effectively dovetailed, but efforts should be devoted to continuing data collection and analysis of the initial employment experiences of recent graduates so that relevant findings can be used to modify the preparatory structure.

If improved preparation is critical, increased opportunity for employment is an equally important dimension of manpower policy. Advanced societies must seek to provide employment opportunities for all who are able and willing to work. No matter how well a society copes with strengthening its preparatory institutions, it will not meet its commitment to provide an environment supportive of an independent citizenry unless it can provide an adequate level of employment affiliation. There is no possible way of placing the onus on the individual to be and remain self-supporting unless the society, through its appropriate agencies, assures that an adequate number of jobs are available.

Several specifications should be noted with respect to the implementation of the principle of full employment. First of all, it is essential that in setting the national target, all persons who desire to work be considered, not just those who meet the selection criteria of employing organizations. A society must therefore experiment with assuring an adequate number of jobs not only for fully qualified members of the labor force but also for the many who are only peripherally attached or who are currently not even counted among the active job seekers. Translated, this means that a full-employment policy must include opportunities for such groups as the large numbers of youths, married women, older persons, and the physically and emotionally handicapped. Members of these groups are not actively looking for work, not because they do not want a job but simply because they believe—and usually correctly—that there are no jobs available for them. In many instances, the jobs that would be most attractive to them would be part-time rather than full-time because of their commitments at home or in school or because of their personal disabilities.

A second specification of a full-employment policy relates to the quality of the jobs that are available. Quality involves such considerations as whether the jobs are intermittent or full-time and whether they provide the incumbent with earnings that will enable him currently, or some time in the future, to maintain himself and his dependents at a generally acceptable standard of living. A third consideration relates to the presumption of employment continuity. If a worker performs competently, he should be able to expect not to be laid off, and he should certainly expect not to lose his job.

Unless the totality of jobs available provides sufficient work, at acceptable pay, with reasonable security for those who meet prevailing standards of performance, it does not fulfill the criterion of a full-employment policy.

The foregoing specifications of an adequate level of job opportunities with respect to both the numbers of potential job applicants and the quality of jobs far exceed the demonstrated capabilities of even the most successful of the advanced economies in meeting the employment challenge. In pointing directions for manpower policy, however, we must acknowledge that a major commitment of effort and resources will be required, as well as a series of carefully designed interventions with room for subsequent modifications to be made on the basis of experience, in order to approximate the full-employment goal here specified.

Important as an improved preparatory system and an adequate level of employment opportunities are, an ambitious manpower policy must also aim at realizing a third principle, which can be defined as facilitating the continued growth in the skills and competences of those who are employed. In part, this growth is currently provided by the increasing efforts of large employing organizations to assure an adequately trained work force and managerial cadre through in-service training, successive assignments geared to career development, and various types of educational programming, both in house and on the outside.

These several efforts fall far short, however, of providing an adequate response. They do not provide sufficient opportunities for all employees of large organizations to expand their skills and continue to gain in competence. Much less is done for the large numbers who are employed in small organizations where employers are able to provide few, if any, training opportunities.

If opportunity for continuing growth is to be realized, considerably greater encouragement for mobility will be required. This implies that, when a worker reaches a point beyond which his present employer cannot train or promote him, he should be able to shift to another employer; a new environment, new tasks, and new challenges would lead to new learning, new experiences, and skills.

A second desideratum is strengthened adult educational and training opportunities under public auspices for different groups of workers: for those who failed to acquire skills while they were in the preparatory system, for those who do not have sufficient training to realize specific occupational goals they have set, and for those who, for reasons of a change in themselves or in the employment situation, seek new skills. While every advanced economy has pieces of an adult educational-training structure in place, no advanced society supports a manpower infrastructure which fully meets this target.

These are a few of the steps required if manpower development is to be transformed from a goal into a reality. Before leaving this theme we should note that the recommendation that the adult educational and training structure be expanded does not assume that all workers, or necessarily even the majority, want to enhance their skills and competence. The foregoing formulation merely implies that the current shortfall in institutional arrangements creates a substantial deficit in opportunities for large numbers who would take advantage of these opportunities if they were available.

We are now ready to assess the last of the basic principles that should inform manpower policy, that of equity. By way of background we should note that this principle runs into strong opposition from a host of social forces, starting with the determination of people to protect their property and power, the efforts of parents to provide special advantages for their children, and the influence of endowment or acquired characteristics in helping competitive persons pursue the limited prizes that a society makes available. Because of these forces and others, such as the protection the law offers to those who own property and the manipulation of public opinion that helps the privileged to maintain their position, all societal efforts directed at establishing greater equity in opportunity and rewards are strongly opposed.

Nevertheless, efforts to achieve greater equity are basic to strengthening manpower policy. We noted earlier that the effective development of a person's potential requires that he have access to a range of institutions and supports. The same conditions were implicit with respect to access to employment opportunities and to institutional supports which enable people to increase their skills and competences during their adult years. On each front—development, utilization, and adult growth—individuals require access to opportunity. Contrariwise, those who do not have access to critical institutions or who are prevented from making an effective affiliation will be left with underdeveloped or underutilized potentials and skills.

Since certain groups are more likely to have limited access to opportunity than others, the thrust toward equity in the manpower arena should first be directed at improving their positions. The largest group in modern societies which is at risk consists of those at the lower end of the income distribution, particularly their children who, having been born into families with limited means, are most likely to be handicapped during their long years of preparation for adulthood.

Overlapping those with the lowest income are the members of groups that are discriminated against by the society, most frequently on grounds of race or ethnicity, less frequently because of religion or ideology. As with the poor, the victims of discrimination inevitably have a distorted developmental cycle with sequelae which encroach on their later employment and career progression. Discrimination is the most corrosive of all societal arrangements which detract from the full development and utilization of human potential and skill.

A heavy toll also continues to be extracted in all societies from discrimination based on sex. Since women constitute the majority of the total population in all modern societies, the reduction and elimination of pervasive discrimination based on sex will lead to marked gains in the size and quality of the human resources pool. We can also look forward to valuable secondary consequences from a reduction in this type of discrimination through a favorable long-term impact on males. Discrimination extracts a high price, not only from its victims but also from its perpetrators, whose personalities and performance become skewed as a result of the special advantages that accrue to them from exploiting others.

Although the inequities that have characterized modern societies have been substantially reduced during the twentieth century, large groups still face major barriers to the full development and utilization of their potentials and skills. Accordingly, a society concerned with reducing manpower waste has no option but to attempt to broaden opportunities for those who presently lack them.

The expansion of opportunities for all involves reinforcements for families which are handicapped in caring for themselves and particularly in providing their children with the essentials for sound development; access to educational and training institutions of comparable quality for all groups; second-chance opportunities for those young people who encounter difficulties during their developmental phase; avoiding shunting those with inadequate preparation into the jobs without opportunities to acquire skills; and finally, a structure whereby the rewards and benefits that people earn from work do not deprive the low earners from participating meaningfully in their society.

The broadening of equity, therefore, involves policies directed at making access to opportunities more nearly equal; ensuring that the outcomes from the development process do not rigidly control what happens later in the employment arena; modifying the tendency of the marketplace to reward liberally those with special talent, skill, or power by placing an income floor beneath those who are in a poor position to compete; and finally, reducing and eliminating the distortions that are embedded in discriminatory policies and practices.

The four principles that should inform manpower policy have been delineated: strengthening the developmental process, assuring adequate employment for all who seek to work, providing opportunities for adults to increase their skills and competences, and enhancing the degree of equity that prevails. It is now necessary to point out the limits that bound these efforts.

It must be recognized that in attempting to strengthen the developmental process, it is difficult to compensate for major weaknesses in the family. It is impractical, therefore, to expect child-directed programs, no matter how imaginative and supportive, to compensate for the family's inabilities to discharge its major responsibilities. Accordingly, a long-range strategy must be sensitive to the interrelations between the generations and must respond to the need to help adults emerge from ignorance and poverty and remove the burden of prejudice from those on whom it rests. This underscores the importance of speeding the expansion of desirable employment opportunities for adults who are on the periphery of the labor force.

Having stressed the critical contribution that a high level of employment, with an expanded proportion of good jobs, can make to enhancing the development and utilization of a nation's human resources, we must now raise a warning about the need to balance this effort with a concern for maintaining an employment environment conducive to enhancing productivity. Unless the work that people engage in contributes to increasing the amount of surplus available to a society, the additional resources required to strengthen the critical institutions involved in manpower development and utilization will not be available. A progressive society needs not only more jobs but also better jobs for its people, and both rest on continuing gains in productivity.

Manpower policy directed at optimal development and the principle of equity can give rise to conflict. Public investments in higher education and specialized training will be reflected in higher personal incomes. There is no simple formula for determining how much money a society should invest in the expansion of the educational-training structure and how the costs should be allocated among the society, the student, and his family. To charge students only a fraction of the total tuition, as do most medical schools, can result in a foolish subsidy of the potentially wealthy. To ask students to cover the full costs of a medical education on the theory that they will recapture their outlay through later earnings also is a limited postulate because of the distortions that would be introduced into the career plans of those who graduate with heavy debts. On balance, it is probably better to seek fiscal justice and equity by adjusting the tax structure than through attempting to forge complex links among tuition, parental capacity to pay, and the graduate's potential lifetime earnings.

The risks inherent in a manpower policy which underwrites education and training make up only one side of the coin. The other consists of the benefits that accrue from the more effective development and utilization of human potential. The gains to be achieved cannot be foreseen, and certainly their value cannot be calculated. The limitless frontier of human achievement should serve as the spur to manpower policy.

Even the search for greater equity is not free of risk. In a democratic society the strength of such an effort depends on the support, at least the tolerance, of the majority, who must be willing to make adjustments if those with restricted opportunities are to improve their positions. This means that the amount of taxes that taxpayers are willing to bear to support a higher level of income transfers to the poor is a factor; that the extent to which they are willing to see their control over preferred jobs reduced so that previously excluded groups can have improved access is a factor; and that the extent to which they are willing to modify the arrangements governing how they interact with people previously discriminated against (and the strains to which they are willing to expose their children) affect the rate at which an advanced society can move to expand equity. As was suggested in the discussion of the welfare state in Chapter 4, liberally oriented societies may have a lower boiling point than their leaders had initially assumed.

This brief discussion of the parameters within which manpower policy must be developed and implemented calls attention once again to the several themes that permeate this work. The first stresses the determining role that institutions play in shaping the lives of individuals. While the endowment with which a person is born plays a part in his later development and accomplishments, more important are the cumulative experiences he undergoes in different institutions, from his parental family to his employing organization. What happens to human beings is the direct outcome of their exposures and experiences.

Secondly, since multiple, powerful forces of change operate on all advanced societies, they have no option but to make adjustments in their principal systems and institutions. If a society is to survive the new threats that it confronts, and if it is to take advantage of the new opportunities that change presents, it must modify its institutions. They cannot remain intact.

All efforts at societal intervention to modify existing systems and institutions represent a risk, and if the interventions are ambitious, if they are introduced speedily, and if the phenomena that are to be altered are complex, the likelihood of failure multiplies. The costs of failure can be high and sometimes overwhelming. Consequently, if a society has garnered understanding about how its critical institutions perform and interact, if it has accumulated experience in adjusting to the forces of change, and if it has established feedback mechanisms that can facilitate modifications in the changes it is seeking to introduce, it is likely that the costs of change can be contained. The highest cost of all would follow an attempt to maintain the status quo in a world of never ending change.

SOURCES AND READING NOTES

THESE READING NOTES have been prepared to assist the interested reader in locating the research findings of the Conservation of Human Resources Project published during the last three and one-half decades and which support the analysis presented in this book, chapter by chapter. I also wish to call the reader's attention to a limited number of books which deal with the same or a related theme and in which the author illuminates an important aspect of the subject.

Each chapter's reading notes cite the numbers given to the references in the bibliography which follows.

PROSPECTUS

CONSERVATION OF HUMAN RESOURCES PUBLICATIONS

1. *Grass on the Slag Heaps,* especially chaps. 7 and 8
2. *The Unemployed,* chaps. IX and X
34. *The Development of Human Resources,* "Foreword"
39. *Manpower Agenda for America,* "Foreword" and chap. 1
70. *The Manpower Connection,* chaps. 7 through 10 on changing aspects of work; chap. 11 on educated manpower in the United States in the 1970s; chaps. 18 and 22 on the interface of manpower and economic policies
87. *Womanpower,* chap. V
302. "The Building of a National Manpower Policy" in *Developing the Nation's Workforce,* pp. 19–38

READING NOTES

137. Bereday, *Universities for All*
163. Davis and Cherns, *The Quality of Working Life*
177. Fermi, *Illustrious Immigrants*
181. Fried, *The Exploitation of Foreign Labor by Germany*
192. Harris, *The Anguish of Change*
264. Price, *The Scientific Estate*
280. Rosow, *The Worker and the Job*
322. Zuckerman, *Scientists and War*

CHAPTER I

CONSERVATION OF HUMAN RESOURCES PUBLICATIONS

  3. *The Labor Leader*, part three
 22. *The American Worker in the Twentieth Century*, chaps. I, III, VI, IX, XII
 23. *Democratic Values and the Rights of Management*, part Three
 29. *The Pluralistic Economy*, chaps. 1, 2, 9
 50. *Career Guidance*, chap. 14
 54. See essay by Kenneth Boulding, "Man as a Commodity," pp. 35–49
 70. *The Manpower Connection*, chap. 7

READING NOTES

134. Becker, *Human Capital*
143. Bok and Dunlop, *Labor and the American Community*
155. Clark, *Alternative to Serfdom*
166. Doeringer and Piore, *Internal Labor Markets and Manpower Analysis*
179. Freud, *Civilization and its Discontents*
188. Gordon, *Theories of Poverty and Unemployment*
193. Harrison, *Education, Training and the Urban Ghetto*
207. Kerr, *Labor and Management in Industrial Society*
208. Keynes, *General Theory of Employment, Interest and Money*
212. Kreps and Clark, *Sex, Age and the Allocation of Work*
271. Reynolds, *The Structure of Labor Markets*
296. Smith, *The Wealth of Nations*
314. Veblen, *The Instinct of Workmanship*

CHAPTER 2

CONSERVATION OF HUMAN RESOURCES PUBLICATIONS

  1. *Grass on the Slag Heaps*, chap. 8
 20. *The Optimistic Tradition and American Youth*, chaps. 2, 3, 4
 23. *Democratic Values and the Rights of Management*, Part 4
 37. *The Middle-Class Negro in the White Man's World*, chaps. 6 through 9
 65. *The Great Society*, "Introduction" and chap. 11
 70. *The Manpower Connection*, part 3
 92. *Studies in the Economics of the Bible*, sec. III, The Jubilee Year
 93. *The House of Adam Smith*, part two

READING NOTES

157. Clark, *Preface to Social Economics*
183. Friedman, *Essays in Positive Economics*
197. Hook, *Human Values and Economic Policy*
224. MacIver, *Politics and Society*
234. Marx, *Capital*
238. Medvedev, *On Socialist Democracy*
245. Mitchell, *The Backward Art of Spending Money*
248. Myrdal, *An American Dilemma*, app. 1
250. ———, *The Political Element in the Development of Economic Theory*

262. Phelps, *Economic Justice*
267. Rawls, *A Theory of Justice*
274. Rickert, *Science and History*
277. Robinson, *Economic Philosophy*
287. Schumpeter, *Capitalism, Socialism, and Democracy*
293. Simkhovitch, *Approaches to History*
313. Veblen, *The Higher Learning*
290. Weber, *On the Methodology of the Social Sciences*

CHAPTER 3

CONSERVATION OF HUMAN RESOURCES PUBLICATIONS

16. *The Ineffective Soldier*, especially vol. III
17. *The Nation's Children*, especially vol. I
24. *Economic Growth and Employment Opportunities for Minorities*, chaps. I, II, IX
51. *Manpower for Development*, chaps. 1, 3, 4, 19
75. *Bridges to Work*, chap. 1
85. *A Policy for Skilled Manpower*, chap. 2

READING NOTES

130. Adelman and Morris, *Economic Growth and Social Equity in Developing Countries*
144. Boulding, *The Image*
147. Bronfenbrenner, *Two Worlds of Childhood*
152. Chandhuri, *The Autobiography of an Unknown Indian*
202. International Labour Organization, *Towards Full Employment: A Programme for Colombia*
317. Whyte and Williams, *Toward an Integrated Theory of Development*

CHAPTER 4

CONSERVATION OF HUMAN RESOURCES PUBLICATIONS

23. *Democratic Values and the Rights of Management*, chap. 12
26. *The Troublesome Presence*, chaps. 10 through 12
29. *The Pluralistic Economy*, chap. 9
65. *The Great Society*, chaps. 1, 2, 11
67. *The Future of the Metropolis*, chaps. 1, 2, 8
70. *The Manpower Connection*, chaps. 19 and 21
94. *The Illusion of Economic Stability*, chap. IX
100. *Manpower in Israel*

READING NOTES

135. Bell, *The Coming of the Post-Industrial Society*
149. Bryant, *Health and the Developing World*
154. Churchward, *The Soviet Intelligentsia*
172. Edwards, *Employment in Developing Nations*
205. Jenkins, *Sweden and the Price of Progress*
215. Kuznets, *Modern Economic Growth*
238. Medvedev, *On Socialist Democracy*

CHAPTER 5

CONSERVATION OF HUMAN RESOURCES PUBLICATIONS

7. *The Uneducated,* parts I and III
9. *Psychiatry and Military Manpower Policy,* chaps. 4 and 5
16. *The Ineffective Soldier,* vol. II
17. *The Nation's Children,* vol. II
21. *A Psychiatrist's Views on Social Issues,* chaps. 4, 9, 10, 11
41. *The Process of Work Establishment,* chaps. 1, 5, 6
47. *Education and Jobs,* chaps. I, II, IX
49. *Changing Careers after 35,* chaps. 1 and 7
50. *Career Guidance,* chap. 5
70. *The Manpower Connection,* part one
116. *Manpower Research and Management in Large Organizations*

READING NOTES

137. Bereday, *Universities for All*
142. Bloom, *Stability and Change in Human Characteristics*
146. Bray, Campbell, and Grant, *Formative Years in Business*
147. Bronfenbrenner, *Two Worlds of Childhood*
222. Lidz, *The Person*
278. Rohrer et al., *The Eighth Generation*
301. Spitz, *The First Year of Life*

CHAPTER 6

CONSERVATION OF HUMAN RESOURCES PUBLICATIONS

6. *Occupational Choice,* chaps. 11, 12, 13, 16
12. *The Negro Potential,* chap. 5
17. *The Nation's Children,* vol. III
36. *Manpower Strategy for Developing Countries,* chaps. 2 and 7
50. *Career Guidance,* chaps. 6, 10, 18
58. *The Labor Market,* chaps. 4, 6, 7
61. *Desegregation and Career Goals,* chaps. 2 and 8
64. *The Urban Labor Market,* chaps. 1, 5, 8
67. *The Future of the Metropolis,* chaps. 5 and 6
75. *Bridges to Work,* chaps. 4, 5, 6

READING NOTES

141. Blau and Duncan, *The American Occupational Structure*
161. Conant, *Slums and Suburbs*
172. Edwards, *Employment in Developing Nations*
190. Grant, *Soviet Education*
218. Levitan, Johnson, and Taggart, *Still a Dream*
261. Pennar, Bakalo, and Bereday, *Modernization and Diversity in Soviet Education*
266. Ramati, *Economic Growth in Developing Countries*
270. Reischauer and Hartman, *Reforming School Finance*

CHAPTER 7

CONSERVATION OF HUMAN RESOURCES PUBLICATIONS

  6. *Occupational Choice*, chaps. 14 and 15
 10. *Issues in the Studies of Talent*, chaps. II and V
 11. *What Makes an Executive?*
 27. *Talent and Performance*, chaps. 1, 4, 5, 11
 30. *Scientific and Managerial Manpower in Nuclear Industry*, chaps. I, VI, VII
 31. *Life Styles of Educated Women*, chaps. 6, 7, 10, 11
 35. *Electronic Data Processing in New York City*, chap. V
 52. *Upgrading Blue Collar and Service Workers*, chaps. 5, 6, 7
110. *Mobility in the Negro Community*

READING NOTES

165. Dobzhansky, *Mankind Evolving*
196. Herrnstein, *I.Q. in the Meritocracy*
206. Jensen, *Genetics and Education*
219. Levitan and Cleary, *Old Wars Remain Unfinished*
226. McPherson, *A Political Education*
247. Moran, *The Anatomy of Courage*

CHAPTER 8

CONSERVATION OF HUMAN RESOURCES PUBLICATIONS

 29. *The Pluralistic Economy*, chaps. 3, 6, 9
 36. *Manpower Strategy for Developing Countries*, chaps. 9 and 10
 38. *Manpower Strategy for the Metropolis*, "Introduction," chaps. 1 and 11, and "Afterword"
 46. *The Metropolitan Economy*, chaps. 2, 10, 11
 51. *Manpower for Development*, chaps. 1, 2, 19
 55. *Unemployment in the Urban Core*, chaps. 7, 8
 59. *Employment Expansion and Metropolitan Trade*, chaps. 1, 4, 7, 8
 65. *The Great Society*, chaps. 2 and 11
 77. *Manpower Goals for American Democracy*
100. *Manpower in Israel*
115. *Perspectives on Indian Manpower, Employment and Income*

READING NOTES

229. *Manpower Reports of the President*, 1963–1975
227. Maddison, *Class Structure and Economic Growth*
225. McNamara, "Address to the Board of Governors," IBRD, 1975
276. Robinson, *The Accumulation of Capital*
298. Solomon, *Mao's Revolution*

CHAPTER 9

CONSERVATION OF HUMAN RESOURCES PUBLICATIONS

36. *Manpower Strategy for Developing Countries*, chaps. 5, 6

41. *The Process of Work Establishment,* chap. 5
52. *Upgrading Blue Collar and Service Workers,* chaps. 2 through 6
56. *New York Is Very Much Alive,* chaps. 5, 6, 7
61. *Desegregation and Career Goals,* chap. 7
74. *Labor Markets,* chaps. II, V, VIII

READING NOTES

153. Chinoy, *Automobile Workers and the American Dream*
209. Kirsch, *Soviet Wages*
218. Levitan, Johnson, and Taggart, *Still a Dream*
221. Lewis, *The Theory of Economic Growth*
223. Lipset and Bendix, *Social Mobility in Industrial Society*

CHAPTER 10

CONSERVATION OF HUMAN RESOURCES PUBLICATIONS

29. *The Pluralistic Economy,* chap. 9
30. *Scientific and Managerial Manpower in Nuclear Industry,* chaps. III, VI, VII
45. *The Hard-to-Employ,* chaps. V through XI
47. *Education and Jobs,* chap. III
51. *Manpower for Development,* chaps. 6, 10, 14, 19
67. *The Future of the Metropolis,* chap. 6
69. *Work and Welfare in New York City,* "Foreword" and chaps. 4 and 7
70. *The Manpower Connection,* part three
72. *Suburbanization and the City*
115. *Perspectives on Indian Manpower, Employment and Income*

READING NOTES

184. Galbraith, *The New industrial State*
255. Okun, *Equality and Efficiency*
303. Sundquist, *Dispersing Population*
306. Third Bellagio Conference on Population, *Working Papers*
308. Ulman and Flanagan, *Wage Restraint*

CHAPTER 11

CONSERVATION OF HUMAN RESOURCES PUBLICATIONS

11. *What Makes an Executive?,* chaps. II and V
13. *Effecting Change in Large Organizations,* chaps. 6 and 7
16. *The Ineffective Soldier,* vol. III, chaps. 7, 8, 14
23. *Democratic Values and the Rights of Management,* chaps. 2, 5, 10
30. *Scientific and Managerial Manpower in Nuclear Industry,* chaps. II, IV, V
35. *Electronic Data Processing in New York City,* chaps. VIII and IX
40. *Business Leadership and the Negro Crisis,* chap. 15
62. *High-Level Manpower and Technological Change,* chaps. 4 through 6
71. *The Impact of Large Public Programs,* "Foreword"
116. *Manpower Research and Management in Large Organizations*

READING NOTES

133. Barnard, *Organization and Management*
140. Berle and Means, *The Modern Corporation and Private Property*
148. Brown, *The Human Nature of Organizations*
156. Clark, *Competition as a Dynamic Process*
162. Cyert and March, *A Behavioral Theory of the Firm*
173. Eichner, *The Megacorp and Oligopoly*
230. March and Simon, *Organizations*
231. Marris, *The Economic Theory of Managerial Capitalism*
257. Parkinson, *Parkinson's Law*
268. Reedy, *The Presidency in Flux*
279. Rommel, *The Rommel Papers*
294. Simon, *Administrative Behavior*
295. Sloan, *My Life at General Motors*
300. Speer, *Inside the Third Reich*
307. Townsend, *Up the Organization*
316. Wavell, *Soldiers and Soldiering*

CHAPTER 12

CONSERVATION OF HUMAN RESOURCES PUBLICATIONS

3. *The Labor Leader*, parts three and four
22. *The American Worker in the Twentieth Century*, parts four and five
23. *Democratic Values and the Rights of Management*, chap. 11
41. *The Process of Work Establishment*, chaps. 3 and 4
43. *The Peripheral Worker*, chaps. 5 and 6
47. *Education and Jobs*, chaps. 7 and 8
52. *Upgrading Blue Collar and Service Workers*, chap. 7
55. *Unemployment in the Urban Core*, chap. 2
64. *The Urban Labor Market*, chap. 2
70. *The Manpower Connection*, part two
74. *Labor Markets*, chap. V

READING NOTES

186. Gardner, *Self-Renewal*
220. Lewellen, *Executive Compensation in Large Industrial Corporations*
233. Marshall and Briggs, *The Negro and Apprenticeship*
235. Maslow, *Motivation and Personality*
260. Patton, *Men, Money and Motivation*
304. "Symposium on the Economics of Internal Organization," *Bell Journal*
318. Widick, *Auto Work and Its Discontents*

CHAPTER 13

CONSERVATION OF HUMAN RESOURCES PUBLICATIONS

23. *Democratic Values and the Rights of Management*, chap. 12
25. *Technology and Social Change*, chap. 6

27. *Talent and Performance*, chaps. 8 through 12
30. *Scientific and Managerial Manpower in Nuclear Industry*, chap. VII
31. *Life Styles of Educated Women*, chaps. 11 and 12
40. *Business Leadership and the Negro Crisis*, part five
49. *Changing Careers after 35*, chaps. 4 and 7
57. *Corporate Lib*, chaps. 1, 2, 12, 13

READING NOTES

143. Bok and Dunlop, *Labor and the American Community*
198. Hoopes, *The Limits of Intervention*
283. Sampson, *The Sovereign State of ITT*
318. Widick, *Auto Work and Its Discontents*

CHAPTER 14

CONSERVATION OF HUMAN RESOURCES PUBLICATIONS

6. *Occupational Choice*, part two, chap. 13
16. *The Ineffective Soldier*, vol. III, chap. 11
27. *Talent and Performance*, chaps. 4 and 10
31. *Life Styles of Educated Women*, chaps. 6, 8, 10, 11
41. *The Process of Work Establishment*, chaps. 1 and 6
43. *The Peripheral Worker*, chap. IV
47. *Education and Jobs*, chaps. II and IV
49. *Changing Careers after 35*, chap. 1
50. *Career Guidance*, chaps. 5 and 14
70. *The Manpower Connection*, chaps. 5 and 7

READING NOTES

134. Becker, *Human Capital*
166. Doeringer and Piore, *Internal Labor Markets*
171. Education Commission of the States, *Update on Education*
189. Gordon, *Higher Education and the Labor Market*
256. Parker, *The Future of Work and Leisure*
299. Sowell, *Black Education*

CHAPTER 15

CONSERVATION OF HUMAN RESOURCES PUBLICATIONS

6. *Occupational Choice*, chaps. 14 through 16
8. *European Impressions of the American Worker*
12. *The Negro Potential*, chap. VI
15. *Women and Work in America*, chap. IV
23. *Democratic Values and the Rights of Management*, chap. 12
29. *The Pluralistic Economy*, chap. 9
39. *Manpower Agenda for America*, "Afterword"
51. *Manpower for Development*, chap. 19
70. *The Manpower Connection*, part three

READING NOTES

131. Bach, *The New Inflation*
135. Bell, *The Coming of the Post-Industrial Society*
167. Downs, *Inside Bureaucracy*
175. Erikson, *Dimensions of a New Identity*
182. Friedman, *Capitalism and Freedom*
184. Galbraith, *The New Industrial State*
195. Heilbroner, *The Future as History*
213. Kristol, *On the Democratic Idea in America*
252. Nisbet, *The Social Philosophers*
255. Okun, *Equality and Efficiency*
267. Rawls, *A Theory of Justice*
306. Third Bellagio Conference on Population, *Working Papers*

CHAPTER 16

CONSERVATION OF HUMAN RESOURCES PUBLICATIONS

14. *Human Resources,* chap. VII
16. *The Ineffective Soldier,* vol. III, part V
36. *Manpower Strategy for Developing Countries,* chap. 10
38. *Manpower Strategy for the Metropolis,* "Afterword"
39. *Manpower Agenda for America,* part three
45. *The Hard-to-Employ,* chap. XIV
53. *Manpower Advice for Government*
55. *Unemployment in the Urban Core,* chaps. 7 and 8
56. *New York Is Very Much Alive,* part IV
68. *Federal Manpower Policy in Transition*
69. *Work and Welfare in New York City,* "Foreword" and chap. 7
70. *The Manpower Connection,* part three

See also "Bibliography," nos. 82 through 91 and nos. 100 through 128, all of which address manpower policy issues.

READING NOTES

129. Adams, *The Brain Drain*
138. Bergson, *The Economics of Soviet Planning*
193. Harrison, *Education, Training and the Urban Ghetto*
215. Kuznets, *Modern Economic Growth*
218. Levitan, Johnson, and Taggart, *Still a Dream*
238. Medvedev, *On Socialist Democracy*
292. Shultz and Weber, *Strategies for the Displaced Worker*
320. Wolfbein, *Manpower Policy*

BIBLIOGRAPHY

CONSERVATION OF HUMAN RESOURCES PUBLICATIONS

BOOKS

1. Eli Ginzberg: *Grass on the Slag Heaps: The Story of the Welsh Miners,* Harper, New York, 1942.
2. Eli Ginzberg, Ethel L. Ginsburg, Dorothy L. Lynn, L. Mildred Vickers, and Sol W. Ginsburg, M.D.: *The Unemployed: I. Interpretation, II. Case Studies.* Harper, New York, 1943.
3. Eli Ginzberg, assisted by Joseph Carwell: *The Labor Leader: An Exploratory Study,* Macmillan, New York, 1948.
4. The Committee on the Function of Nursing, Eli Ginzberg, Chairman: *A Program for the Nursing Profession,* Macmillan, New York, 1948.
5. Eli Ginzberg: *A Pattern for Hospital Care,* Columbia, New York, 1949.
6. Eli Ginzberg, Sol W. Ginsburg, M.D., Sidney Axelrad, and John L. Herma: *Occupational Choice: An Approach to a General Theory,* Columbia, New York, 1951.
7. Eli Ginzberg and Douglas W. Bray: *The Uneducated,* Columbia, New York, 1953.
8. Robert W. Smuts: *European Impressions of the American Worker,* Kings Crown Press, Columbia, New York, 1953.
9. Eli Ginzberg, Sol W. Ginsburg, M.D., and John L. Herma: *Psychiatry and Military Manpower Policy—A Reappraisal of the Experience of World War II,* Kings Crown Press, Columbia, New York, 1953.
10. Douglas W. Bray: *Issues in the Studies of Talent,* Kings Crown Press, Columbia, New York, 1954.
11. Eli Ginzberg, Chairman: *What Makes an Executive? Report of a Round Table on Executive Potential and Performance,* Columbia, New York, 1955.
12. Eli Ginzberg, with the assistance of James K. Anderson, Douglas W. Bray, and Robert W. Smuts: *The Negro Potential,* Columbia, New York, 1956.
13. Eli Ginzberg and Ewing W. Reilley, assisted by Douglas W. Bray and John L. Herma: *Effecting Change in Large Organizations,* Columbia, New York, 1957.

14. Eli Ginzberg: *Human Resources: The Wealth of a Nation,* Simon and Schuster, New York, 1958.
15. Robert W. Smuts: *Women and Work in America,* Columbia, New York, 1959.
16. Eli Ginzberg, James K. Anderson, Sol W. Ginsburg, M.D., and John L. Herma: *The Ineffective Soldier: Lessons for Management and the Nation,* vol. I, *The Lost Divisions,* Columbia, New York, 1959. Eli Ginzberg, John B. Miner, James K. Anderson, Sol W. Ginsburg, M.D., and John L. Herma: *The Ineffective Soldier: Lessons for Management and the Nation,* vol. II, *Breakdown and Recovery,* Columbia, New York, 1959. Eli Ginzberg, James K. Anderson, Sol W. Ginsburg, M.D., John L. Herma, Douglas W. Bray, William Jordan, and Major Francis J. Ryan: *The Ineffective Soldier: Lessons for Management and the Nation,* vol. III, *Patterns of Performance,* Columbia, New York, 1959.
17. Eli Ginzberg (ed.): *The Nation's Children,* vol. I, *The Family and Social Change,* vol. II, *Development and Education,* vol. III, *Problems and Prospects,* Columbia, New York, 1960.
18. Eli Ginzberg (ed.), with "Foreword" by John W. Gardner: *Values and Ideals of American Youth,* Columbia, New York, 1961.
19. Eli Ginzberg and Peter Rogatz, M.D.: *Planning for Better Hospital Care,* Kings Crown Press, Columbia, New York, 1961.
20. Eli Ginzberg, James K. Anderson, and John L. Herma: *The Optimistic Tradition and American Youth,* Columbia, New York, 1962.
21. Sol W. Ginsburg, M.D.: *A Psychiatrist's Views on Social Issues,* Columbia, New York, 1963.
22. Eli Ginzberg and Hyman Berman: *The American Worker in the Twentieth Century: A History through Autobiographies,* Free Press, New York, 1963.
23. Eli Ginzberg and Ivar E. Berg, with John L. Herma and James K. Anderson: *Democratic Values and the Rights of Management,* Columbia, New York, 1963.
24. Dale L. Hiestand: *Economic Growth and Employment Opportunities for Minorities,* Columbia, New York, 1964.
25. Eli Ginzberg (ed.): *Technology and Social Change,* Columbia, New York, 1964.
26. Eli Ginzberg and Alfred S. Eichner: *The Troublesome Presence: American Democracy and the Negro,* Free Press, New York, 1964.
27. Eli Ginzberg and John L. Herma, with Ivar E. Berg, Carol A. Brown, Alice M. Yohalem, James K. Anderson, and Lois Lipper: *Talent and Performance,* Columbia, New York, 1964.
28. Eli Ginzberg (ed.): *The Negro Challenge to the Business Community,* McGraw-Hill, New York, 1964.
29. Eli Ginzberg, Dale L. Hiestand, and Beatrice G. Reubens: *The Pluralistic Economy,* McGraw-Hill, New York, 1965.
30. James W. Kuhn: *Scientific and Managerial Manpower in Nuclear Industry,* Columbia, New York, 1966.
31. Eli Ginzberg, Ivar E. Berg, Carol A. Brown, John L. Herma, Alice M. Yohalem, and Sherry Gorelick: *Life Styles of Educated Women,* Columbia, New York, 1966.
32. Eli Ginzberg and Alice M. Yohalem: *Educated American Women: Self-Portraits,* Columbia, New York, 1966.
33. Harry I. Greenfield: *Manpower and the Growth of Producer Services,* Columbia, New York, 1966.
34. Eli Ginzberg: *The Development of Human Resources,* McGraw-Hill, New York, 1966.
35. Boris Yavitz and Thomas M. Stanback, Jr.: *Electronic Data Processing in New York City: Lessons for Metropolitan Economics,* Columbia, New York, 1967.
36. Eli Ginzberg and Herbert A. Smith: *Manpower Strategy for Developing Countries,* Columbia, New York, 1967.

37. Eli Ginzberg, with Vincent Bryan, Grace T. Hamilton, John L. Herma, and Alice Yohalem: *The Middle-Class Negro in the White Man's World*, Columbia, New York, 1967.

38. Eli Ginzberg and the Conservation of Human Resources Staff: *Manpower Strategy for the Metropolis*, Columbia, New York, 1968.

39. Eli Ginzberg: *Manpower Agenda for America*, McGraw-Hill, New York, 1968.

40. Eli Ginzberg (ed.): *Business Leadership and the Negro Crisis*, McGraw-Hill, New York, 1968.

41. Marcia Freedman with Gretchen Maclachlan: *The Process of Work Establishment*, Columbia, New York, 1969.

42. Harry I. Greenfield with Carol Brown: *Allied Health Manpower: Trends and Prospects*, Columbia, New York, 1969.

43. Dean Morse: *The Peripheral Worker*, Columbia, New York, 1969.

44. Eli Ginzberg with Miriam Ostow: *Men, Money and Medicine*, Columbia, New York, 1969.

45. Beatrice G. Reubens: *The Hard-to-Employ: European Programs*, Columbia, New York, 1970.

46. Thomas M. Stanback, Jr., and Richard Knight: *The Metropolitan Economy: The Process of Employment Expansion*, Columbia, New York, 1970.

47. Ivar E. Berg: *Education and Jobs: The Great Training Robbery*, Praeger, New York, 1970.

48. Eli Ginzberg and the Conservation of Human Resources Staff: *Urban Health Services: The Case of New York*, Columbia, New York, 1971.

49. Dale L. Hiestand: *Changing Careers after 35*, Columbia, New York, 1971.

50. Eli Ginzberg: *Career Guidance: Who Needs It, Who Provides It, Who Can Improve It*, McGraw-Hill, New York, 1971.

51. Eli Ginzberg: *Manpower for Development: Perspectives on Five Continents*, Praeger, New York, 1971.

52. Charles Brecher: *Upgrading Blue Collar and Service Workers*, Johns Hopkins, Baltimore, 1972.

53. Eli Ginzberg, Chairman: *Manpower Advice for Government: Letters of the National Manpower Advisory Committee*, U.S. Department of Labor, Washington, D.C., 1972.

54. Ivar E. Berg (ed.): *Human Resources and Economic Welfare: Essays in Honor of Eli Ginzberg*, Columbia, New York, 1972.

55. Stanley Friedlander with Robert Shick: *Unemployment in the Urban Core: An Analysis of 30 Cities with Policy Recommendations*, Praeger, New York, 1972.

56. Eli Ginzberg and the Conservation of Human Resources Staff: *New York Is Very Much Alive: A Manpower View*, McGraw-Hill, New York, 1973.

57. Eli Ginzberg and Alice M. Yohalem (eds.): *Corporate Lib: Women's Challenge to Management*, Johns Hopkins, Baltimore, 1973.

58. Boris Yavitz and Dean Morse: *The Labor Market: An Information System*, Praeger, New York, 1973.

59. Richard Knight: *Employment Expansion and Metropolitan Trade*, Praeger, New York, 1973.

60. Charles M. Brecher: *The Impact of Federal Anti-Poverty Policies*, Praeger, New York, 1973.

61. Alice M. Yohalem with Captain Quentin B. Ridgley: *Desegregation and Career Goals: Children of Air Force Families*, Praeger, New York, 1974.

62. Dale L. Hiestand: *High-Level Manpower and Technological Change: The Steel Industry*, Praeger, New York, 1974.

63. Charles Brecher: *Where Have All the Dollars Gone? Public Expenditures for Human Resources Development in New York City 1961–71*, Praeger, New York, 1974.

64. David Lewin, Raymond Horton, Robert Shick, and Charles Brecher: *The Urban Labor Market: Institutions, Information, Linkages*, Praeger, New York, 1974.

65. Eli Ginzberg and Robert M. Solow (eds.): *The Great Society: Lessons for the Future,* Basic Books, New York, 1974.
66. Eli Ginzberg and Alice M. Yohalem (eds.): *The University Medical Center and the Metropolis,* Josiah Macy, Jr., Foundation, 1974.
67. Eli Ginzberg (ed.): *The Future of the Metropolis: People, Jobs, Income,* Olympus, 1974.
68. Eli Ginzberg, Chairman: *Federal Manpower Policy in Transition,* Letters of the National Manpower Advisory Committee, U.S. Department of Labor, Washington, D.C., 1974.
69. Miriam Ostow and Anna Dutka: *Work and Welfare in New York City,* Johns Hopkins, Baltimore, Md., 1975.
70. Eli Ginzberg: *The Manpower Connection: Education and Work,* Harvard, Cambridge, Mass., 1975.
71. Jerome Schnee, James W. Kuhn, and Boris Yavitz: *The Impact of Large Public Programs: The NASA Story,* Olympus, 1976.
72. Thomas Stanback, Jr., and Richard Knight: *Suburbanization and the City,* 1976.
73. Dale L. Hiestand with Miriam Ostow: *Health Manpower Information for Policy Guidance,* 1976.
74. Marcia Freedman with Gretchen Maclachlan: *Labor Markets: Segmentation and Shelters,* 1976.
75. Beatrice G. Reubens: *Bridges to Work: International Comparisons of Transition Services,* 1976.
76. Dean Morse: *Pride Against Prejudice: Labor Market Experiences of Young Puerto Ricans and Older Blacks,* 1976.
77. Eli Ginzberg (ed.): *Manpower Goals for American Democracy.* Prentice-Hall, Englewood Cliffs, N.J., 1976.
78. Eli Ginzberg (ed.): *Regionalization and Health Policy,* National Library of Medicine, 1976.
79. Ivar Berg and Marcia Freedman: *Work and Values,* 1976.
80. David Lewin, Raymond D. Horton, and James W. Kuhn: *Manpower Utilization and Collective Bargaining in Local Government,* 1976.
81. Alfred S. Eichner, and Charles M. Brecher: *Large City Budgeting for Human Resources Expenditures,* 1976.

The Conservation staff contributed to the following publications of the National Manpower Council, all of which were published by Columbia University Press.

82. *Student Deferment and National Manpower Policy,* 1952.
83. *A Policy for Scientific and Professional Manpower,* 1953.
84. *Proceedings of a Conference on the Utilization of Scientific and Professional Manpower,* 1954.
85. *A Policy for Skilled Manpower,* 1954.
86. *Improving the Work Skills of the Nation,* 1955.
87. *Womanpower,* 1957.
88. *Work in the Lives of Married Women,* 1958.
89. *Education and Manpower,* Henry David (ed.), 1960.
90. *Government and Manpower,* 1964.
91. *Public Policies and Manpower Resources,* 1964.

OTHER BOOKS BY ELI GINZBERG

92. *Studies in the Economics of the Bible,* Jewish Publication Society, New York, 1932.
93. *The House of Adam Smith,* Columbia, New York, 1934.

94. *The Illusion of Economic Stability*, Harper, New York, 1939.
95. *Report to American Jews: On Overseas Relief, Palestine and Refugees in the U.S.*, Harper, New York, 1942.
96. *Agenda for American Jews*, Columbia, New York, 1950.
97. *Keeper of the Law: Louis Ginzberg*, Jewish Publication Society, Philadelphia, 1966.

REPORTS

98. *Work Load Studies for Personnel Strength Control*, (Eli Ginzberg), Army Service Forces, 1943.
99. *Report to the Secretary of State of Five Power Conference on Reparation for Non-Repatriable Victims of German Action*, U.S. Representative, Eli Ginzberg, June 1946.
100. *Reports: Manpower in Israel*, Eli Ginzberg, Department of State, Washington, D.C., and Government of Israel, Jerusalem, Israel, 1953, 1956, 1961, 1964, 1967, 1971.
101. *Manpower for Government: A Decade's Forecast*, Eli Ginzberg and James K. Anderson, Public Personnel Association, Chicago, 1958.
102. *Manpower for Aviation: Final Report to the Aviation Human Resources Study Board*, Federal Aviation Agency, Eli Ginzberg, Dale L. Hiestand, and Samuel B. Richmond, Conservation of Human Resources, Columbia University, New York, 1964.
103. *The Social Order and Delinquency*, Eli Ginzberg, Ivar E. Berg, Marcia K. Freedman, and John L. Herma: The Report of the President's Commission on Crime in the District of Columbia, Appendix volume, 1966.
104. *A Manpower Strategy for Ethiopia*, Eli Ginzberg and Herbert A. Smith, USAID, Addis Ababa, July 1966.
105. *Manpower for Library Services*, Eli Ginzberg and Carol A. Brown, Conservation of Human Resources, Columbia University, New York, September 1967.
106. *White Collar Employment Opportunities for Minorities in New York City*, Dale L. Hiestand, Office of Research and Reports, U.S. Equal Employment Opportunity Commission, 1967.
107. *Federal Manpower Programs, An Evaluation*, National Manpower Advisory Committee (Eli Ginzberg, Chairman), U.S. Department of Labor, 1968.
108. *People and Progress in East Asia*, Eli Ginzberg, Columbia University, 1968.
109. *Perspectives and Policies on Employment Problems of Youth and Juvenile Delinquency*, Conservation of Human Resources, Columbia University, December 2, 1968, Task Force on Individual Acts of Violence, National Commission on the Causes and Prevention of Violence, Washington, D.C., 1968.
110. *Mobility in the Negro Community*, Eli Ginzberg and Dale L. Hiestand, U.S. Commission on Civil Rights, Clearinghouse Publication, no. 11, June 1968.
111. *One-Fifth of the World: Manpower Reports on Iran and South Asia*, Eli Ginzberg, Conservation of Human Resources, Columbia University, New York, 1969.
112. *Discrimination in Employment: An Appraisal of the Research*, Dale L. Hiestand, Institute of Labor and Industrial Relations, University of Michigan-Wayne State, no. 16, Ann Arbor, February 1970.
113. *Special Job Creation for the Hard-to-Employ in Western Europe*, Beatrice G. Reubens, Manpower Research Monograph 14, U.S. Department of Labor, 1970.
114. *State Development Agencies and Employment Expansion*, Alfred S. Eichner, Institute of Labor and Industrial Relations, University of Michigan Wayne State, no. 18, Ann Arbor, November 1970.
115. *Perspectives on Indian Manpower, Employment and Income*, Eli Ginzberg, Ford Foundation, New Delhi, and Conservation of Human Resources, Columbia University, New York, 1971.

116. *Manpower Research and Management in Large Organizations: A Report of the Task Force on Manpower Research,* Eli Ginzberg, Chairman, Defense Science Board, U.S. Department of Defense, June 1971.

117. *Private and Public Manpower Policies to Stimulate Productivity,* Prepared for the U.S. National Commission on Productivity, Eli Ginzberg, with James W. Kuhn and Beatrice G. Reubens, June 1971.

118. *The Job Crisis for Black Youth,* The Twentieth Century Task Force on Employment Problems of Black Youth (Eli Ginzberg, Chairman), Praeger, New York, 1971.

119. *The Manpower Reach of Federal Policies,* Eli Ginzberg, chap. 1, *Manpower Report of the President,* March 1972.

120. *Federation Responsibility for Central Services for Jewish Education in Greater New York,* Eli Ginzberg, Federation of Jewish Philanthropies, New York, April 1972.

121. *Manpower Policies and Programming: An Evaluation,* Eli Ginzberg, a working paper prepared for the National Manpower Advisory Committee, September 1972.

122. *New York's Future: A Manpower View,* Eli Ginzberg with Charles Brecher, *City Almanac,* October 1972.

123. *Economic Policy for New York City: Outlines of a Strategy,* Prepared for Twentieth Century Fund, Task Force on Prospects and Priorities for New York City, Conservation of Human Resources Staff, New York, August 1973.

124. *Vocational Education for ALL in High School,* Beatrice G. Reubens, in *Work and the Quality of Life: Resource Papers for Work in America,* James O'Toole (ed.), M.I.T., Cambridge, Mass., 1974.

125. *Where Have All the Dollars Gone?,* Charles Brecher, *City Almanac,* August 1974.

126. *Manpower Impact of Government Policy and Procurement,* James W. Kuhn, in *Manpower Report of the President,* 1975, chap. 6.

127. *The Implications of National Health Insurance for Ambulatory Care Services in New York City,* Charles Brecher, Karen Brudney, and Miriam Ostow, *Bulletin of the New York Academy of Medicine,* New York, in press.

128. *Current Responses to Youth Unemployment and Longer-Term Problems and Strategies in OECD Countries,* Beatrice G. Reubens, 1976.

SUPPLEMENTARY BIBLIOGRAPHY

129. Adams, Walter (ed.): *The Brain Drain,* Macmillan, New York, 1968.

130. Adelman, Irma, and Cynthia Taft Morris: *Economic Growth and Social Equity in Developing Countries,* Stanford University Press, Stanford, 1973.

131. Bach, George L.: *The New Inflation: Causes, Effects, Cures,* Brown, Providence, R.I., 1973.

132. Banfield, Edward: *The Unheavenly City: The Nature and Future of Our Urban Crisis,* Little, Brown, Boston, 1970.

133. Barnard, Chester I.: *Organization and Management, Selected Papers,* Harvard, Cambridge, Mass., 1948.

134. Becker, Gary S.: *Human Capital: A Theoretical and Empirical Analysis, with Special Reference to Education,* National Bureau of Economic Research, distributed by Columbia University Press, New York, 1964.

135. Bell, Daniel: *The Coming of the Post-Industrial Society: A Venture in Social Forecasting,* Basic Books, New York, 1973.

136. Bennett, Harry H. (as told to Paul Marcus): *We Never Called Him Henry,* Fawcett, New York, 1951.

137. Bereday, George Z. F.: *Universities for All,* Jossey-Bass, San Francisco, 1973.

138. Bergson, Abram: *The Economics of Soviet Planning,* Yale, New Haven, 1964.

139. _____: *Planning and Productivity under Soviet Socialism,* Columbia, New York, 1968.
140. Berle, Adolf A., and Gardiner C. Means: *The Modern Corporation and Private Property* (1933), rev. ed., Harcourt Brace Jovanovich, New York, 1968.
141. Blau, Peter M., and Otis Dudley Duncan: *The American Occupational Structure,* Wiley, New York, 1967.
142. Bloom, Benjamin S.: *Stability and Change in Human Characteristics,* Wiley, New York, 1964.
143. Bok, Derek C., and John T. Dunlop: *Labor and the American Community,* Simon and Schuster, New York, 1970.
144. Boulding, Kenneth E.: *The Image: Knowledge in Life and Society,* The University of Michigan Press, Ann Arbor, Mich., 1956.
145. Bowen, William G., and T. Aldrich Finegan: *The Economics of Labor Force Participation,* Princeton, Princeton, N.J., 1969.
146. Bray, Douglas W., Richard J. Campbell, and Donald L. Grant: *Formative Years in Business: A Long-Term AT&T Study of Managerial Lives,* Wiley-Interscience, New York, 1974.
147. Bronfenbrenner, Urie, with the assistance of J. C. Condry, Jr.: *Two Worlds of Childhood: U.S. and U.S.S.R.,* Russell Sage, New York, 1970.
148. Brown, J. Douglas: *The Human Nature of Organizations,* AMACOM, New York, 1973.
149. Bryant, John: *Health and the Developing World,* Cornell, Ithaca and London, 1969.
150. Cain, Glen: *Married Women in the Labor Force,* The University of Chicago Press, Chicago, 1966.
151. Cairnes, John: *Some Leading Principles of Political Economy Newly Expounded,* Harper, New York, 1874.
152. Chandhuri, Nirod C.: *The Autobiography of an Unknown Indian,* University of California Press, Berkeley, 1968.
153. Chinoy, Ely: *Automobile Workers and the American Dream,* Doubleday, Garden City, N.Y., 1955.
154. Churchward, Lloyd G.: *The Soviet Intelligentsia: An Essay in the Social Structure and Role of Soviet Intellectuals during the 1960's,* Routledge, London and Boston, 1973.
155. Clark, John M.: *Alternative to Serfdom,* Knopf, New York, 1948.
156. _____: *Competition as a Dynamic Process,* Brookings, Washington, D.C., 1961.
157. _____: *Preface to Social Economics: Essays on Economic Theory and Social Problems,* Farrar & Rinehart, New York, 1936.
158. _____: *Studies in the Economics of Overhead Costs,* The University of Chicago Press, Chicago, 1923.
159. _____: *The Economics of Planning Public Works,* U.S. Government Printing Office, Washington, D.C., 1935.
160. Commission on Population Growth and the American Future, J. D. Rockefeller, 3rd, (Chairman): *Population and the American Future,* U.S. Government Printing Office, Washington, D.C., 1972.
161. Conant, James B.: *Slums and Suburbs: A Commentary on Schools in Metropolitan Areas,* McGraw-Hill, New York, 1961.
162. Cyert, Richard M., and James G. March: *A Behavioral Theory of the Firm,* Prentice-Hall, Englewood Cliffs, N.J., 1963.
163. Davis, Louis E., and A. B. Cherns (eds.): *The Quality of Working Life,* 2 vols., Free Press, New York, 1975.
164. Djilas, Milovan: *The New Class: An Analysis of the Communist System,* Praeger, New York, 1957.
165. Dobzhansky, Theodosius G.: *Mankind Evolving: The Evolution of the Human Species,* Yale, New Haven, 1961, 1967.

166. Doeringer, Peter B., and Michael J. Piore: *Internal Labor Markets and Manpower Analysis*, Heath, Boston, 1971.

167. Downs, Anthony: *Inside Bureaucracy*, Rand Corporation Research Study, Little, Brown, Boston, 1967.

168. Dunlop, John T. (ed.): "The Theory of Wage Determination," *Proceedings of a Conference Held by the International Economics Association*, Macmillan and London, New York, 1957.

169. Dunlop, John T., Frederick H. Harbison, Clark Kerr, and Charles A. Myers: *Industrialism and Industrial Man Reconsidered*, Princeton: The Inter-University Study of Human Resources in National Development, 1957.

170. Easterlin, Richard A.: *Population, Labor Force, and Long Swings in Economic Growth*, National Bureau of Economic Research, New York, 1968.

171. Education Commission of the States: *Update on Education: A Digest of the National Assessment of Educational Progress*, Denver, 1975.

172. Edwards, Edgar O. (ed.): *Employment in Developing Nations*, report on a Ford Foundation study, Columbia, New York and London, 1974.

173. Eichner, Alfred S.: *The Megacorp and Oligopoly: Micro Foundations of Macro Dynamics*, Cambridge, New York, 1976.

174. Epstein, Cynthia Fuchs: *Woman's Place: Options and Limits in Professional Careers*, University of California Press, Berkeley and Los Angeles, 1970.

175. Erikson, Erik H.: *Dimensions of a New Identity: The 1973 Jefferson Lectures in the Humanities*, Norton, New York, 1974.

176. Fei, John C. H., and Gustav Ranis: *Development of the Labor Surplus Economy: Theory and Policy*, Irwin, Homewood, Ill., 1964.

177. Fermi, Laura: *Illustrious Immigrants: The Intellectual Migration from Europe, 1930–1941*, The University of Chicago Press, Chicago, 1968.

178. Freud, Anna: *The Ego and the Mechanisms of Defense*, International Universities Press, New York, 1966.

179. Freud, Sigmund: *Civilization and Its Discontents* (1930), Norton, New York, 1962.

180. ———: *The Ego and the Id* (1927), James Strachey (ed.), Norton, New York, 1962.

181. Fried, John H.: *The Exploitation of Foreign Labour by Germany*, International Labour Office, Studies and Reports, Series C., no. 25, Montreal, 1945.

182. Friedman, Milton: *Capitalism and Freedom*, The University of Chicago Press, Chicago, 1962.

183. ———: *Essays in Positive Economics*, The University of Chicago Press, Chicago, 1953.

184. Galbraith, John K.: *The New Industrial State*, 2d rev. ed., Houghton Mifflin, Boston, 1972.

185. Galenson, Walter, and Harvey Leibenstein: "Investment Criteria, Productivity and Economic Development," *Quarterly Journal of Economics*, vol. LXIX, no. 3, pp. 343–370, August 1955.

186. Gardner, John W.: *Self-Renewal: The Individual and the Innovative Society*, Harper & Row, New York, 1964.

187. Glazer, Nathan, and Daniel P. Moynihan: *Beyond the Melting Pot*, M.I.T., Cambridge, Mass., 1963.

188. Gordon, David M.: *Theories of Poverty and Underemployment: Orthodox, Radical and Dual Labor Market Perspectives*, Lexington Books, Lexington, Mass., 1972.

189. Gordon, Margaret S. (ed.): *Higher Education and the Labor Market*, a report of the Carnegie Commission on Higher Education, McGraw-Hill, New York, 1973.

190. Grant, Nigel: *Soviet Education*, Penguin, Baltimore, 1964.

191. Greenwood, Michael J.: "Research on Internal Migration in the United States. A Survey," *Journal of Economic Literature*, vol. XIII, no. 2, pp. 397–433, June 1975.

192. Harris, Louis: *The Anguish of Change*, Norton, New York, 1973.

193. Harrison, Bennett: *Education, Training and the Urban Ghetto*, Baltimore: Johns Hopkins, 1972.
194. Harrod, Roy F.: *The Life of John Maynard Keynes*, Harcourt, Brace, New York, 1951.
195. Heilbroner, Robert L.: *The Future as History: The Historic Currents of Our Time and the Direction in Which They Are Taking America*, Harper, New York, 1960.
196. Herrnstein, Richard J.: *I.Q. in the Meritocracy*, Little, Brown, Boston, 1973.
197. Hook, Sidney (ed.): *Human Values and Economic Policy: Proceedings of a Symposium Conducted by the New York University Institute of Philosophy*, New York University Press, New York, 1967.
198. Hoopes, Townsend: *The Limits of Intervention*, McKay, New York, 1969.
199. Howenstine, E. Jay: *Compensatory Employment Programmes*, Organization for Economic Cooperation and Development, Paris, 1968.
200. Hughes, H. Stuart: *Consciousness and Society, The Reorientation of European Social Thought, 1890–1930*, Vintage Books, New York, 1961.
201. International Labour Office: *Matching Employment Opportunities and Expectations: A Programme of Action for Ceylon*, Geneva, 1971.
202. _____: *Towards Full Employment: A Programme for Colombia Prepared by an Inter-Agency Team Organized by the International Labour Office*, Geneva, 1970.
203. _____: *Employment and Income Policies for Iran*, Geneva, 1973.
204. _____: *Employment, Incomes and Equality: A Strategy for Increasing Productive Employment in Kenya*, Geneva, 1972.
205. Jenkins, David: *Sweden and the Price of Progress*, Coward–McCann, New York, 1968.
206. Jensen, Arthur R.: *Genetics and Education*, Harper & Row, New York, 1972.
207. Kerr, Clark: *Labor and Management in Industrial Society*, Anchor Books, Doubleday, Garden City, N.Y., 1964.
208. Keynes, John Maynard: *The General Theory of Employment, Interest and Money*, Harcourt, Brace, New York, 1936.
209. Kirsch, Leonard Joel: *Soviet Wages: Changes in Structure and Administration Since 1956*, M.I.T., Cambridge, Mass., 1972.
210. Knight, Frank H.: *The Ethics of Competition*, Harper, New York and London, 1935.
211. Kosa, John, Aaron Antonovsky, and Irving K. Zola (eds.): *Poverty and Health, A Sociological Analysis*, Harvard, Cambridge, Mass., 1969.
212. Kreps, Juanita, and Robert Clark: *Sex, Age and the Allocation of Work*, Johns Hopkins, Baltimore, 1976.
213. Kristol, Irving: *On the Democratic Idea in America*, Harper & Row, New York, 1972.
214. Kuznets, Simon: *Economic Growth and Structure: Selected Essays*, Norton, New York, 1965.
215. _____: *Modern Economic Growth: Rate, Structure, and Spread*, Yale, New Haven and London, 1966.
216. Lester, Richard A.: *The Economics of Labor*, 2d ed., Macmillan, New York, 1964.
217. Leveson, Irving: "Nonfarm Self-Employment in the United States," unpublished Ph.D. dissertation, Columbia University, New York, 1968.
218. Levitan, Sar, William B. Johnson, and Robert Taggart: *Still a Dream: The Changing Status of Blacks Since 1960*, Harvard, Cambridge, Mass., 1975.
219. _____, and Karen A. Cleary: *Old Wars Remain Unfinished: The Veterans Benefits System*, Johns Hopkins, Baltimore, 1973.
220. Lewellen, Wilbur G.: *Executive Compensation in Large Industrial Corporations*, National Bureau of Economic Research, distributed by Columbia, New York, 1968.
221. Lewis, William Arthur: *The Theory of Economic Growth*, Irwin, Homewood, Ill., 1955.
222. Lidz, Theodore: *The Person: His Development throughout the Life Cycle*, Basic Books, New York, 1968.
223. Lipset, S. M., and R. Bendix: *Social Mobility in Industrial Society*, University of California Press, Berkeley, 1959.

224. MacIver, Robert M.: *Politics and Society,* David Spitz (ed.), Atherton, New York, 1969.
225. McNamara, Robert S.: "Address to the Board of Governors," International Bank for Reconstruction and Development, Washington, D.C., September 1, 1975.
226. McPherson, Harry: *A Political Education,* Little, Brown, Boston, 1972.
227. Maddison, Angus: *Class Structure and Economic Growth: India and Pakistan Since the Moghuls,* Norton, New York, 1971.
228. Malthus, Thomas R.: *An Essay on Population* (1798), Dent, London, 1958.
229. *Manpower Report of the President,* U.S. Government Printing Office, Washington, D.C., annually since 1963.
230. March, James G., and Herbert A. Simon, with the collaboration of Harold Guetzkow: *Organizations,* Wiley, New York, 1958.
231. Marris, Robin L.: *The Economic Theory of Managerial Capitalism,* Free Press, New York, 1964.
232. Marshall, Alfred: *Principles of Economics* (1920), 8th ed., Macmillan, London and New York, 1961.
233. Marshall, F. Ray, and Vernon M. Briggs: *The Negro and Apprenticeship,* Johns Hopkins, Baltimore, 1967.
234. Marx, Karl: *Capital* (1867), Friedrich Engels (ed.), Modern Library, New York, 1906.
235. Maslow, Abraham A.: *Motivation and Personality* (1954), 2d ed., Harper & Row, New York, 1970.
236. Mason, Edward S.: *Economic Concentration and the Monopoly Problem,* Atheneum, New York, 1964.
237. Mazlish, Bruce: *James and John Stuart Mill,* Basic Books, New York, 1975.
238. Medvedev, Roy A.: *On Socialist Democracy,* Knopf, New York, 1975.
239. Meidner, Rudolf, and Rolf Anderson: "The Overall Impact of an Active Labor Market Policy in Sweden," in Lloyd Ulman (ed.), *Manpower Programs in the Policy Mix,* Johns Hopkins, Baltimore, 1973, pp. 117-158.
240. Merton, Robert K., George G. Reader, and Patricia L. Kendall (eds.): *The Student-Physician,* Harvard, Cambridge, Mass., 1957.
241. Mill, John Stuart: *Principles of Political Economy with Some of Their Applications to Social Philosophy* (1848), Longmans, London, 1926.
242. Mills, C. Wright: *The Sociological Imagination,* Oxford University Press, New York, 1959.
243. Mincer, Jacob: *Schooling, Experience, and Earnings,* Columbia, New York, 1974.
244. Mishan, E. J.: *The Costs of Economic Growth,* Praeger, New York, 1967.
245. Mitchell, Wesley C.: *The Backward Art of Spending Money and Other Essays,* A. M. Kelley, New York, 1950.
246. —— (ed.): *What Veblen Taught: Selected Writings of Thorstein Veblen,* Viking, New York, 1936.
247. Moran, Lord: *The Anatomy of Courage,* Eyre & Spottiswoode, London, 1945.
248. Myrdal, Gunnar: *An American Dilemma: The Negro Problem and Modern Democracy* (1944), 2 vols., Harper, New York, 1962.
249. ——: *Asian Drama: An Inquiry into the Poverty of Nations,* Twentieth Century Fund, New York, 1968.
250. ——: *The Political Element in the Development of Economic Theory,* Harvard, Cambridge, Mass., 1954.
251. National Commission on Technology, Automation and Economic Progress: *Technology and the American Economy,* report with 6 appendix vols., U.S. Government Printing Office, Washington, D.C., 1966.
252. Nisbet, Robert A.: *The Social Philosophers: Community and Conflict in Western Thought,* Crowell, New York, 1970.
253. Nozick, Robert: *Anarchy, State and Utopia,* Basic Books, New York, 1968.

254. Oksenberg, Michel (ed.): "China's Developmental Experience," *Proceedings of the Academy of Political Science,* vol. 31, no. 1, Academy of Political Science, New York, March 1973.

255. Okun, Arthur M.: *Equality and Efficiency, The Big Tradeoff,* Brookings, Washington, D.C., 1975.

256. Parker, Stanley: *The Future of Work and Leisure,* Praeger, New York, 1971.

257. Parkinson, Cyril N.: *Parkinson's Law and Other Studies in Administration,* Houghton Mifflin, Boston, 1957.

258. Parnes, Herbert S., et al.: U.S. Department of Labor, Manpower Research Monograph 13, *The Pre-Retirement Years;* Monograph 16, *Career Thresholds;* Monograph 21, *Dual Careers;* Monograph 24, *Years for Decision.* Each multi-volumed. Washington, D.C., 1968-75.

259. Patten, Thomas H., Jr.: *Manpower Planning and the Development of Human Resources,* Wiley-Interscience, New York, 1971.

260. Patton, Arch: *Men, Money and Motivation: Executive Compensation as an Instrument of Leadership,* McGraw-Hill, New York, 1961.

261. Pennar, Jaan, Ivan I. Bakalo, and George Z. F. Bereday: *Modernization and Diversity in Soviet Education,* Praeger, New York, 1971.

262. Phelps, Edmund S. (ed.): *Economic Justice,* Penguin, Baltimore, 1973.

263. Platt, The Lord, and A. S. Parkes (eds.): *Social and Genetic Influences on Life and Death,* Third Eugenics Society symposium, Oliver & Boyd, Edinburgh and London, 1967.

264. Price, Don K.: *The Scientific Estate,* The Belknap Press, Harvard, Cambridge, Mass., 1965.

265. Purcell, Thomas V., and Gerald F. Cavanagh: *Blacks in the Industrial World: Issues for the Manager,* Free Press, New York, 1972.

266. Ramati, Yohanan (ed.): *Economic Growth in Developing Countries—Material and Human Resources,* Praeger, New York, 1975.

267. Rawls, John: *A Theory of Justice,* Harvard, Cambridge, Mass., 1971.

268. Reedy, George E.: *The Presidency in Flux,* Columbia, New York, 1973.

269. Rehn, Gösta: "The Problem of Stability: An Analysis and Some Public Proposals," in Ralph Turvey (ed.), *Wages Policy under Full Employment,* William Hodge and Co., London, 1952.

270. Reischauer, Robert D., and Robert W. Hartman: *Reforming School Finance,* Brookings, Washington, D.C., 1973.

271. Reynolds, Lloyd G.: *The Structure of Labor Markets,* Harper, New York, 1951.

272. _____: "China As a Less Developed Economy," *American Economic Review,* vol. LXV, no. 3, pp. 418-428, June 1975.

273. Ricardo, David: *The Principles of Political Economy and Taxation* (1817), Irwin, Homewood, Ill., 1963.

274. Rickert, Heinrich: *Science and History: A Critique of Positivist Epistemology,* Van Nostrand, Princeton, N.J., 1962.

275. Robbins, Lionel: *The Theory of Economic Policy in English Classical Political Economy,* Macmillan, London, 1952.

276. Robinson, Joan: *The Accumulation of Capital,* Macmillan, New York, 1956.

277. _____: *Economic Philosophy,* Aldine, Chicago, 1962.

278. Rohrer, John H., and Munro S. Edmonson (eds.), Harold Lief, Daniel Thompson, and William Thompson (co-authors): *The Eighth Generation,* Harper, New York, 1960.

279. Rommel, Erwin: *The Rommel Papers,* B. H. Liddell-Hart (ed.), Harcourt, Brace, New York, 1953.

280. Rosow, Jerome R. (ed.): *The Worker and the Job: Coping with Change,* Prentice-Hall, Englewood Cliffs, N.J., 1974.

281. Ross, Arthur M., and Herbert Hill (eds.): *Employment, Race and Poverty,* Harcourt, Brace and World, New York, 1967.

282. Ruttenberg, Stanley H., and associates: *Needed: A Constructive Foreign Trade Policy,* AFL-CIO Industrial Union Department, Washington, D.C., 1971.

283. Sampson, Anthony: *The Sovereign State of I.T.T.,* Stein and Day, New York, 1973.

284. Samuelson, Paul A.: *Economics,* 9th ed., McGraw-Hill, New York, 1973.

285. Schlesinger, Arthur M.: *The Age of Roosevelt,* vol. 3, *The Politics of Upheaval,* Houghton Mifflin, Boston, 1960.

286. Schlesinger, James R.: *The Political Economy of National Security: A Study of the Economic Aspects of the Contemporary Power Struggles,* Praeger, New York, 1960.

287. Schumpeter, Joseph A., *Capitalism, Socialism and Democracy,* 2d ed., Harper, New York, 1947.

288. _____ : *History of Economic Analysis,* Oxford University Press, New York, 1954.

289. Senior, Nassau W.: "Letter on the Factory Act, as It Affects the Cotton Manufacture, March 28, 1837," *Selected Writings in Economics by Nassau W. Senior, A Volume of Pamphlets, 1827–1835,* A. M Kelley, New York, 1966, pp. 10–17.

290. Shils, Edward A., and Henry A. Finch (eds. and trans.): *Max Weber on the Methodology of the Social Sciences,* Free Press, Glencoe, Ill., 1949.

291. Shotwell, James T. (ed.): *The Origins of the International Labour Organization,* 2 vols., Columbia, New York, 1934.

292. Shultz, George P., and Arnold R. Weber: *Strategies for the Displaced Workers: Confronting Economic Change,* Harper & Row, New York, 1968.

293. Simkhovitch, Vladimir G.: *Approaches to History,* 6 parts in 1 vol., New York Academy of Political Sciences, New York, 1929–1936.

294. Simon, Herbert A.: *Administrative Behavior: A Study of Decision-Making Processes in Administrative Organization,* 2d ed., Macmillan, New York, 1957.

295. Sloan, Alfred P.: *My Life at General Motors,* Doubleday, Garden City, N.Y., 1964.

296. Smith, Adam: *An Inquiry into the Nature and Causes of the Wealth of Nations* (1776), Modern Library, New York, 1937.

297. The Social Science Institute: *Reshaping Britain: A Programme of Economic and Social Reform,* vol. XL, Broadsheet 548, PEP, London, 1974.

298. Solomon, Richard R.: *Mao's Revolution and the Chinese Political Culture,* University of California Press, Berkeley, 1971.

299. Sowell, Thomas: *Black Education: Myths and Tragedies,* McKay, New York, 1972.

300. Speer, Albert: *Inside the Third Reich: Memoirs,* Macmillan, New York, 1970.

301. Spitz, Rene: *The First Year of Life,* International Universities Press, New York, 1965.

302. Strong, Merle E. (ed.): *Developing the Nation's Workforce,* Yearbook 5, American Vocational Association, Washington, D.C., 1975.

303. Sundquist, James L.: *Dispersing Population: What America Can Learn from Europe,* Brookings, Washington, D.C., 1975.

304. "Symposium on the Economics of Internal Organization," *The Bell Journal of Economics,* vol. 6, pp. 163–278, Spring 1975.

305. Third Bellagio Conference on Population: *Working Papers,* The Rockefeller Foundation, New York, 1974.

306. Tobin, James: *The New Economics, One Decade Older,* Princeton, Princeton, N.J., 1974.

307. Townsend, Robert: *Up the Organization,* Knopf, New York, 1970.

308. Ulman, Lloyd, and Robert J. Flanagan: *Wage Restraint: A Study of Incomes Policies in Western Europe,* University of California Press, Berkeley, 1971.

309. U.S. Department of Health, Education and Welfare, Office of Education: *Higher Education in the U.S.S.R.,* Washington, D.C., 1963.
310. U.S. Department of Labor, Bureau of Labor Statistics: *Seniority in Promotions and Transfer Provisions,* Bulletin 1425-11, March 1970.
311. _____: *The Skilled Work Force of the United States,* Washington, D.C., 1955.
312. Veblen, Thorstein: *Absentee Ownership and Business Enterprise in Recent Times: The Case of America,* B. W. Huebsch, New York, 1923.
313. _____: *The Higher Learning in America: A Memorandum on the Conduct of Universities by Business Men,* B. W. Huebsch, New York, 1918.
314. _____: *The Instinct of Workmanship and the State of the Industrial Arts,* B. W. Huebsch, New York, 1914.
315. _____: *The Theory of the Leisure Class: An Economic Study of Institutions,* Modern Library, New York. 1934.
316. Wavell, Archibald P., Earl: *Soldiers and Soldiering,* Cape, London, 1953.
     Weber, Max: *see* Shils & Finch.
317. Whyte, William F., and Lawrence K. Williams: *Toward an Integrated Theory of Development: Economic and Noneconomic Variables in Rural Development,* ILR Paperback 5, New York State School of Industrial and Labor Relations, Cornell University, Ithaca, 1968.
318. Widick, B. J.: *Auto Work and Its Discontents,* Johns Hopkins, Baltimore, 1976.
319. Wilcock, Richard C., and Walter H. Franke: *Unwanted Workers: Permanent Layoffs and Long-Term Unemployment,* Free Press, New York, 1963.
320. Wolfbein, Seymour L. (ed.): *Manpower Policy: Perspectives and Prospects,* Temple University School of Business Administration, Philadelphia, 1973.
321. Wolfle, Dael L.: *America's Resources of Specialized Talent: A Current Appraisal and a Look Ahead,* report prepared for the Commission on Human Resources and Advanced Training, Harper, New York, 1954.
322. Zuckerman, Sir Solly: *Scientists and War: The Impact of Science on Military and Civil Affairs,* Hamish Hamilton, London, 1966.

Index